普通高等教育材料成型及控制工程系列规划教材

焊接科学与工程专业英语

吴志生　柏艳红　黎穗琼　主编

化学工业出版社

·北京·

本教材主要介绍焊接技术与工程专业的基础知识和专业知识英语文献。该教材内容大部分选自国外原版教材，教材共分九章，内容包括焊接技术与工程专业知识的诸多方面的英语文献。内容涉及现代工程结构材料、金属材料的力学性能及热物理性能、钢的热处理、电弧物理等焊接技术基础知识，以及弧焊电源、焊接方法及设备、焊接冶金学、焊接工艺、焊接应力与变形、焊接自动化及焊接质量检验等焊接专业知识。

本书为高等院校焊接专业学生专用教材，也可以供从事焊接技术与工程领域工作的工程技术人员参考。

图书在版编目（CIP）数据

焊接科学与工程专业英语/吴志生，柏艳红，黎穗琼主编. —北京：化学工业出版社，2012.11（2025.2重印）
普通高等教育材料成型及控制工程系列规划教材
ISBN 978-7-122-15458-3

Ⅰ.①焊… Ⅱ.①吴… ②柏… ③黎…Ⅲ.①焊接-英语-高等学校-教材 Ⅳ.①H31

中国版本图书馆 CIP 数据核字（2012）第 234440 号

责任编辑：彭喜英　　　　　　　　　　　装帧设计：杨　北
责任校对：顾淑云

出版发行：化学工业出版社（北京市东城区青年湖南街 13 号　邮政编码 100011）
印　　装：北京天宇星印刷厂
787mm×1092mm　1/16　印张 12½　字数 342 千字　2025 年 2 月北京第 1 版第 6 次印刷

购书咨询：010-64518888　　　　　　　　售后服务：010-64518899
网　　址：http://www.cip.com.cn
凡购买本书，如有缺损质量问题，本社销售中心负责调换。

定　　价：48.00 元

本书编写人员

主编： 吴志生　博士/教授　　　　　　太原科技大学

柏艳红　博士/副教授　　　　太原科技大学

黎穗琼　博士/博士后/研究员　奥本大学（美国）

参编： 李志勇　博士/教授　　　　　　中北大学

程方杰　博士/副教授　　　　天津大学

陈少平　博士/副教授　　　　太原理工大学

赵　菲　博士　　　　　　　　太原科技大学

苏允海　博士　　　　　　　　沈阳工业大学

张　鑫　博士　　　　　　　　河南科技大学

序

材料成型及控制工程专业是 1998 年国家教育部进行专业调整时，在原铸造专业、焊接专业、锻压专业及热处理专业基础上新设立的一个专业，其目的是为了改变原来老专业口径过窄、适应性不强的状况。新专业强调"厚基础、宽专业"，以拓宽专业面，加强学科基础，培养出适合经济快速发展需要的人才。

但是由于各院校原有的专业基础、专业定位、培养目标不同，也导致在人才培养模式上存在较大差异。例如，一些研究型大学担负着精英教育的责任，以培养科学研究型和科学研究与工程技术复合型人才为主，学生毕业以后大部分攻读研究生，继续深造，因此大多是以通识教育为主。而大多数教学研究型和教学型大学担负着大众化教育的责任，以培养工程技术型、应用复合型人才为主，学生毕业以后大部分走向工作岗位，因此大多数是进行通识与专业并重的教育。而且目前我国社会和工厂企业的专业人才培训体系没有完全建立起来；从人才市场来看，许多工厂企业仍按照行业特征来招聘人才。如果学生在校期间的专业课学得过少，而毕业后又不能接受继续教育，就很难承担用人单位的工作。因此许多学校在拓宽了专业面的同时也设置了专业方向。

针对上述情况，教育部高等学校材料成型及控制工程专业教学指导分委员会于 2008 年制定了《材料成型及控制工程专业分类指导性培养计划》，共分四个大类。其中第三类为按照材料成型及控制工程专业分专业方向的培养计划，按这种人才培养模式培养学生的学校占被调查学校的大多数。其目标是培养掌握材料成形及控制工程领域的基础理论和专业基础知识，具备解决材料成形及控制工程问题的实践能力和一定的科学研究能力，具有创新精神，能在铸造、焊接、模具或塑性成形领域从事设计、制造、技术开发、科学研究和管理等工作，综合素质高的应用型高级工程技术人才。其突出特色是设置专业方向，强化专业基础，具有较鲜明的行业特色。

由化学工业出版社组织编写和出版的这套"材料成型及控制工程系列规划教材"，针对第三类培养方案，按照焊接、铸造、塑性成形、模具四个方向来组织教材内容和编写方向。教材内容与时俱进，在传统知识的基础上，注重新知识、新理论、新技术、新工艺、新成果的补充。根据教学内容、学时、教学大纲的要求，突出重点、难点，力争在教材中体现工程实践思想。体现建设"立体化"精品教材的宗旨，提倡为主干课程配套电子教案、学习指导、习题解答的指导。

希望本套教材的出版能够为培养理论基础和专业知识扎实、工程实践能力和创新能力强、综合素质高的材料成形及加工的专业性人才提供重要的教学支持。

教育部高等学校材料成型及控制工程专业教学指导分委员会主任

李春峰

2010 年 4 月

前　言

本教材是普通高等教育材料成型及控制工程系列规划教材之一，适用于焊接技术与工程专业，以及材料成型及控制工程、机械制造工程和材料科学与工程等专业的焊接方向。

焊接技术是国内外重大装备制造业的关键技术之一，广泛应用于工程机械制造业、航空航天、海洋资源开发、舰船制造业、交通车辆及兵器制造业等。同时，世界经济正在全球化，世界市场在一体化，焊接加工的产品遍布世界各地，某重大装备各个焊接部件可能在不同国家进行焊接加工，并促成不同国家焊接工程技术人员的交流。英语是国际通用语言之一，使用范围广泛，因此，掌握焊接专业英语是国际化焊接工程师必备的素质之一，是了解国际先进焊接技术及发展前沿的工具。

本教材旨在提高学生焊接专业英语阅读和翻译能力，通过学习与焊接专业相关的科技英语文献提高学生在该领域的英语应用能力；了解科技英语的特点和结构；理解科技英语的常用语法、专业术语、词汇和缩写；能以英语为工具与国外工程技术人员交流以完成国际焊接工程。

教材共分九章，选材新颖，覆盖面广，内容涵盖了焊接技术与工程专业知识的各个方面。内容涉及现代工程结构材料、金属材料的力学性能及热物理性能、钢的热处理、电弧物理等焊接技术基础知识，以及弧焊电源、焊接方法及设备、焊接冶金学、焊接工艺、焊接应力与变形、焊接自动化及焊接质量检验等焊接专业知识。

该教材由太原科技大学吴志生、柏艳红和美国奥本大学黎穗琼主编。第 1 章由吴志生和黎穗琼编写，第 2 章由黎穗琼和柏艳红编写，第 3 章由赵菲编写，第 4 章由李志勇编写，第 5 章由程方杰和柏艳红编写，第 6 章由苏允海编写，第 7 章由张鑫和吴志生编写，第 8 章由柏艳红编写，第 9 章由陈少平编写。

由于编者水平有限，时间仓促，书中难免有错误和不足之处，恳请广大读者和同行批评指正。

编者

2012 年 10 月

CONTENTS

Chapter 1　Welding Technology Fundamental ·············· 1

1. 1　Modern Engineering Structural Material ··· 1
1. 2　Mechanical Property of Metal Material ······ 3
1. 3　Thermophysical Property of Metal Material ·············· 4
　1. 3. 1　Specific Heat ·············· 4
　1. 3. 2　Thermal Expansion ·············· 5
　1. 3. 3　Thermal Conductivity ·············· 5
　1. 3. 4　Melting Point or Melting Range ········ 5
　1. 3. 5　Thermionic Work Function ·············· 6
1. 4　Principal Types of Heat Treatment of Steel ·············· 6
1. 5　Arc Physics ·············· 6
　1. 5. 1　Stability of Electric Arc ·············· 6
　1. 5. 2　Stability of AC Arc ·············· 8

Chapter 2　Arc Welding Power Source ·············· 16

2. 1　Classification of Power Source ·············· 16
　2. 1. 1　AC Power Supplies ·············· 16
　2. 1. 2　DC power supplies ·············· 19
　2. 1. 3　Inverse Source of Arc Welding ······ 20
2. 2　Electrical Characteristics of Power Source ·············· 21
　2. 2. 1　Constant Voltage ·············· 21
　2. 2. 2　Constant Current ·············· 21
　2. 2. 3　Combined Constant-Current and Constant-Voltage Characteristics ······ 22
2. 3　Selecting and Specifying a Power Source ·············· 22

Chapter 3　Arc Welding Process ·············· 25

3. 1　Shielded Metal-Arc Welding ·············· 25
3. 2　Gas Shielded-Arc Welding ·············· 27
　3. 2. 1　Specific Advantages of Gas-shielded Arc ·············· 28
　3. 2. 2　Types of Gas-Shielded Arc Processes ·············· 28
　3. 2. 3　Gas Tungsten Arc-Tig ·············· 28
　3. 2. 4　Gas Metal Arc-Mig ·············· 31
　3. 2. 5　CO_2 Welding ·············· 34
　3. 2. 6　Pulsed Arc Welding ·············· 35
3. 3　Submerged Arc Welding Fundamentals of the process ·············· 36
　3. 3. 1　Definition and general description ··· 36

3. 3. 2　Principles of operation ·············· 37
3. 4　Plasma Arc Welding ·············· 38
　3. 4. 1　Keyhole Action ·············· 39
　3. 4. 2　Arc Shaping ·············· 39
　3. 4. 3　Operating Data ·············· 39
　3. 4. 4　Applications ·············· 40
　3. 4. 5　Summary ·············· 40

Chapter 4　Other Welding Methods ·············· 41

4. 1　Resistance Welding ·············· 41
　4. 1. 1　Introduction ·············· 41
　4. 1. 2　Resistance Spot Welding (RSW) ······ 42
　4. 1. 3　Projection Welding ·············· 44
　4. 1. 4　Resistance Seam Welding (RSEW) ·············· 45
　4. 1. 5　Upset Butt Welding ·············· 46
　4. 1. 6　Flash Butt Welding ·············· 47
4. 2　Friction Stir Welding ·············· 49
　4. 2. 1　Introduction ·············· 49
　4. 2. 2　Principles ·············· 50
　4. 2. 3　Friction Stir Tool ·············· 51
　4. 2. 4　Friction Stirring Imperfections ········ 55
4. 3　Laser Beam Welding ·············· 56
　4. 3. 1　Introduction ·············· 56
　4. 3. 2　Principles ·············· 58
　4. 3. 3　Metals Welded ·············· 60
　4. 3. 4　Machines ·············· 60
　4. 3. 5　Parameters and Technology ·············· 62
4. 4　Electron Beam Welding ·············· 63
　4. 4. 1　Introduction ·············· 63
　4. 4. 2　Principles ·············· 64
　4. 4. 3　Variations ·············· 66
　4. 4. 4　Equipment ·············· 67
　4. 4. 5　Safety ·············· 68

Chapter 5　Welding Metallurgy ·············· 69

5. 1　Chemical Reactions in Welding ·············· 69
　5. 1. 1　Overview ·············· 69
　5. 1. 2　Gas-Metal Reactions ·············· 70
　5. 1. 3　Slag-Metal Reactions ·············· 79
5. 2　Weld Metal Solidification ·············· 85
　5. 2. 1　Epitaxial Growth at Fusion Boundary ·············· 85
　5. 2. 2　Nonepitaxial Growth at Fusion Boundary ·············· 86
　5. 2. 3　Competitive Growth in Bulk

Fusion Zone ·················· 87

5. 2. 4　Effect of Welding Parameters on
　　　　 Grain Structure ·············· 88

5. 2. 5　Weld Metal Nucleation
　　　　 Mechanisms ················· 89

5. 2. 6　Grain Structure Control ·········· 94

5. 3　The Microstructure and Properties
　　　of Heat-affected Zone ············ 97

5. 3. 1　Welding Thermal Cycle ·········· 98

5. 3. 2　The Microstructure Changes
　　　　 in the HAZ ················· 98

5. 3. 3　Hardness Distribution in the
　　　　 HAZ ··················· 101

5. 3. 4　Welding Cracks in the HAZ ········ 105

Chapter 6　Weldability of Material ····· 109

6. 1　Weldability of Material and Testing
　　　Method ··················· 109

6. 1. 1　Weldability of Material ·········· 109

6. 1. 2　Weldability Evaluation and Test
　　　　 Method ·················· 112

6. 2　Weldability of low carbon steel ········ 114

6. 2. 1　Metallurgy of the liquid weld
　　　　 metal ··················· 114

6. 2. 2　Solidification and solidification
　　　　 cracking ················· 119

6. 2. 3　Stress intensification, embrittlement
　　　　 and cracking of fusion welds below
　　　　 the solidus ··············· 121

6. 2. 4　Lamellar tearing ············· 124

6. 2. 5　Reheat Cracking ············· 125

6. 3　Weldability of Magnesium and Its Alloys ··· 128

6. 3. 1　Alloys and Welding Procedures ····· 128

6. 3. 2　Oxide Film Removal ··········· 128

6. 3. 3　Cracking ················· 128

6. 3. 4　Mechanical Properties ·········· 129

6. 3. 5　Corrosion Resistance and Fire
　　　　 Risk ··················· 129

**Chapter 7　Residual Stresses, Distortion
　　　　　　 and Fatigue** ·············· 130

7. 1　Residual stresses ·············· 130

7. 1. 1　Development of residual stresses ···· 130

7. 1. 2　Analysis of Residual Stresses ······· 131

7. 2　Distortion ················· 133

7. 2. 1　Cause ·················· 133

7. 2. 2　Remedies ················ 133

7. 3　Fatigue ·················· 134

7. 3. 1　Mechanism ··············· 134

7. 3. 2　Fractography ·············· 135

7. 3. 3　S-N Curves ··············· 135

7. 3. 4　Effect of Joint Geometry ········ 135

7. 3. 5　Effect of Stress Raisers ·········· 136

7. 3. 6　Effect of Corrosion ············ 137

7. 3. 7　Remedies ················ 137

7. 4　Case Studies ················ 138

7. 4. 1　Failure of a Steel Pipe Assembly ··· 138

7. 4. 2　Failure of a Ball Mill ·········· 138

Chapter 8　Automation of Welding ······ 140

8. 1　Introduction of Automatic Welding
　　　System ·················· 140

8. 2　Flexible Automation of Welding ········ 143

8. 3　ARC Welding Robots ············· 145

8. 3. 1　Introduction ·············· 145

8. 3. 2　Robot Manipulator Configuration ··· 147

8. 3. 3　Robot Welding Application ········ 151

8. 3. 4　Buying a Welding Robot ········· 154

8. 3. 5　Robot Safety ·············· 154

8. 4　Controls for Automatic Arc Welding ······ 156

8. 4. 1　Automatic Welding Controllers ····· 156

8. 4. 2　Robot Controllers ············ 159

8. 4. 3　Teaching the Robot ··········· 159

8. 4. 4　Robot Memory ············· 161

8. 4. 5　Weld Execution ············· 161

8. 5　Sensors and Adaptive Control ········· 162

8. 5. 1　Introduction ·············· 162

8. 5. 2　Contact Sensors ············ 164

8. 5. 3　Noncontact Sensor Systems ······· 165

8. 6　Tooling and Fixtures ············· 168

Chapter 9　Welding Quality Inspection ··· 171

9. 1　Welding Defects ··············· 171

9. 1. 1　Definition and Types ··········· 171

9. 1. 2　Cracks ················· 171

9. 1. 3　Porosity ················· 172

9. 1. 4　Solid Inclusion ············· 172

9. 1. 5　Lack of Fusion and Inadequate or
　　　　 incomplete penetration ·········· 173

9. 1. 6　Imperfect Shape ············· 173

9. 2　Non-destructive Testing ············ 174

9. 2. 1　Radiographic Testing ··········· 174

9. 2. 2　Ultrasonic Testing (UT) ·········· 177

9. 2. 3　Magnetic Particle Inspection (MPI) ··· 178

9. 2. 4　Liquid Penetrant Testing (PT) ····· 179

9. 3　Destructive Test ··············· 182

9. 3. 1　Tension Tests ·············· 182

9. 3. 2　Bend Tests ··············· 182

9. 3. 3　Charpy Tests ·············· 183

9. 3. 4　Hardness Testing ············· 183

9. 4　Radiograph Interpretation ··········· 184

9. 4. 1　General Welding Discontinuities ····· 184

9. 4. 2　Other Discontinuities ··········· 188

References ···················· 190

Chapter 1　Welding Technology Fundamental

1. 1　Modern Engineering Structural Material

Manufacturing is essentially the art of transforming raw materials or, very often, semifinished product into goods and articles (whether they are means of production or articles of consumption).

The designer chooses materials to satisfy criteria which can be, very broadly, grouped into three sets (Table 1. 1).

Table 1. 1　Performance Criteria of Materials

Physical and Chemical properties	Mechanical Properties	Shape and Size
Electrical and thermal(conductivity insulation)	Strength(static,dynamic,fatigue)	Geometry
	Ductility	Dimensions
Chemical reactivity(corrosion)	Toughness(crack resistance)	Tolerances
Optical(color,transparency,fluorescence)	Wear resistance	Surface finish
Magnetic		Surface appearance
Change of state(softening,melting)		Weight

All the performance criteria must be satisfied, however, at a cost that is commensurate with the willingness of the potential customer to pay for the finished article. Since the cost of raw materials is usually a smaller part of the total cost, all decisions regarding materials of construction must be made with an eye on the feasibility of manufacture.

Voluminous handbooks exist, which show various properties of materials, usually classified according to the material composition. Since there are thousands of potential materials to be considered, such classifi-cations are of little value unless some more generally applicable guideline can be brought to bear on the problem. Such guidelines allow the designer to consider the broadest possible groups of materials without prematurely restricting the choice to one or two materials and thus immediately limiting the possibilities of manufacture. A premature decision may set a cost that will make the final product uneconomical or non-competitive, no matter how ingenious the design may be.

Because manufacturing processes aim at creating a usable end product or component, the starting materials are often the result of prior operations. While many possible routes of primary processing are available, as a few indicated in Figure 1. 1, the same starting materials may often be obtained through a number alternative routes (Some of them much shorter than others.) to form raw material for semi fabricated product. It would, however, be too hasty to conclude that the more complex processes are necessarily more expensive. Very often, economy is a matter of scale; thus, it is still possible to buy steel strip at a lower price than powder, partly because of the vast quantities produced in strip form.

Metals are the most generally employed engineering materials, and the growth of their production (especially that of steel) has often been taken as an indicator of industrial development. With

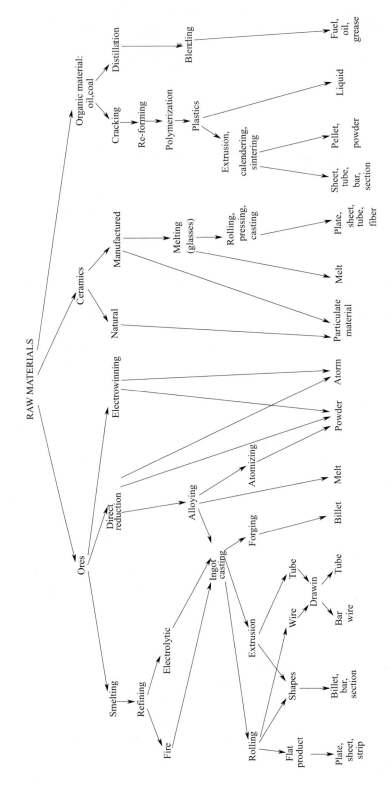

Figure 1.1 Alternative processing routes for the staring materials of manufacturing unit processes

the increasing sophistication of many products and the increasing use of plastic, these relationships are not valid any more, particularly in the industrialized states. Nevertheless, metals remain in-dis-pensable. Steel still represents an overwhelming portion of total metal production (Table 1. 2), but other metals offer unique properties and some of them (notably Mg and Ti) would become much more important if they could be extracted with a smaller energy outlay. Polymers (plastics) play an increasingly important role and, while some readjustment is necessary during raw material (oil) shortages, their position is not likely to suffer greatly. Although they are not shown in Table 1. 2, the various natural and manufactured ceramics represent a vast source of engi-neering material, many of them used also in the manufacturing industries.

Table 1. 2 Selected production data and properties for materials of manufacturing

Material	World Production /$\times 10^6$ metric tons	Melting Point /℃	Density /(kg/m³)	Elastic Modulus /$\times 10^3$MPa	Resistivity at 20℃ /$\times 10^{-8}$Ω·m	Thermal Conductivity at 20℃/[J/(m·s·℃)]
Iron	634(steel)	1536	7900	210	9. 7	75
Aluminum	11. 0	660	2700	70	2. 7	240
Copper	7. 0	1083	8900	122	1. 7	400
Zinc	5. 2	419	7100	90	5. 9	115
Lead	3. 6	327	11300	16	21. 0	35
Nickel	0. 6	1455	8900	210	6. 8	90
Magnesium	0. 26	649	1700	44	4. 0	160
Tin	0. 2	232	5800	42	11. 0	65
Titanium	0. 06	1670	4500	106	6. 8	25
Plastics	43. 3		900~2200	3~10	10^{12}	0. 2

1. 2 Mechanical Property of Metal Material

Mechanical properties are measures of how materials behave under applied loads. Another way of saying this is how strong a metal is when it comes in contact with one or more forces. If you know the strength properties of a metal, you can build a structure that is safe and sound. Likewise, when a welder knows the strength of his weld as compared with the base metal, he can produce a weldment that is strong enough to do the job. Hence strength is the ability of a metal to withstand loads without breaking down.

Strength properties are commonly referred to as tensile strength, bending strength, compres-sive strength, torsional strength, shear strength, fatigue strength and impact strength. An expla-na-tion of these terms as well as other terms that are associated with mechanical properties is includ-ed in the following paragraphs.

① Stress is the internal resistance a material offers to being deformed and is measured in terms of the applied load.

② Strain is the deformation that results from a stress and is expressed in terms of the amount of deformation per inch or centimeter.

③ Elasticity is the ability of a metal to return to its original shape after being elongated or dis-torted, when the forces are released. A rubber band is a good example of what is meant by elasticity. If the rubber is stretched, it will return to its original shape after you let it go. However if the rubber is pulled beyond a certain point, it will the same way?

④ Elastic limit is the last point at which material maybe stretched and still be return to its un-deformed condition upon release of the stress.

⑤ Modulus of elasticity is the ratio of stress to strain within the elastic limit. The less a material deforms under a given stress the higher the modulus of elasticity. By checking the modulus of elasticity the comparative stiffness of different materials can readily be ascertained. Rigidity or stiffness is very important for many machine and structural applications.

⑥ Tensile strength is that property which resists forces acting to pull the metal apart. It is one of the more important factors in the evaluation of a metal.

⑦ Compressive strength is the ability of a material to resist being crushed. Compression is the opposite of tension with respect to the direction of the applied load. Most metals have high tensile strength and high compressive strength. However, brittle materials such as cast iron have high compressive strength but only a moderate tensile strength.

⑧ Bending strength is that quality witch resists forces from causing a member to bend or deflect in the direction in which the load is applied. A bending stress is a combination of tensile and compressive stresses.

⑨ Torsional strength is the ability of a metal to withstand forces that cause a member to twist.

⑩ Shear strength refers to how well a member can withstand two equal forces acting in opposite directions.

⑪ Fatigue strength is the property of a material to resist various kinds of rapidly alternating stresses. For example, a piston rod or an axle undergoing complete reversal of stresses from tension to compression until it breaks is an example of fatigue strength.

⑫ Impact strength is the ability of a metal to resist loads that are applied suddenly and often at high velocity. The higher the impact strength of a metal the greater the energy required to break it. Impact strength may be seriously affected by welding since it is one of the most structure sensitive properties.

⑬ Ductility refers to the ability of metal to stretch, bend, or twist without breaking or cracking. A metal having high ductility, such as copper or soft iron, will fail or break gradually as the load on it is increased. A metal of low ductility, such as cast iron, fails suddenly by cracking when subjected to a heavy load.

⑭ Hardness is that property in steel which resists indentation or penetration. Hardness is usually expressed in terms of the area of an indentation made by a special ball under a standard load or the depth of a special indenter under a specific load.

⑮ Cryogenic properties of metal represent behavior characteristics under stress in environments of very low temperatures. In addition to being sensitive to crystal structure and processing conditions metals are also sensitive to low and high temperatures. Some alloys which perform satisfactorily at room temperatures may fail completely at low or high temperatures. The changes from ductile to brittle failure occur rather suddenly at low temperatures.

1.3　Thermophysical Property of Metal Material

Thermal properties of metals being joined affect either the efficiency or applicability the welding processes. The thermal properties that should be given proper considerations in welding operation include specific heat, thermal expansion, thermal conductivity, melting point or melting range, and thermionic work function. Most of the thermal properties are temperature-dependent, which means their value will vary with the temperature at which they are measured.

1.3.1　Specific Heat

The specific heat is the amount of energy required to raise the temperature of a unit weight of a material by one degree. It indicates the ability of a material to absorb heat. A metal with large specific heat, such as aluminum, requires more energy to bring it to its melting temperature. The specific heat of a material is temperature-dependent. An abnormal increase in the specific heat is observed in ferromagnetic metals, such as iron, around the Curie temperature. At Curie temperature, ferromagnetic materials become paramagnetic, requiring additional heat to randomize the orientations of the magnetic moments. The abnormity of the specific heat may also be observed when an allotropic phage change occurs.

1.3.2 Thermal Expansion

Metals change in volume when they are heated or cooled. Thermal expansion of a material can be described by the change in either its volume or dimensions. From the engineering point of view, the dimension change of a metal is more important. Therefore, the thermal expansion is measured by the linear coefficient of thermal expansion, which is defined as the change in the dimensions per unit length when the temperature of the material is changed by one degree.

The coefficient of thermal expansion is determined by the strength of the atomic bonds. Therefore, the coefficient is strongly affected by the crystalline structure of a metal. For a material with single crystalline structure or preferred orientations, its thermal expansion is anisotropic. Met-als show considerable changes in their coefficients of thermal expansion at different temperatures. The temperature range should be noted when analyzing the thermal expansion of a metal.

Thermal expansion has essentially effect on the distortion of welded metals. Higher coefficient of thermal expansion means greater amounts of expansion and subsequent contraction when a metal is welded, generating thermal stress in the welds and increasing the possibility of distortion. This problem is more severe in welding large rigid structures, such as bridges or cranes. The distortion of a weld is also sensitive to the yield strength of the base metal. Thermal stresses in metals with lower yield strength tend to be released through plastic deformation, thus reducing the possibility of distortion. Conversely, higher yield strength results in large residual stress in the welded material and severe distortion.

1.3.3 Thermal Conductivity

Thermal conductivity is the rate at which heat is transferred through a material. It is expressed as

$$\frac{Q}{A} = k \frac{\Delta T}{\Delta x}$$

Where k is the thermal conductivity, Q is the heat passes a given plane of area A per second, and $\Delta T / \Delta x$ is the temperature gradient. Thermal conductivity is dependent on temperature.

Metals transfer heat mainly through two mechanisms: free electron transfer and lattice vibrations. Different valence band and lattice structures of metals lead to very different thermal conductivities for different metals. For example, copper shows excellent thermal conductivity, making it a good candidate as "heat sink." However, high thermal conductivity results in a large amount of heat flowing away the heat source at high rate during welding, which makes it is difficult to weld copper using a relatively low-temperature heat source. On the other hand, iron shows a poor thermal conductivity among metals. This partially contributes to the good weldability of steels. However, a relatively low thermal conductivity results in a steep temperature gradient when welding, which increases the risk of distortion.

1.3.4 Melting Point or Melting Range

Melting point is the temperature at which a material changes its state from solid to liquid. Elements and compounds melt at a fixed temperature - melting point; while alloys melt over a range of temperatures. Welding a metal with higher melting point or range normally requires a larger heat input to melt a given volume of the metal. It is difficult to weld two metals with large difference in their melting points or ranges.

1. 3. 5 Thermionic Work Function

Thermionic work function is the energy that is required to remove an electron out of the metal surface. This energy plays an important role in arc welding. A lower thermionic work function means it is easier to start and maintain an arc.

1. 4 Principal Types of Heat Treatment of Steel

The principal types of heat treatment can be described in the constitutional diagram in the following manner.

Annealing is a structural recrystallization of heating above Ac_3 and subsequent slow cooling. With heating above Ac_1 but below Ac_3, full recrystallization will not occur and the procedure is called partial annealing. The state of annealed steel is close to the state of structual equilibrium and its structure is pearlite + ferrite, pearlite, or pearlite + cementite.

If a steal is heated above Ac_3 and then cooled in the air, this will be first step to change it to a state farther from the structural equilibrium. This type of heat treatment is called normalizing and is an intermediate stage between the second-group procedure (annealing) and the third-group proce-dure (hardening).

Hardening is heating above the critical point, Ac_3, followed by quick cooling. With slow cooling, austenite decomposes into ferrite + cementite at Ar_1. With increasing cooling rate, the transformation occurs at lower temperatures. As the Ar_1 point is lowered, the ferrite-cementite mixture becomes more and more fine-disperse and hard. If the cooling rate is so high and the undercooling so substantial that the precipitation of cementite and ferrite dose not take place, there will be no decomposition of the solid solution and austenite (r-solid solution) will transform into martensite (supersaturated solid solution of carbon in a-iron). Incomplete hardening is heat treatment procedure with heating the metal above Ac_1 but below Ac_3 (Ac_{cm}), after which the steel structure retains hypoeutectoid ferrite (hypoeutectoid cementite).

Tempering is a procedure of heating a harden steel to a temperature below Ac_1 and then cooling to room temperature at certain cooling rate.

Steels can be subjected to various types of chemical heat treatment, depending on the element that diffuses in steel.

The saturation of steel in carbon is called carburizing, in nitrogen, nitriding, in aluminium, alitizing, in chromium, chromizing, etc.

Thermomechanical treatment of steal consists of heating the metal to austenitic state, deforming in that state (above Ac_3 in stable state or in unstable undercooled state) and final cooling which is associated with the transformation of the strain hardened austenite.

1. 5 Arc Physics

1. 5. 1 Stability of Electric Arc

To use an arc for welding metals, it must have the required energy characteristics and sufficient stability.

The term 'stability' usually refers to the capacity of an arc for long-term burning after ignition. Arcing conditions which can exist for an unlimited time in the absence of perturbations and are characterized by a specific feature are referred to as equilibrium. If the deviation or the conditions from the initial equilibrium under the effect of perturbations over the period under examination does not exceed the permissible value, the equilibrium regime is regarded as stable in relation to the given perturbation.

When analyzing stability, it is usually sufficient to know only the integral quantities e. g. arc voltage and current, which determine the energy state of the arc, and identical quantities determi-ning its spatial position, from and movement (length, diameter, travel speed).

Arc stability is determined by one or two conditions: the capacity of the emission processes, ensuring a current at the arc cathode, to take place under conditions with a limited current whose value is determined by the circuit parameters. For arcs in any media, with the exception of vacuum both these conditions are important.

In the arc, the total voltage drop at the discharge can be considerable and may reach the voltage of the external circuit. Consequently, the condition for stable arcing is not fulfilled and the discharge may stop.

The arc processes can be stabilized to a certain degree (arc stability can be increased and the extent of metal splashing reduced) by selecting suitable electrical parameters of the current source and welding circuit. This is achieved by setting a specific from of the volt-ampere characteristic of the current source and its dynamic properties. This method can be referred to as an external method of regulating the technological properties of the arc. Another method is based on exerting an active effect on the welding processes in the arc itself by adding various compounds to the arc. These compounds can be divided into three groups: easily ionized, electronegative and elements increasing the emissivity of the electrode.

The duration of a discharge is determined mainly by the nature of emission processes taking place on the arc cathode and has not been completely explained. In practice, it is often necessary to consider the dynamic equilibrium states of arcs. In the literature on welding arcs where attention is given to the effect on the arc of different materials and welding conditions with no reference to the characteristics of the power source, this state is often referred to as 'stable arcing' and 'stability'.

There are a large number of interfering factors in the welding arc: voltage fluctuations determined by the power source, continuous displacement of the arc to new-sections of the weld component, metal melting and transfer, alternation of the polarity of AC non-uniformity and heterogeneity of the flow of particles travelling into the arc gap, etc.

Melting and transfer of metal through the column are the reason for disruption of the stability of the welding process, whereas short circuits cause splashing of electrode metal. Oxide and other films on the cathode may both increase and reduce arc stability.

The presence of easily ionized elements in the arc discharge atmosphere stabilities the position of the cathode spot and changes the nature of the discharge. If the concentration of these elements is sufficiently high, the discharge can be diffusion-coupled with the cathode. This greatly influences the nature of melting and transfer of electrode metal.

The initial attempts to explain the mechanism of the effect of easily ionized additions on arc stability and electrode metal transfer were made as early as 1936—1938. The positive effect of stabilizing compounds is caused by an increase of the intensity of the electron emission at the cathode as a result of a reduction of the work function of the electrons. The effect of stabilizing compounds on arc stability is caused by evaporation of a given compound, dissipation of products of evaporation in the arc, and thermal ionization of gases and metallic vapors. This effect is caused by the fact that the atoms of alkaline elements situated in the arc gap are the first to receive (as a result of large collision sections with electrons) the energy of the electric field generated by the electrons in collisions with these atoms. The stability of an AC arc can be increased by influencing both process determining the course of arc reignition, i. e. the process of ionization of the gas in the volume, and the residual thermionic emission. An increase of duration of resistance of the residual conduction of the arc gap, which is a characteristic of arc stability, as a result both of adding vapors of easily ionized elements to the arc column and increasing the emissivity of the cathode, was also reported. Therefore, it appears that in the absence of suitable experimental data, the two hypotheses should not contradict each other. In all likelihood, the two hypotheses explain different representations of the same process of maintaining arcing and their effect differs depending on the specific conditions.

The emissivity of the cathode with the presence of the atoms of alkaline elements in the atmosphere of the arc gap can play very significant role in an AC arc. Whose stability is determined by the variation of the electrical parameters of the arc gap from the instant at which current passes through zero to the ignition phase . as well as by their value and reproducibility in each half cycle.

Regardless of the relatively large number of studies concerned with arc stability, there are still many assumptions requiring additional examination and clarification, especially when using multi-component welding materials.

1. 5. 2 Stability of AC Arc

The arc is ignited in each new half cycle after passage of the current through zero when the voltage at the electrodes reaches a critical value. The current in the arc gap at ignition I rapidly increase to arc current I, whereas the voltage decreases to U. Throughout the remaining part of the half cycle, the arc voltage remains almost constant, whereas the current continuously increases. This result in a change in the dimensions of the arc column and its temperature, the intensity of the gas flows in the arc, and the size and temperature of active spots. At the end of a half cycle, volt-age and current, approaching zero, decrease to such an extent that the arc is extinguished. The residual plasma in the arc gap starts to cool down rapidly. This is accompanied by a reduction of its conduction which is detected even after the passage of current through zero. In subsequent stages, energy supply increases, the plasma is heated and its conduction increase. At a specific voltage an arc discharge forms in a new half cycle.

The nature of variation of the electrical parameters of the arc gap from the instant at which current passes through zero to the ignition phase, as well as their magnitude and reproducibility in each subsequent half cycle, determines the stability of arcing as a whole.

The stable process of AC welding is characterized by low peaks of ignition voltage at the start of each half cycle or even by complete absence of these peaks, relatively high pre-arc current and rate of its increase, and by higher conduction and duration of existence of residual plasma.

An unstable process is indicated by a high ignition voltage, which may reach the open circuit voltage of the power source (in an extreme case, the arc does not form) , a low pre-arc current and a low rate of its increase, and a low conduction of residual plasma.

Over a period of many years, investigators have carried out semi-quantitative evaluations of the stability of the process in a direct link with the examined welding materials or power sources. It is proposed to characterize the stabilizing properties of electrodes by the stability coefficient which takes into account the frequency of natural breaks of the arc in AC welding. The method is simple and was also used by other investigators. Someone improved the using method using a special device for automatic arc ignition after its separation.

The method is used most extensively for this application. It is based on determining the mean arc length at separation during multiple repetition of the same experiment. The method makes it possible to determine the effect of a large number of different chemical compounds on the breaking arc length. As shown later, arc elongation is accompanied by unavoidable changes of its thermal and electrical characteristics, so that a number of additional perturbations are introduced into the arc process when using this method.

It is proposed to measure the arc voltage separately in half cycles with straight and reverse polarity. In this case, the ignition voltage is added up with the arc voltage. The method makes it possible to evaluate arc stability to a certain extent and does not require complicated equipment.

After arc extension during the subsequent passage of current through zero, the residual plasma and its conduction drop. The duration of existence of residual plasma rapidly cools down and its conduction determine the nature and parameters of arc reignition and, it is believed, can be used as a sufficiently objective criterion for evaluating arc stability.

Someone measured the conduction of residual plasma in relation to the welding conditions and the composition of electrode coatings using the method of probing the arc gap. When examining the process of welding with thick coated electrodes, there were considerable procedural problems when using this method because of the short arc length and the presence of a deep 'sleeve' produced from the coating.

It is more convenient to probe the arc gap using the open circuit voltage of the power source. However, a higher voltage may heat the residual plasma, thus distorting the experimental results.

It is proposed to evaluate arc stability on the basis of the rate of increase of current during arc reignition in each half cycle. The rate of increase of current is recorded on the screen of an oscilloscope in the form of phase trajectories. The di/dt derivative does not change its sign but during transition through zero its value rapidly decreases. Non-linear shunts greatly increase the accuracy of measuring the current at low values. However it is showed that the method cannot be used to compare arc stability in welding under different welding currents, since the rate of current variation (di/dt) during the passage of current through zero is determined by its amplitude value (at constant frequency) , i. e. a reduction of current reduces the value of di/dt. This means that at low currents the arc cannot burn. However, this is not confirmed by experiment. Consequently, the authors proposed to evaluate the stability of reignition (on the basis of phase trajectories) using the relationship

$$K_i = \frac{di_2/dt}{di_1/dt} 100\%$$ (1. 1)

Where K_i is the parameter of reignition of the AC arc; di_1/dt tis the maximum rate of variation of welding current during arc reignition.

Assume that coefficient K_i can be used efficiently because it is not necessary to calibrate devices and measure the absolute values of derivatives. However, to obtain accurate values of K_i, it is necessary to examine phase trajectories for a long period of time (welding with three to five elec-trodes). Unfortunately, there are no specific examples of using the method, so that it is difficult to evaluate its reliability and efficiency. The method requires a device for synchronizing operations with equipment for filming the oscilloscope screen, as well as a system for switching on the beams.

The rate of passage of current through zero is determined only by the power source characteristic and consequently, the effect of the properties of welding materials on di/dt is only slight.

Combining in a single coefficient the parameters of metal transfer, arc reignition, and the properties of the plasma-forming gas and welding transformers:

$$K = \frac{I_{cr}}{\tau} = \frac{\omega}{2\arcsin\frac{U_i}{U_m}}\left(I_m\sin\varphi - 2en_{oe}r_c\sqrt{\frac{8\pi KT}{m_i}}\right) \tag{1.2}$$

Where I_{cr} is the arc current below which the arc can be extinguished during the passage of an electrode metal droplet through it; τ is the time during which the voltage in the arc gap is lower than the ignition voltage; r_c is the radius of the electrode metal droplets; n_{oe} is the electron concentration in the arc column; m_i is the mass of the atom of the plasma-forming gas; T is the plasma temperature in the arc column; U_m and I_m are the amplitude values of the open circuit voltage of the transformer and welding current.

It is reported that this parameter can be used only if metal transfer takes place without short circuiting.

To determine parameter K it is necessary to: carry out high-speed filming of the arc and synchronous loop oscillographic recording of arc voltage and current; measure U_i; determine τ; determine the grain size composition of electrode metal droplets; measure the dimensions of droplets r_c flying through the arc gap at the end of a half cycle i. e. in the period from $\tau/2$ to the end half cycle; take into account m_i; measure concentration n_{oe}; determine the values of U_m and I_m.

The authors believe that this method is highly laborious and this will prevent its wide application.

Taking into account that parameter K was developed for welding without short circuiting, it should be mentioned that it cannot be used for manual arc welding with coated electrodes, because in this case, metal transfer takes place mainly with short circuits. In addition, the presence of a lip from the coating at the electrode tip prevents the use of filming for determining r_c and the instant of droplet separation form the electrode. Therefore, this parameter cannot be used even if metal transfer in coated electrode welding takes place without short circuits (welding with rutile coated electrodes under 'forced' conditions).

In the method, the stabilizing properties of welding electrodes are evaluated on the basis of the extent of distortion of the welding current curve determined as the ratio of the tangent of the angles β and α:

$$A = \frac{\tan\beta}{\tan\alpha} \tag{1.3}$$

Arc stability increases with an increase of this ratio to unity. The extent of distortion of the current curve depends on both the electrical properties of the arc and the design feature of the transformer, and the criterion takes this into account. In fact, this criterion can be represented in the from

$$A = \frac{\sqrt{2}\,U_{o.c}\sin\varphi - U_a}{\sqrt{2}\,U_{o.c}\sin\varphi + U_a} \tag{1.4}$$

It can be seen that criterion A includes the characteristics of transformer design $U_{o.c}$, and arc U_a. Investigations carried out to determine A show that the criterion reflects with sufficient reliability the effect of characteristics of welding materials and the transformer. However, an accurate determination of the position of the tangents on the current oscillograms is difficult. The high error of calculating the values of A is a serious disadvantage of the method. Methods of increasing the accuracy of the position of the tangents, increase the accuracy of evaluation but, at the sane time, make the procedure more complicated because it is necessary to determine the transformer parameters under idling conditions.

It is proposed to evaluate arc stability in welding with DC and AC on the basis of the area of the 'working field' of the characteristic $U_a = f(I_w)$, obtained on a cathode oscilloscope (display, graph plotter) by superimposing a set of curves $U_a = f(I_w)$ on each other during a specific welding period. This results in the formation of an illuminated 'working field'. Arc stability increases with a reduction of this field. However, a contradiction is detected in the actual results. For example, the working field for arc voltage in basic electrodes is smaller than for rutile electrodes, regardless of the higher stabilizing properties of the former.

The method based on determining the minimum open circuit voltage of the welding transformer $U_{o.c}^{min}$ at which the arc still runs without breaks satisfies quite efficiently the practical requirements. It is proposed to use a transformer with a regulated voltage $U_{o.c}$. In the initial stage, the value of $U_{o.c}^{min}$ for a specific electrode is determined and, knowing the open circuit voltage of the transformer, it is possible to evaluate the 'reserve' of open circuit voltage $\Delta U_{o.c}$ which determines the reliability of reignition with the electrode coating properties (on the basis of $U_{o.c}^{min}$) and the transformer properties (on the basis of $U_{o.c}$) also taken into account:

$$U_{o.c} = U_{o.c} - U_{o.c}^{min} \tag{1.5}$$

One of the disadvantages of the method is that it is necessary to record arc breaks which are clearly visible when an arc is finally extinguished or extinguished and then again ignited spontaneously after a period exceeding $0.2 \sim 0.5s$. Because of the specific features of the human eye, arc extension in a time equal to one or several half cycles cannot be recorded visually. The number of half cycles in which the arc does not ignite but there is no final in the arc can reach, according to our data, up to 20% of the total number of half cycles. This arcing process cannot be regarded as stable. It is therefore necessary to determine voltage $U_{o.c}^{min}$ on the basis of the principle of absence of both final arc breaking and half cycles with no arcing. To solve this problem, it is necessary to use the methods of quantitative evaluation of the electrical and time parameters of arc reignition.

It is proposed a method of determining voltage $U_{o.c}^{min}$, using the mean value of the arc reignition voltage in the half cycles with reverse polarity $+U_i^n$, and the curves linking parameter $U_{o.c}^{min}$ and U_i^n, in relation to the properties of the welding circuit (on the basis of the oscillograms arc voltage). This approach is justified and, the authors believe, reflects the state of the arc gap in the most important pre-arc period.

The method is also interesting. It is based on using a nonlinear shunt for measuring the pre-arc current, which characteristics the residual conduction of plasma and, consequent, the ignition process.

Thus, the stability of AC arcs is determined by the processes taking place in the transition Period. The arc is stable if the heat losses into the surrounding space are compensated by the electric power supplied.

The condition of dynamic stability of the arc gap in the range of zero currents is described by the inequality

$$1/(CR_0) > 1/\theta \tag{1.6}$$

where R_0 is the resistance of the arc gap; θ is the time constant of the arc ($\theta = Q_0/P_0$), i. e. the time during which the energy of bodies Q_0, situated in the arc gap, is fully scattered and the mean power of the loss is equal to P_0.

Inequality (1.6) shows that arc stability is characterized most efficiently by the parameters reflecting the resistance (or conduction) of the arc gap.

Arc reignition will now be examined. In each new half cycle there is a specific period during which the power supplied to the electrode reaches the level required to restore the arc discharge. If U_i and I_i are the voltage at the electrodes and the current in the inter electrode space at discharge restoration, the parameter of arc stability ($\Omega^{-1} \cdot s^{-1}$) can be written in the form

$$B_i = I_i / U_i t_i \tag{1.7}$$

The ignition voltage can be expressed as follows

$$U_i - U_{o.c} \sqrt{?} \sin(\omega t_i + \phi) \tag{1.8}$$

Where ϕ is the shift phase angle between the current and open circuit voltage. This equation gives

$$t_i = \frac{\arcsin \dfrac{U_i}{U_{o.c} \sqrt{2}} - \phi}{\omega} \tag{1.9}$$

ω will be replaced by $2\pi f$ and Ep (1.9) substituted into Ep (1.7). Finally, the following is obtained:

$$B_i = \frac{2\pi f I_i}{U_i \left(\arcsin \dfrac{U_i}{U_{o.c} \sqrt{2}} - \varphi\right)} \tag{1.10}$$

Parameter B_i includes the main parameters of the electric circuit and reflects their effect on arc stability. Its value increases with an increase of current I, frequency, voltage $U_{o.c}$, angle ϕ and a reduction of voltage U_i.

In the initial stage of the investigations a method was developed of evaluating the stability of AC arcs using an 8SO-4 loop oscilloscope (Germany) and a non-linear shunt High frequency gal-va-nometers (intrinsic oscillation frequency 0.5×10^4 and 1×10^4 Hz) were used. Aerial photo film with a sensitivity of 1200 units to GOST 1069 120 mm wide was used. The recording speed was 9m/s.

The measurement circuit is shown in Figure 1.2. The arc voltage was fed through the resistance box R4 to the galvanometer G3. A voltage proportional to the welding current was recorded from the inductionless water-cooled shunt R_s. Welding was carried out using a TSD-500 trans-former ($U_{o.c} = 80$V) with a switched-off choke coil and an RB-300 ballast rheostat connected in series. Since ignition currents I_i, for different electrodes can differ by more than an order of magnitude, I_i was recorded using two variants of parallel non-linear shunts with different sensitivity. The signals from the shunts travelled to two galvanometers in the same group (G1 and G2). A typical oscillo-gram is shown in Figure 1.3.

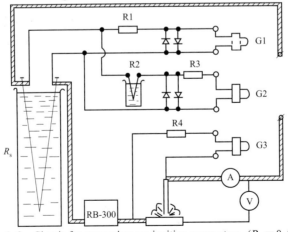

Figure 1.2 Circuit for measuring arc ignition parameters ($R_s = 0.078\Omega$)

A typical histogram of the distribution of voltage at arc ignition for electrodes with rutile and calcium flurion coatings [Figure 1.4 (b)] shows that their stabilizing properties greatly differ. In welding with rutile coated electrodes which ensure stable arcing, the value of U_i is low and slightly differs from the statistically most probable values. In welding with calcium fluorine-coated elec-trodes U_i is high. At the same time, the range over which the voltage varies widens. The distribu-tions of current [Figure 1. 4 (a)] and arc ignition time [Figure 1. 4 (c)] are similar.

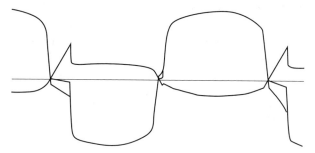

Figure 1. 3   Typical oscillogram of the AC welding process obtained using non-linear shunts.

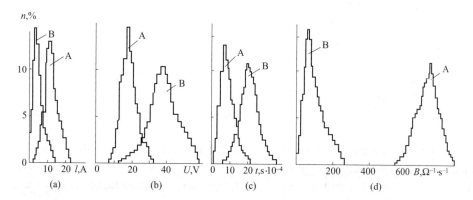

Figure 1. 4   Distribution of the probability density of current (a) and voltage (b) at arc ignition, the duration of the pre arc period (c) and stability parameter Bi (d)：A) rutile electrode; B) basic electrodes.

The stability parameter can be represented by the resultant values of the distributions for U_i, I_i or t separately. However, parameter B_i is more suitable in a number of cases. This parameter combines the above parameters and characteristics the conduction of the arc gap. For example, for electrode types with rutile and calcium fluorine coatings, examined by the authors of this work, B_i is respectively 710 and 43 $(\Omega^{-1} \cdot s^{-1})$.

In the first stage of development of the method investigations were carried out on electrodes with a different ratio of $CaCO_3$ to ferrite in the coating. The total content of the compounds was constant (52%). The remaining part of the coating consisted of rutile, ferromanganese, ferrosilicium and iron powder. The ratio of these components was not varied. Some of the electrodes were produced using sodium water glass, others with potassium water glass. The electrode diameter was 4mm. the coating thickness per side 1.1mm. The power source was represented by TSD-500 and STE transformers connected in series, with the total $U_{o.c} = 135V$.

To examine the processes in greater detail, the choke coils of the transformers were switched off and the welding current was regulated with ballast rheostats.

The arc stability parameter increases with a reduction of the CaF_2, content of the coating. An especially large increase of B_i is detected in series K electrodes, which contain a potassium compound in the coating.

For the same composition of the coating, parameter B_i is lower in the half cycle in which the cathode forms on the pool. This difference increases with a reduction of the stabilizing properties of the coating. This conclusion was confirmed when testing electrodes of many experimental and industrial grades with tulle and calcium fluorine coatings. The resultant relationship between current and voltage for any half cycle with the same current polarity can be expressed by the equation $P = U_i I_i$ const, and this confirms the assumption according to which the arc reignition power is constant. However, if different current half cycles are compared, this power is no longer different. For a positive current half cycle (positive on the electrode), the relationship between U_i and I_i is described accurately by the empirical expression:

$$+U_i = \frac{100}{+I_i} + 20 \tag{1.11}$$

and for a negative half cycle it has the form

$$-U_i = \frac{25}{-I_i} + 10 \tag{1.12}$$

Consequently, in the current half cycle in which the cathode forms on the pool, the supplied power, required for restoring an arc discharge, is considerably higher as a result of a simultaneous increase of U_i and I_i. At the same time, the points determining the values of U_i and I_i for different current half cycles (in the same experiment) are usually distributed along a straight line directed to the origin of the co-ordinates. The cotangent of the angle of inclination of these straight lines represents the conduction of the arc gap at arc reignition, and it has the same value for direct and reverse current half cycles. The value of B_i for different half cycles differs, since the same conduction is reached more rapidly in the case in which the cathode is represented by the electrode and not the pool.

The asymmetry of parameter B_i in half cycles with different polarity confirms that formation of the cathode on the pool is more complicated from the energy viewpoint than on the electrode. It is evident that this is associated with a lower mean temperature of the molten pool metal and a higher cooling rate of active spots as a result of heat removal into the workpiece.

The effect of welding current on B_i is studied Welding was carried out with electrodes 4mm in diameter with a basic coating and the power was supplied by an STSh-500-80 transformer ($U_{o.c} = 80V$). B_i increases in proportion to welding current at both polarities, but is again lower when the cathode forms on the pool.

An increase of welding current increases the temperature and mass of molten metal. This increases the thermal inertia of the electrodes and energy of the bodies situated in the arc gap. The time constant of the arc, which increases as a result of this process, reduces the resistance of the arc gap and facilitates arc reignition.

The experiments show that for power sources without a choke coil, the threshold value of the stability parameter in the positive half cycle in which arc breaks start to take place, equals approximately $150 \pm 20 \Omega^{-1} \cdot s^{-1}$.

It was reported that, to ensure reliable arc reignition, the voltage applied to the arc gap must be higher than the maximum ignition voltage U_i^{max}. B E Paton recommends to take into account voltage U_i^{max} and the arc is excited not only in half cycles in which the consumable electrode acts as the cathode. To verify this assumption the authors carried out experiments using the following proce-dure. The parameters U_a and $U_{o.c}$ were recorded in a loop oscilloscope during multiple elongation of the arc to breaking. The oscillographic data were used to determine the value of U_i in the last half cycle prior to arc breaking. The value was then compared with the amplitude values of open circuit voltage $U_{o.c}^a$. As shown by the experiments, in most cases, the arc did not ignite in the half cycle with reverse polarity.

Thus, the condition for reliable arc reignition in AC welding has the form

$$U_{o.c}^a \geqslant +U_i^{max} \tag{1.13}$$

Consequently, to evaluate the reliability of arc reignition, It is necessary to determine the voltage $+U_i^{max}$. This can be carried out by selecting the highest values of $+U_i$ recorded during the experiment. However, the values of $+U_i^{max}$, determined by this procedure, vary greatly from experiment to experiment (by 10-15V). The investigations show that the distribution of voltage $+U_i$ in welding with electrodes is usually governed by a normal law. Consequently, using the rule of three sigma $+U_i^{max}$ is determined with a reliability of 99.7% using the following equation

$$+U_i^{max} = U_i^m + 3\sigma \tag{1.14}$$

Where σ is the root mean square deviation of the distribution of probability densities of the parameter $+U_i$.

Knowing the value $+U_i^{max}$ and taking into account condition (1.13). it is possible to calculate the minimum open circuit voltage of a welding transformer at which the arc should run without break:

$$U_{o.c}^{min} = \frac{+U_i^{max}}{\sqrt{2}} = \frac{+U_i^m + 3\sigma}{\sqrt{2}} \tag{1.15}$$

In developing the procedure, it was determined that voltage U_i is almost independent of the experimental conditions: welding conditions, open circuit voltage, inductance of the transformer. The values of $+U_i$ can be used as a simple and suitable characteristic of the stabilizing properties of the welding material (electrode).

The proposed parameters B_i, U_i and $U_{o.c}^{min}$ have certain advantages and disadvantages. The stability parameter B_i can be used for a quantitative evaluation of the effect of the composition of electrode coatings, welding conditions and the characteristics of power sources on arc stability. However, in this case, it is required to standardize the experimental conditions. For example, the same power source should be used when examining electrodes and welding conditions or, vice versa, the same electrode grade and welding conditions should be studied when testing transformers.

It is often convenient to use the initial voltage as a stability parameter (or a derivative of this voltage, $U_{o.c}^{min}$), since U_i is almost independent of the open circuit voltage of the transformer and depends only slightly on the inductance of the welding circuit and welding current.

If loop oscilloscopes are available, these parameters can be utilized in almost any laboratory. However, the high labour content of statistical processing the oscillograms must be taken into account.

Chapter 2　Arc Welding Power Source

2. 1　Classification of Power Source

Arc welding power sources provide the required voltage and current for the welding operation. There are many types of welding power sources due to the unique requirements related to different welding processes. Welding power sources can be classified according to certain output features. A power source can supply alternating current (AC), direct current (DC), or both. The output of a power source can also be classified as constant current, constant voltage, or both. A power source may also provide a pulsing output mode.

2. 1. 1　AC Power Supplies

2. 1. 1. 1　Welding Transformer

Arc welding requires low-voltage and high-current between an electrode and the work piece. The voltage provided through the utility power line is too high to use directly in arc welding. A transformer is usually used to convert the high voltage and low current utility electricity into a high current and low voltage power, typically between 20 to 80 volts.

Figure 2. 1 shows the basic elements of a welding transformer. For a transformer, the relationship between the winding turns and the input/output voltages can be expressed as follows:

$$\frac{N_1}{N_2} = \frac{E_1}{E_2} = \frac{I_2}{I_1} \tag{2.1}$$

Where N_1 and N_2 are the numbers of turns on the primary and secondary winding of the transformer, respectively. E_1 is the input voltage, E_2 is the output voltage. I_1 and I_2 are the input and output current, respectively. Based on equation 2. 1, when the number of turns in the secondary winding is decreased, the output voltage is reduced. On the other hand, a large secondary current can be obtained since the primary-secondary current ratio is inversely proportional to the ratio of number of turns in the primary and secondary winding.

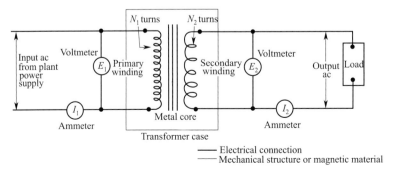

Figure 2. 1　Basic electrical elements of a welding transformer.

The output current of a transformer power supply is controlled by changing the magnetic coupling between the primary and secondary coil or by adjusting the inductance of the circuit. The output of a transformer may be directly applied for proper welding conditions. However, generally an impedance is inserted in series with the transformer and the work load. The electrical characteristics for welding are adjusted by the impedance.

There are several transformer designs to provide desired output volt-ampere characteristics for an arc welding condition, including tapped secondary coil control, movable-coil control, movable-shunt control, movable-core reactor, saturable reactor control. These designs are briefly described as follows.

(1) Tapped secondary coil control

The configuration of the tapped secondary coil transformer can be represented by Figure 2. 1. In this type of transformer, a set of taps are installed in the secondary winding coil. By choosing different tapes, the number of turns in the secondary winding can be changed, which will directly adjust the output volt-current characteristics for a proper welding condition. Reducing the secondary turns decreases the open circuit voltage and increases welding current. Tapped secondary coil transforms are cheap and the most widely used welding power supplies.

(2) Movable-Coil Control

In a movable-coil transform, both primary and secondary coils are located on an elongated metal core. On the core, one of the coils is fixed, while the other coil is movable. For most cases, the position of secondary coil is fixed. The primary coil is normally attached on a movable compo-nent; therefore, the coil can be adjusted to move closer or farther away from the secondary coil.

Changing the distance between the primary and secondary coil adjusts the inductive coupling between the two coils. When the two coils are farther apart, the output voltage-current curve becomes more vertical, resulting a smaller maximum short-circuit current value. Conversely, when the coils are closer, a larger maximum short-circuit current and a flatter voltage-current curve are obtained.

(3) Movable-Shunt Control

In this type of transformer, the primary and secondary coils are fixed on a metal core. A movable shunt between the primary and secondary coil is used to block the magnetic coupling of the primary/secondary coils. The magnetic shunt is made of the same material as that used for the metal core. The output is controlled by the amount of blocking from the shunt.

As the shunt is moved into the position between the primary and secondary coil, it blocks and diverts the magnetic flux path from the primary coil to the secondary coil. This causes the slope of the output voltage-current curve to decrease. Conversely, the voltage-current slope increases as the shunt is moved out, and the maximum output current is obtained when the shunt is completely separated from the primary and secondary coils.

(4) Movable-Core Reactor

Figure 2. 2 shows the basic design of movable-core reactor transformer. In this design, a reactor is connected in series with the transformer and the working piece. The inductance of the re-actor is varied by moving a movable metal section into or out of the reactor core. As the movable section withdraws from the reactor core, the inductive reactance reduces due to the air gap, allowing a large welding current. As the movable section moves into the reactor core, the inductive reactance increases, which causes a decrease in the welding current.

(5) Saturable Reactor Control

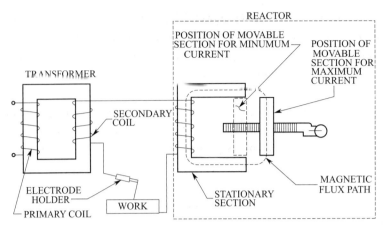

Figure 2. 2   Movable-core reactor type AC power supply.

In this design, the output voltage-current characteristics of the power supple is regulated by a saturable reactor connect to the main transformer. As shown in Figure 2. 3, a DC circuit is connected to the control coils of the saturable reactor. When a direct current flows through the coils, it controls the current flowing in the main coils that are connected to the main transformer. Therefore, the welding current is controlled by adjusting the DC current in the control coils.

The saturable reactor consists of coils in pairs that are wound in opposite direction. This design is used to cancel out the instantaneous voltage and current, reducing the circulating current in the circuit. Saturable reactors tend to cause distortion of the sinusoid wave from the main transformer. This may cause a problem in gas tungsten welding. Introducing air gaps in the reactor cores can reduce this distortion.

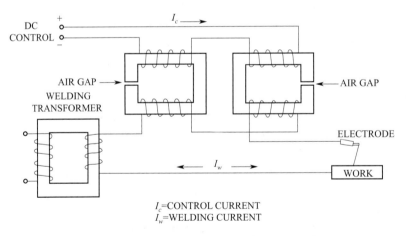

I_c=CONTROL CURRENT
I_w=WELDING CURRENT

Figure 2. 3   Saturable reactor type AC power supply.

2. 1. 1. 2   Square Wave Power Supply

AC power supplies generally provide 60 Hz alternating current with a sinusoidal waveform. After each half cycle, the current reaches zero and changes its direction. With sinusoidal waveforms, this reversal occurs slowly. At this zero-crossing, the low current will cause the lost of the arc and the welding arc requires reignition, which requires high open-circuit voltage that can be as high as 80 V. Some power supplies are installed with a high frequency reignition system that generates a high frequency spark and encourages the reignition. Even then, the instantaneously available current might be too low to assure a reliable arc ignition.

18

This problem can be solved by using a power supply with a square-wave form current output (Figure 2. 4). The square wave cycle passes through the zero point many times faster than that with a sinusoidal wave. Because of the rapid build up of current to current reversal, the reignition is enhanced even to the extant that deionization may not occur. With square wave current, the high-frequency reignition system is not necessary, removing the risks of high frequency radiation and damaging sensitive electronic equipment.

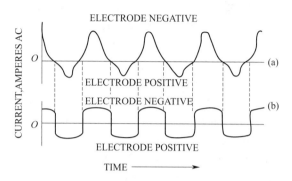

Figure 2. 4   Comparison of arc current waveform of
(a) AC magnetic amplifier and (b) square wave power supply.

There are various power supplies that can produce square wave forms. Most modern power supplies use a solid state circuit to generate a square wave AC current. The inverter-based power supply is a novel power supply that can provide a highly controlled square-wave output. More details about inverter-based power supply are discussed in section 2. 3. These power supplies can be adjusted to vary the wave frequency and the balance of positive and negative current. Increasing the current frequency results in a more focused arc, deeper penetration and faster travel speed. Biasing the square wave towards the positive half cycle will reduce penetration, which is desired when welding thin materials. On the other hand, reducing the positive portion will increase the penetration and give faster travel speed. Increasing the electrode negative portion also reduces the tungsten spitting.

2. 1. 2   DC power supplies

Most of the consumable electrode welding processes are done with DC power supplies. There are several types of DC power supplies, such as motor generator, transformer-rectifier, and inverter power supply. The most common DC power supplies are transformer-rectifier power supplies. This type of power supply converts the AC signal from the transformer into the DC signal through the rectifier.

A rectifier is an electrical device that converts AC, where the current periodically reverses the flow direction, to DC which flows in only one direction. There are many types of rectifiers, in-clu-ding vacuum tube, mercury arc valves and silicon-controlled rectifiers (SCR). With the advances in the semiconductor industry, solid state rectifiers, such as the SCR, have become the most impor-tant rectifier used in DC power supplies. The current flowing through a SCR is controlled by the voltage applied on the "gate." In the normal "off" state, the current is blocked by the SCR. When a positive signal applied to the gate and the gate-to-cathode voltage exceeds a certain threshold, the SCR turns "on" and current flows. The current will continue to flow until the voltage applied to the anode becomes negative with respect to the cathode. The SCR will only be turned "on" again if another gate signal is received.

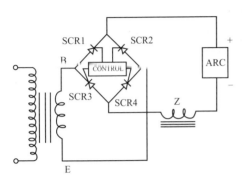

Figure 2. 5   DC power supply using an SCR bridge for control.

Figure 2. 5 shows a typical circuit of DC power supple with SCR. A full wave bridge SCR rectifier is connected to the transformer. In Figure 2. 5, when the voltage at point B is positive with respect to point E (positive half wave cycle), a gate signal is applied to SCR1 and SCR4, turning on the SCRs and allowing the current to flow through the load. When the polarity of point B and E reverses (negative half wave cycle), SCR1 and SCR4 are turned off, blocking the current. At the same time, a gate signal is applied to SCR2 and SCR3, which allows the current to flow through SCR2 and SCR3. By this way, the current flowing through the load is in the same direction even though the input AC current changed direction at each positive and negative half cycle. In Figure 5, it is necessary to precisely control the time that the gate signal is applied at any given half cycle.

The output from the rectifier still contains too much waviness. The current goes to zero every time a half wavereverses. Generally, a large inductance, Z, is connected to the circuit to filter the output wave shape. Theoretically, the output waviness can be totally smoothed with an infinitely large inductance. However, the bigger the filter inductor, the more expensive it is. In a three phage transformer-rectifier system, the phases are turned on by the SCRs at different times so the output waveform never goes to zero, thus the requirement for the size of the inductor is significantly reduced. Therefore, DC welding power supplies are generally three-phase SC systems. Normally, capacitor filters are also used to further reduce the ripple and obtain steadier DC output.

DC power supplies can be divided into constant-voltage and constant-current power supply. Constant-voltage power supplies are characterized by their typically flat voltage-current output curve (typical output from Figure 2. 5). Constant-voltage power supplies are commonly used for GMAW, FCAW, and SAW. The typical output of constant-current power supplies is characterized as droo-ping voltage-current curve (Figure 2. 7 shown in next section). Generally, a reactor is introduced between the transformer and the rectifier to obtain the drooping characteristics. Constant-current power supplies are typically used for SMAW, GTAW, PAC, PAW, and SAW.

2. 1. 3   Inverse Source of Arc Welding

Conventional welding power supplies are very heavy and large due to the huge magnetic parts in the power supply, such as the main transformer or the filter inductor. The novel inverter-based welding power drastically reduces the size and weight of these components as well as their electrical loss.

The inverter power supply is designed based on high power semiconductors such as the insulated gate bipolar transistor (IGBT). The IGBT is a three-terminal power semiconductor device that can provide fast switching. In an inverter power supply, the incoming power (50/60 Hz) is converted to DC by a full wave rectifier, then the IGBT switch (inverts) the DC power into high-frequency square wave AC power. The switching frequency is typically 10 kHz or higher. Since transformer size is inversely proportional to the applied frequency, the high frequency AC power allows the use of a much smaller transformer to produce the desired welding voltage or current. Inverter power supplies are compact, light and more efficient.

Inverter power supplies can provide constant-current, constant-voltage, or pulsed outputs.

The higher switching and control frequencies enable faster response time, resulting in more stable arcs and superior arc performance. Nowadays, IGBT-based inverter power supplies are controlled by a microcontroller. The electrical characteristics of the power are controlled precisely by software in real time. Software control allows advanced features for welding, such as power protection, variable frequencies, variable ratios and current densities through a welding cycle.

2.2 Electrical Characteristics of Power Source

Welding power supplies provide proper power for the welding arc. The output of a power supply can be characterized by the curve of output voltage versus current. There are two typical voltage vs. current curves that are used to describe the electrical characteristics of power sources: constant voltage output and constant current output.

2.2.1 Constant Voltage

For an ideal power supply (No resistance exists inside the power supply), the output voltage vs. current curve can be represented by a flat line. Theoretically, there is no limit to the amount of current that the power source can supply. No matter what current is drawn, the voltage remains constant. However, in reality, power sources do not provide constant output voltage at all currents. The internal resistance/impedance of the welding circuit will cause the output voltage to drop as the current increases.

Figure 2.6 shows a typical voltage-current curve for a constant-voltage power supply. The curve has a negative slope due to the internal resistance/impedance. Changing this resistance/impedance can adjust the slope of the voltage-current curve. The slope of the curve determines how much the current will change because of the fluctuation in the voltage. For example, when the voltage increases from point B (20V) to A (25V), the current decreases by 100 A (50%). This voltage-current characteristic can self-regulate arc length in welding process with constant electrode feeding, such as gas metal arc, flux cored arc, and submerged arc welding. During these welding processes, a slight change in arc length alters the voltage across the arc, which will cause a large change in welding current. An increase in arc length results in a large decrease in current thus decreases the electrode melting rate, and vice versa. This will automatically adjust the arc length back to original length.

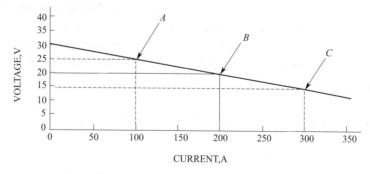

Figure 2.6　Voltage-current output for a constant voltage power supply.

2.2.2 Constant Current

When a power supply has a substantial internal resistance/impedance, its output voltage-current curve will have a very steep slope. A typical voltage-current output curve for a constant current power supply is shown in Figure 2. 7. This kind of voltage-current curve sometimes is referred as "drooper" because of the large downward (negative) slope of the curve. As shown in Figure 2. 7, a large change in the voltage only causes a small change in the current due to the steep slope. This voltage-current characteristic provides relatively constant current output.

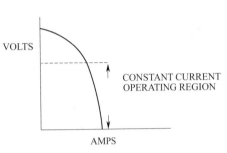

Figure 2. 7   Typical voltage-current output for a constant current power supply.

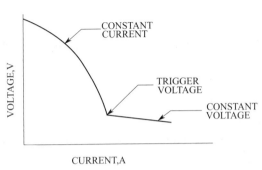

Figure 2. 8   Combination of constant voltage and constant current output.

Due to the stability of the current from a constant current power supply, the melting rate of a consumable electrode will remain relatively constant with a slight change in arc length. Power supplies with nearly constant current are typical used in covered electrode and gas tungsten arc welding. Constant current output offers benefit to less skilled welders, allowing greater changes in voltage with minor changes in current.

2. 2. 3   Combined Constant-Current and Constant-Voltage Characteristics

The electrical characteristics, the shape and slope of the output voltage-current curve, of power supplies are very important to the welding performance. Power supplies that can provide a combination of constant-voltage and constant-current output can be designed with electric control components, such as feedback circuits, magnetic amplifiers, solid state circuits. The slopes of the output voltage-current curves of these power supplies are adjustable. A power supply with combined electrical characteristics can be used for a variety of welding processes.

Figure 2. 8 shows a typical output curve with a combination of constant current and constant voltage from an electronically controlled power supply. This power supply is designed to be able to automatically change from constant current to constant voltage. The top part of the curve is essentially constant current, while the output switches to constant voltage below a certain trigger voltage. This type of output is generally used for SMAW. The constant current output will assist starting. If the arc length is too short, automatically switching to constant voltage output will avoid the electrode sticking in the melting pool.

2. 3   Selecting and Specifying a Power Source

The type of welding to be done dictates the type of welding machine to be used. This requires an analysis of the weldments to be produced, factors such as thickness of members, size of the weldment, materials involved, and method of application. The following information should be considered in order to make an intelligent power source selection.

① Process selection. The welding process to be used is based on the weldments to be produced.

② Welding current. The welding work determines the welding current type: that is, DC,

AC, steady state, pulsed, and type of pulsed current.

③ Machine rating. This determines the size of the power source. Heavier materials require larger electrode, which indicates a higher welding current. Machines are rated in amperes at a given voltage.

④ Type of power available. If power is not available from utility company, engine-driven generators are required. If utility power is available, the type the number of phases of AC power, and the voltage are specified.

⑤ Auxiliary devices. This includes water and shielding gas control systems, current control systems wire feeders, and any other factor required to allow manual, semiautomatic, or automatic welding.

⑥ Duty cycle. The duty cycle is a measure of the amount of work that the power source will do. Low-duty-cycle equipment is designed for light duty work. High-duty-cycle work equipment is designed for semi-automatic or automatic welding. Duty cycle is the ratio of arc time to total time and is explained below.

Rating of the machine is determined by tests and is related to the static volt-ampere characteristic curves. Machines are rated according to the duty cycle at a specific load voltage. Load voltage standard changes from 28 to 44v, depending on the size of the machine. Tests are run at the duty cycle specified to determine that specific temperatures within the machine are not exceeded. The method for testing and rating welding machines is in accordance with IEC 974-1 Standard.

In general, 20%-duty-cycle machines are designed light-duty work, 60%-duty-cycle machines are designed for manual shielded metal arc work and for some semi-automatic welding, and 100%-duty-cycle machines are designed for automatic welding. Welding machines can be used at higher levels than their duty-cycle rating and/or welding current rating under specific conditions. It may be necessary to use a machine to weld automatically for 100% of a 10-minute cycle, even though it has a 60% duty cycle rating. This is possible if the current is reduced below the rating. In other cases it may be necessary to use the machine at a higher current rating but for a short period of time.

Both of these situations can be resolved by use of the following formula:

$$\text{desired duty cycle } (\%) = \frac{(\text{rated current})^2}{(\text{desired current})^2} \times \text{rated duty current } (\%) \qquad (2.2)$$

For example, a machine rated at 300 A and 60% duty cycle needs to produce 350 A. What is the maximum cycle that can be used?

$$\text{desired duty cycle } (\%) = \frac{(300)^2}{(350)^2} \times 0.60 = \frac{90000}{12500} \times 0.60 = 44\% \qquad (2.3)$$

Thus, to use this machine at 350A, the duty cycle would have to be reduced to 44%. This means welding 4.4 minutes out of every 10 minutes.

In another situation, the same machine, a 300-A, 60%-duty-cycle machine, must be used on an automatic welding application. It must run at 100% duty cycle, or for a full 10 minutes. What output current could safely be obtained from this machine?

$$1.00 = \frac{(300)^2}{(\text{desired current})^2} \times 0.60 \qquad (2.4)$$

$$(\text{desired current})^2 = \frac{(300)^2}{1.00} \times 0.60 = 90000 \times 0.60$$

$$\text{desired current} = \sqrt{54000} = 232A$$

Thus, for an automatic operation running 10 minutes continuously, the machine output must not exceed 232 A. to avoid overloading the power source. These same determinations can be used without using the foregoing formula. Figure 2. 9 is the duty cycle versus rated current plot of this formula. The sloping lines show typical machine ratings, and by drawing a sloping line in parallel to those shown, different duty cycles or different load current requirements can be determined. Manufacturers provide duty cycle versus rated current curves for their machines.

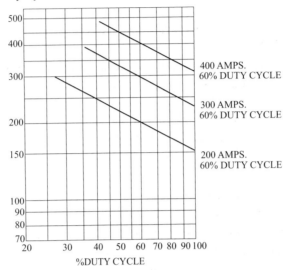

Figure 2. 9 The duty cycle versus rated current.

Specifying the Equipment

To specify a welding power source properly, the following data should be provided:

① Manufacturer's machine designation. This is determined by consulting the manufacturer's catalog or data sheets.

② Manufacturer's catalog number. This is shown in the manufacturer's literature and is usually given as a model number.

③ Rated load voltage. Welding machine for production requirements are rated in accordance with the standard. This system shows that minimum load volts are related to the ampere output of the machine. For example, the 200-A machine has a minimum load of 28V and it increases as the machine ratings are increased.

④ Rated load amperes. This is the rated current that the power source will deliver at the rated volts.

⑤ Duty cycle. Most production welding machines are rated at 60% or 100% duty cycle, in accordance with the standard. The manufacturer's data will provide this information.

⑥ Voltage of incoming power. The welding machine must match the power available at the fuse or circuit breaker box. Most industrial welding machines can be reconnected for specific voltages. The voltage that is available must be specified.

⑦ Frequency of incoming power. This is the frequency of the power provided by the utility company. In North America this is normally 60 Hz. In some locations in the world it is 25, 50, or 60Hz.

⑧ Number of phases of incoming power. For industrial equipment, three-phase power is normally provided. Single-phase power is used for limited input or low-duty-cycle welding machines. Some machines are capable of operating on either single- or three-phase power. For engine-driven welding machines it is wise to specify the maximum speed in rpm at no load. The information outlined above permits accurate specification of the welding power source desired. Probably the most important factor is to specify the precise voltage of power that will be available at the fuse box.

Chapter 3　Arc Welding Process

Welding techniques have become so versatile that it is difficult nowadays to define "welding". Formerly welding was "the joining of metals by fusion", that is, by melting, but this definition will no longer do. Even though fusion methods are still the most common, they are not always used. Welding was next defined as the "joining of metals by heat", but this is no longer a proper defini-tion either. Not only metals can be welded, so can many of the plastics. Furthermore, several welding methods do not require heat, such as cold pressure welding. Besides, we can weld with sound and even with light from the famous laser. Faced with a diversity of welding methods that increase year by year, we must adopt the following definition of welding: "Welding is the joining of metals and plastics by methods that do not employ fastening devices".

Welding activities may not make the newspaper headlines yet the technology of welding embraces a wide area. Even though electronics may owe much of its progress to joining techniques developed by welders, at the same time many electronic circuits are required to control the more intricate welding machines. Even radio frequencies have their applications in welding, in induction brazing and the ultrasonic testing of welds. Photography is also drawn into the scope of welding, for more photographic film is used in the X-raying and gamma graphing of welds than is used for ordinary photography. It is quite possible to use a mile of X-ray film in checking a welding job. Finally, welding has made important contributions to two outstanding technical creations of our time, the nuclear reactor and the aerospace rocket. Indeed, neither reactors nor rockets could be built without welding, for both are weldments. Welding is no longer what it was in time past, the simple matter of running a bead with a gas flame or a stick electrode.

As we know, there are in use about sixty methods of welding. No useful purpose would be served by listing all these methods. Instead, we shall begin a general description of the most availa-ble ones.

3. 1　Shielded Metal-Arc Welding

Shielded metal-arc welding is an arc welding process wherein coalescence is produced by heating with an electric arc between a covered or "coated" metal rod called the electrode and the work. Shielding is obtained from decomposition of the electrode covering, and filler metal is obtained from the electrode's metal core and metallic particles in the covering. The source of the shielding and filler metal varies with electrode design. The shielding and filler metal largely control the mechanical, chemical, metallurgical and electrical characteristics.

Shielded metal-arc welding is by far the most widely used of the various electric arc welding processes. Like the other electric arc welding processes, it employs the heat of the electric arc to bring the work to be welded and a consumable electrode to a molten state. The work is made part of an electric circuit known as the welding circuit (Figure 3. 1). This circuit includes a source of power, welding cables, an electrode holder, a ground clamp and the consumable welding elec-

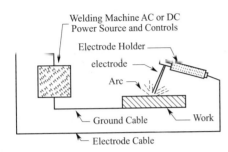

Figure 3. 1　Elements of a typical welding circuit for shielded metal-arc welding.

trode. One cable carrying current from the power source is attached to the work, and another cable is attached to the electrode holder.

Welding begins when an electric arc is formed or struck between the metallic electrode and the work. The intense heat of the arc melts the electrode and the surface of the work adjacent to the arc. Tiny globules of molten metal rapidly form on the tip of the electrode and transfer through the arc into the molten weld pool or weld puddle on the work's surface. If the welds are flat or horizontal, the actual transfer is induced by the force of gravity, molecular attraction and surface tension. Molecular attraction and surface tension are the forces that induce metal transfer from the electrode to the work where the weld is being made in the vertical or overhead position. The arc is moved along the work, melting and fusing the metal as it progresses. Since the arc is one of the hottest commercial sources of heat (temperatures above 9000°F/ 5000℃ have been measured at its center), this melting takes place almost instantaneously as the arc is applied to the metal.

In addition to establishing the arc and supplying filler metal for the weld deposit, the electrode introduces other materials into the arc, around it, or in both areas. Depending upon the type of electrode being used, the electrode covering performs the following functions:

① Help stabilize and direct the arc for effective penetration.

② Provide a gaseous shield to prevent atmospheric contamination.

③ Control surface tension in the pool to influence the shape of the bead formed when the metal freezes.

④ Act as scavengers to reduce oxides.

⑤ Add alloying elements to the weld.

⑥ Form a slag to carry off impurities, protect the hot metal, and slow the cooling rate.

⑦ Electrically insulate the electrodes.

⑧ Minimize spatter of weld metal.

⑨ Form a plasma to conduct current across the arc.

Another development in the evolution of arc welding electrodes has been the addition of iron powder to the covering or core. The iron powder is metal available for deposition in addition to that of the core wire. The presence of iron powder in the covering also makes more efficient use of the available arc energy. The thick covering increases the "crucible" effect at the end of the electrode, concentrating the heat and giving an automatically consistent arc length. When powdered iron is added in relatively large amounts, weld metal deposition rate and welding speed usually increase and weld bead appearance is improved.

Powdered iron covered electrodes also reduce the degree of welder skill needed to run theses electrodes, since the thick covering permits dragging the tip of electrode along the work's surface without shorting out and freezing. For this reason, the heavy powdered iron covered electrodes are frequently called "drag rods".

The arc welding process requires electric current (amperes) sufficient in amount to produce melting of the base and filler metal, and a proper voltage (volts) to maintain an arc. The sizes and types of electrodes currently available for shielded metal-arc welding define arc voltage requirements as 17 to 45 volts and current may be either alternating or direct, but it must be provided through a source that can be controlled to meet the complex variables of the arc welding process.

The most important factor to be considered in a power source is performance. What type of machine will make the job easiest to do and enable better welding to be done at a lower cost? There is one best way to do every welding job. A study of the type of welding to be done will generally tell whether alternating or direct current should be used for the job. This, in turn, will result in the selection of either an a-c or d-c power source or, as applications often justify it, a combination a-c/d-c power source. The performance characteristics of any one of these three power sources, however, must be the constant-current rather than the constant-voltage type. The constant-voltage machine is preferred for certain metal-arc welding processes particularly suited to mechanized welding.

The constant-current type of power source is preferred for manual welding since it is difficult for the welder to hold a constant arc length. The changing arc length causes arc voltage to increase or decrease, which in turn produces a change in welding current.

If the study of the welding application suggests a d-c power source, further consideration must be given to final selection since three different power sources are available-the welding gener-ator, the three-phase rectifier and the combination a-c/d-c, single-phase transformer-rectifier welding machines. This analysis is complicated and involves consideration of all factors, including performance, welding characteristics and equipment maintenance.

The ability of the motor-generator set to maintain a stable welding current output in spite of power line voltage variations is sometimes desired since it results in less interference with the opera-tor's manipulative technique. In certain types of electrodes, and for certain welding jobs, such as sheet metal and pipe welding, power line voltage variations are not tolerable. Using the motor-generator set on these applications will result in better welds at higher speeds.

The three-phase rectifier d-c power source lists among its advantages quiet operation, on mov-ing parts and simple control.

The three-phase rectifier d-c power source has the same application potential as the motor-gen-erator set, unless line voltage variations should constitute a problem.

Selection of power source should also take into consideration the type of input power available. Mo-tor-generator and rectifier-type welding machines normally perform only on three-phase power.

When only single-phase power is available, power source selection is reduced to making a choice between the a-c or combination a-c/d-c welding machines. The combination a-c/d-c source has the same advantages cited above for the three-phase, d-c rectifier since it can supply either straight or reverse polarity, d-c current. In addition, this power source offers alternating current at the output terminals. This greatly enhances the usability of the welding machine. Unfortunate-ly, since the a-c or combination a-c/d-c machine operates on a single-phase power supply, the d-c current arc is not as smooth as that produced by either the motor-generator or the three-phase recti-fier design.

3. 2 Gas Shielded-Arc Welding

The primary consideration in any welding operation is to produce a weld that has the same properties as the base metal. Such a weld can only be made if the molten puddle is completely protected from the atmosphere during the welding process. Otherwise atmospheric oxygen and nitrogen will be absorbed in the molten puddle, and the weld will be porous and weak. In gas-shielded arc welding, a gas is used as a covering shield around the arc to prevent the atmosphere from contaminating the weld.

Originally gas-shielded arc welding was developed to weld corrosion resistant and other difficult-to-weld metals. Today the various gas-shielded arc processes are being applied to all types of metals. Gas-shielded arc welding will eventually displace much of the Shielded Metal-Arc and Oxy-Acetylene production welding due to the superiority of the weld, greater ease of operation, and increased welding speed. In addition to manual welding, the process can be automated, and in either case can be used for both light and heavy gage ferrous and non-ferrous metals.

3. 2. 1　Specific Advantages of Gas-shielded Arc

Since the shielding gas excludes the atmosphere from the molten puddle, welded joints are stronger, more ductile, and more corrosion-resistant than welds made by most other welding processes. The gas-shielded arc particularly simplifies the welding of nonferrous metals, since no flux is required. Whenever a flux is needed, there is always the problem of removing traces of the flux after welding. Furthermore, with the use of flux there is always the possibility that slag inclusions and gas pockets will develop.

Another advantage of the gas-shielded arc is that a neater and sounder weld can be made because there is very little smoke, fumes, or sparks to contend with. Since the shielding gas around the arc is transparent, the welder can clearly observe the weld as it is being made. Even more important, the completed weld is clean and free of the complications often encountered in other forms of metallic-arc welding.

Welding can be done in all positions with a minimum of weld spatter. Inasmuch as the weld surface is smooth, there is a substantial saving in production cost because little or no metal finishing is required. Also, there is less distortion of the metal near the weld.

3. 2. 2　Types of Gas-Shielded Arc Processes

There are two general types of gas-shielded arc welding: Gas Tungsten-Arc (Tig), and Gas Metal-Arc (Mig). Each has certain distinct advantages, however both produce welds that are deep penetrating and relatively free from atmospheric contamination.

Most industrial metals can be welded easily with either the Tig or Mig process. These include aluminum, magnesium, low-alloy steel, carbon steel, stainless steel, copper, nickel, monel, inconel, titanium, and others.

Both welding processes can be semi-automatic or fully automatic. In semi-automatic the operator controls the speed of travel and directional. With the automatic process the weld size, weld length, rate of travel, start and stop are all controlled by the equipment.

3. 2. 3　Gas Tungsten Arc-Tig

In the Gas-Tungsten Arc process, a virtually non-consumable tungsten electrode is used to provide the arc for welding. During the welding cycle a shield of inert gas expels the air from the welding area and prevents oxidation of the electrode, weld puddle, and surrounding heat-affected zone. See Figure 3. 2.

In Tig Welding, the electrode is used only to create the arc. It is not consumed in the weld. In

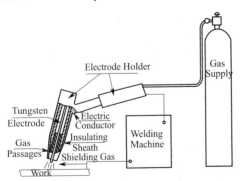

Figure 3. 2　Schematic diagram of gas tungsten arc equipment

28

this way it differs from the regular Shielded Metal-Arc process, where the stick electrode is consumed in the weld. For joints where additional weld metal is needed, a filler rod is fed into the puddle in a manner similar to welding with the Oxy-Acetylene flame process.

3.2.3.1 Welding Machines

Any standard DC or AC arc welding machine can be used to supply the current for Tig welding. However, it is important that the generator or transformer have good current control in the low range. This is necessary in order to maintain a stable arc. It is especially necessary when welding thin gage materials.

An AC machine must be equipped with a high frequency generator to supply an even current. Remember that in an AC welder, the current is constantly reversing its direction. Every time the current flow changes direction, there is a very short interval when no current is flowing. This causes the arc to be unstable, and sometimes go out. With a high frequency generator in the system a more even current flow is possible. This stabilizes the arc.

Both the resistor for the DC machine, and the high frequency generator for the AC welder can be obtained from most welding equipment dealers. Automatic or semi-automatic controls are also manufactured. These can be installed on the machines to regulate the flow of gas and the water supply for cooling.

Specially designed machines for tungsten-inert gas welding with all of the necessary controls are available. Many power supply units are made to produce both AC and DC current.

The choice of an AC or DC machine depends on weld characteristics that may be required. Some metals are joined more easily with AC current while with others better results are obtained when DC current is used. To understand the effects of the two different current an explanation of their behavior in a welding process is necessary.

3.2.3.2 Direct Current Reverse Polarity (DCRP)

With direct current the welding circuit may be either straight or reverse polarity. When the machine is set for straight polarity the flow of electrons from the electrode to the plate exerts considerable heat on the plate. In reverse polarity, the flow of electrons is from the plate to the electrode, thus causing a greater concentration of heat at the electrode.

The intense heat at the electrode tends to melt off the end of the electrode and contaminate the weld. Hence, for any given current DCRP requires a larger diameter electrode than DCSP. For example, a 1/16″ diameter tungsten electrode normally can handle about 125 amperes in a straight-polarity circuit. However, if reverse polarity is used with this amount of current the tip of the electrode would melt off. Consequently a 1/4″ diameter electrode would be required to handle 125 amperes of welding current.

Polarity also affects the shape of the weld. DCSP produces a narrow deep weld whereas DCRP with its larger diameter electrode and lower current forms a wide and shallow weld. For this reason DCRP is never used in gas tungsten-arc welding except in rare occasions for welding aluminum and magnesium.

3.2.3.3 Direct Current Straight Polarity (DCSP)

Direct current straight polarity is used for welding most metals because better welds are achieved. With the heat concentrated at the plate the welding process is more rapid, there is less distortion of the base metal, and the weld puddle is deeper and narrower than with DCRP. Since more heat is liberated at the puddle, smaller diameter electrodes can be used.

3.2.3.4 Alternating current (ACHF)

AC welding is actually a combination of DCSP and DCRP. Notice in Figure 3.3 (a) that half of each complete AC cycle is DCSP and the other half is DCRP. Unfortunately oxides, scale and moisture on the workpiece often tend to prevent the full flow of current in the reverse-polarity direction. If no current whatsoever flowed in the reverse polarity direction, the current wave would resemble something shown in Figure 3.3 (b) During welding operation the partial or complete stop-page of current flow (rectification) would cause the arc to be unstable and sometimes even go out. To prevent such rectification AC welding machines incorporate a high frequency current flow unit. The high-frequency current is able to jump the gap between the electrode and the workpiece, pier-cing the oxide film and forming a path for the welding current to follow.

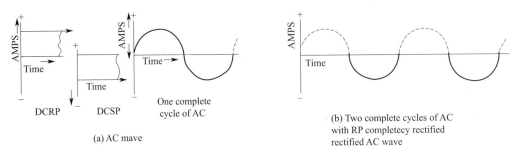

(a) AC mave

(b) Two complete cycles of AC
with RP completecy rectified
rectified AC wave

Figure 3.3   Characteristic of an AC wave.

3.2.3.5   Torches

Manually operated welding torches are constructed to conduct both the welding current and the inert gas to the weld zone. These torches are either air- or water-cooled. Air-cooled torches are designed for welding light gage materials where low current values are used. Water-cooled torches are recommended when the welding requires amperages over 200. A circulating stream of water flows around the torch to keep it from overheating. The tungsten electrode which supplies the welding current is held rigidly in the torch by means of a collet that screws into the body of the torch. A variety of collet sizes are available so different diameter electrodes can be used. Gas is fed to the weld zone through a nozzle which consists of a ceramic cup. Gas cups are threaded into the torch head to provide directional and distributional control of the shielding gas. The cups are inter-changeable to accommodate a variety of gas flow rates. Some torches are equipped with a "gas lens" to eliminate turbulence of the gas stream which tends to pull in air and cause weld contamination. Gas lenses have a permeable barrier of concentric fine-mesh stainless steel screens that fit into the nozzle.

Pressing a control switch on the torch starts the flow of both current and gas. On some equipment the flow of current and gas is energized by a foot control. The advantage of the foot control is that the current flow can be better controlled as the end of the weld is reached. By gradually deceasing the current it is less likely for a cavity to remain in the end of the weld puddle and less danger of cutting short the shielding gas.

Gas cups vary in size. The size to be used depends upon the type and size of torch and the diameter of the electrode.

3.2.3.6   Electrode

Basic diameters of non-consumable electrodes are $1/16''$, $3/22''$, and $1/8''$. They are either pure tungsten, or alloyed tungsten. The alloyed tungsten electrodes usually have one to two per cent thorium or zirconium. The addition of thorium increases the current capacity and electron emission, keeps the tip cooler at a given level of current, minimizes movement of the arc around the electrode tip, permits easier arc starting, and the electrode is not as easily contaminated by accidental contact with the workpiece. The two per cent thoria electrodes normally maintain their formed point for a greater period than the one per cent type. The higher thoria electrodes are used primarily for critical sheet metal weldments in aircraft and missile industries. They have little advantage over the lower thoria electrode for most steel welds. The introduction of the "striped" electrode combines the advantage of the pure, low, and high thoriated tungsten electrodes. This electrode has a solid stripe of two per cent thoria inserted in a wedge the full length of the electrode.

The diameter of the electrode selected for a welding operation is governed by the welding current to be used. Larger diameter tungsten electrodes are required with reversed polarity than with straight polarity.

3. 2. 3. 7 Electrode shapes

To produce good welds the tungsten electrode must be shaped correctly. The general practice is to use a pointed electrode with DC welding and a spherical end with AC welding.

It is also important that the electrode be straight, otherwise the gas flow will be off center from the arc.

3. 2. 3. 8 Shielding gas

Shielding gas for gas tungsten-arc welding can be argon, helium, or a mixture of argon and helium. Argon is used more extensively because it is less expensive than helium. Argon is 1. 4 times as heavy as air and 10 times as heavy as helium. There is very little difference between the viscosity of these two gases. Since argon is heavier than air it provides a better blanket over the weld. More-over, there is less clouding during the welding process with argon and consequently it permits better control the weld puddle and arc.

Argon normally produces a better cleaning action especially in welding aluminum and magnesium with alternating current. With argon there is a smoother and quieter arc action. The lower arc voltage characteristic of argon is particularly advantageous in welding thin material because there is less tendency for burning through the metal. Consequently, argon is used most generally for shielding purposes when welding materials up to 1/8″ in thickness both for manual welding and low speed machine welding.

The use of argon also permits better control of the arc in vertical and overhead welding. As a rule, the arc is easier to start in argon than in helium and for a given welding speed the weld produced is narrower with a smaller heat-affected zone.

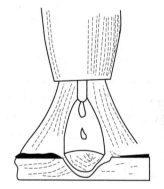

3. 2. 4   Gas Metal Arc-Mig

The Gas Metal Arc welding process (Mig) uses a continuous consumable wire electrode. The molten weld puddle is completely covered with a shield of gas. The wire electrode is fed through the torch at pre-set controlled speeds. The shielding gas is also fed through the torch. See Figure 3. 4.

Figure 3. 4   High temperature electric arc melts advancing wire electrode into a globule of liquid metal. Wire is fed mechanically through the torch. Arc heat is regulated by conditions pre-set on the power supply.

The welding can be completely automatic or semi-automatic. When completely automatic, the wire feed, power setting, gas flow and travel over the workpiece are pre-set and function automatically. When semi-automatic, the wire feed, power setting and gas flow are pre-set, but the torch is manually operated. The welder directs the torch over the weld seam, holding the correct arc-to-work dis-tance and speed.

3. 2. 4. 1 Specific Advantages of Mig Welding

The following are considered to be some of the more important advantages of Mig welding:

① Since there is no flux or slag and very little spatter to remove, there is a considerable saving in total welding cost. Generally speaking, weld cleanup is often more costly than actual welding time.

② Less time is required to train an operator. As a matter of fact welding operators who are proficient in other welding processes can usually master the technique of Mig welding in a matter of hours. All the operator has to do is pull the gun trigger and weld. His main concern is to watch the angle of the welding gun and speed of travel.

③ The welding process is faster especially when compared with metallic arc stick welding. There is no need to start and stop in order to change electrodes. As a rule weld failures are often due to the starting and stopping of welding, since this condition induces slag inclusions, cold lapping and crater cracking.

④ Because of the high speed of the Mig process, better metallurgical benefits are imparted to the weld area. With faster travel there is a narrower heat-affected zone and consequently less molecular disarrangement, less grain growth, less heat transfer in the parent metal, and, even more important, greatly reduced distortion.

⑤ Although originally Tig welding was considered more practical for welding thin sheet, because of its lower current, the development of the short circuiting transfer technique now makes it possible to weld thin stock equally as effectively with the Mig process.

⑥ Since Mig welding has deep penetrating characteristics, narrower beveled joint design can be used. Furthermore, the size of fillet welds is reduced by comparison to other welding methods.

3. 2. 4. 2　Welding current

Different welding currents have a profound effect on the results obtained in gas metal-arc welding. Optimum efficiency is achieved with direct current reverse polarity (DCRP). The heat in this instance is concentrated at the weld puddle and therefore provides deeper penetration at the weld. Furthermore, with DCRP there is greater surface cleaning action which is important in weld-ing metals having heavy surface oxides such as aluminum and magnesium.

Straight polarity (DCSP) is very impractical with Mig welding because weld penetration is wide and shallow, spatter is excessive, and there is no surface cleaning action. The ineffectiveness of straight polarity largely results from the pattern of metal transfer from the electrode to the weld puddle. Whereas in reverse polarity the transfer is in the form of a fine spray, with straight polarity the transfer is largely of the erratic globular type. The use of AC current is never recommended since the burn-offs are unequal on each half-cycle.

3. 2. 4. 3　Types of Metal Transfer

When welding with consumable wire electrodes, the transfer of metal is achieved by three methods spray transfer, globular transfer, and short circuiting transfer. The type of metal transfer that occurs will depend on electrode wire size, shielding gas, arc voltage, and welding current.

(1) Spray transfer

In spray transfer very fine droplets or particles of the electrode wire are rapidly projected through the arc plasma from the end of the electrode to the workpiece in the direction in which the electrode is pointed. The droplets are equal to or smaller than the diameter of the electrode. While in the process of transferring through the welding arc, the metal particles do not interrupt the flow of current and there is virtually a constant spray of metal.

Spray transfer requires a high current density. With the higher current, the arc becomes a steady quiet column having a well defined narrow incandescent cone-shape core within which metal transfer takes place. See Figure 3. 5 (a). The use of argon or a mixture of argon and oxygen is also necessary for spray transfer. Argon induces a pinching effect on the molten tip of the electrode,

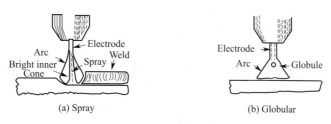

(a) Spray   (b) Globular

Figure 3. 5   Types of metal transfer

permitting only small droplets to form and transfer during the welding process.

With high heat input, heavy wire electrodes will melt readily and deep weld penetration becomes possible. Since the individual drops are small the arc is stable and can be directed where required. Owing to the fact that the metal transfer is produced by an axial force which is stronger than gravity, spray transfer is effective for out-of-position welding. It is not too practical for welding light gage metal because of the resulting burn through.

(2) Globular transfer

This type of transfer occurs when the welding current is low or below what is known as the transition current. The transition range extends from the minimum value where the heat melts the electrode to the point where the high current value induces spray transfer. Notice in Figure 3. 6, only a few drops are transferred per second at low current values, while mangy small drops are transferred at high current values.

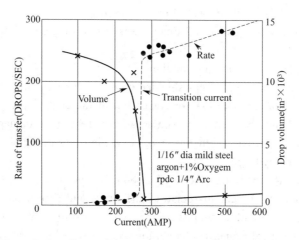

Figure 3. 6   Effect of current on the size and frequency of drops
transferred in an arc shielded by predominantly inert gas.

In globular transfer the molten ball at the tip of the electrode tends to grow in size until its diameter is two or three the diameter of the wire before it separates from the electrode and transfers across the arc to the workpiece. See Figure 3. 5B. As the globule moves across the arc it assumes an irregular shape and rotary motion because of the physical forces of the arc. This frequently causes the globule to reconnect with the electrode and workpiece, causing the arc to go out and then reignite. The result is poor arc stability, shallow penetration, and excessive spatter.

(3) Short circuiting transfer

The short circuiting transfer permits welding thinner sections with greater ease and is extremely practical for welding in all positions.

With this process a shallow weld penetration is obtained. It is generally considered to be the most practical at current levels below 200 amperes with fine wire of 0. 45″ or less in diameters. The use of fine wire produces weld pools that remain relatively small and are easily managed, making all position welding possible.

As the molten wire is transferred to the weld, each drop touches the weld puddle before it has broken away from the advancing electrode wire. The circuit is "shorted", and the arc is extinguished.

Electromagnetic "pinch force" squeezes the drop from the wire. The short circuit is broken and the arc reignites. "Shorting" occurs from 20 to 200 times a second according to preset controls. "Shorting" of the arc pinpoints the effective heat. The result is a small, relatively cool weld puddle which reduces burn-through. Intricate welds are possible in most all of the positions.

In short-arc welding, the shielding gas mixture consists of 25 per cent carbon dioxide, which provides increased heat for higher speeds, and 75 per cent argon which controls spatter. However, considerable usage is now being made of straight CO_2 where bead contour is not particularly important but good penetration is very essential.

3. 2. 5 CO_2 Welding

CO_2 Shielded consumable electrode arc welding is a new welding technique which came into being in 1950's.

As compared with other welding processes, CO_2 welding is high in efficiency, low in cost and ready for automation. It can ease the intensity of labor and improve the quality of welding. CO_2 welding is mainly applied to low-carbon steels, low-alloy steels, stainless steels, high-temperature steels, etc.

With all its advantages CO_2 welding will in many cases displace other types of welding processes. It promises a great prospect in welding 0. 5 to 2. 5mm sheets instead of gas welding and argon shielded arc welding.

3. 2. 5. 1 Carbon Dioxide as a Shielding Medium

Quite early in the development of gas shielded consumable electrode arc welding a search was made for a cheaper gas than argon to use for steel, but of the commercially available gases many could be rejected immediately because they would cause metallurgical damage to the weld, e. g. loss of ductility and gross porosity with nitrogen, oxidation and gross porosity with oxygen and porosity with acetylene or hydrogen.

Apart from the slightly oxidizing nature of carbon dioxide (chemical symbol CO_2), which increases with temperature as the gas dissociates, the gas would appear attractive as it is inexpensive and in plentiful supply. With a suitable filler wire composition it would be expected to deposit weld metal of good mechanical properties like argon-oxygen shielding. Moreover, the flow characteristics of CO_2 are such that the gas would issue in a non-turbulent manner from a MIG gun and effectively sweep the area to prevent contamination by the air. A suitable filler wire would therefore only have to be effective in compensating for oxygen and possibly carbon, instead of nitrogen, hydrogen and oxygen of the air.

The absence of a "finger" type penetration characteristic with CO_2 shielding would obviously be an added advantage over argon-oxygen mixtures for deep penetration welding.

There were however a number of problems which prevented CO_2 being used as a cheap alter-native shielding gas for steel. At the time these limitations seemed characteristic of the gas for welding and were not really thought to be surmountable. The need to combat rising labor costs and also to produce more welders focused the need36 for a semi-automatic welding process for steel, and the potential of CO_2 led to considerable research activity.

Three basic problems had to be solved before CO_2 could be rise for gas shielded metal arc welding of steel and "CO_2 welding" became an every-day welding process.

Porosity in the Welded Metal

If a reactive gas such as CO_2 shielding was used with the rimming steel filler wire normally used for flux covered electrodes, the weld metal contained extensive porosity. This was caused by the evolution of bubbles of carbon monoxide, which resulted from the reaction in the molten metal of the carbon in the steel with iron oxide or oxygen from the CO_2 atmosphere.

CO_2 welding wires now contain sufficient silicon, manganese and other elements to provide an "overkilled" weld composition so that porosity is not caused when CO_2 is used for gas shielded metal arc welding of steel.

3. 2. 5. 2   The Problems of Spatter

The manner in which droplets of metal are detached from the electrode in an atmosphere of CO_2 differs markedly from that in argon or argon-oxygen mixtures for the same welding conditions. Whereas in argon-oxygen the droplet rate is very rapid, and achieved at fairly low currents, droplets are only infrequently transferred in CO_2 and in a non-axial manner. By increasing the current to around 400A (with 1/16 in. diameter wire) an improvement is obtained, but these currents cannot be used for welding sheet thicknesses because abnormally high welding speeds would be required.

The "short circuiting arc" or "dip transfer" has now effectively improved the metal transfer characteristics in CO_2 at low currents.

3. 2. 5. 3   Positional Welding

Where CO_2 welding was first tried for vertical and overhead welding, the high currents required to produce a smooth metal transfer resulted in a weld pool too large for the operator to control, so that metal ran out of the joint.

The "short circuiting arc" has now made positional CO_2 welding a simple procedure because low currents can be used to make a small, quickly freezing weld pool; filler metal is added each time the wire tip automatically touches the weld pool (about 100 times a second).

These three problems were sufficient to inhibit the application of CO_2 welding in the early 1950s but have now all been overcome by developments in filler wire composition and power source design. Industry all over the world has not been slow to apply this new process and it has now become the most popular semi-automatic process for welding steel. The overwhelming success of the semi-automatic form arises from its high metal deposition rate coupled with excellent arc visibility—a combination not previously achieved by any other semi-automatic system for welding steel.

CO_2 welding is not, however, the universal process that is intended to replace more established conventional methods of welding steel. If a prospective purchaser of additional welding equipment had already built up years of experience in submerged arc welding and wished to augment his capacity for mechanized downhand welding of pressure vessels he would certainly not be advised to buy CO_2 welding equipment, since the submerged arc process retains its superiority for high quality welding over a range of plate thicknesses; thereafter electro-slag welding becomes more attractive. If, however, fully mechanized machines were being designed to weld ferrules into sheet metal domestic radiators or put nozzles into vessels by multi-pass welding, or if there was a considerable amount of semi-automatic welding of brackets, stiffeners and details that could not be mechanized, then CO_2 welding would be an attractive welding method.

3. 2. 6   Pulsed Arc Welding

Pulsed arc welding is a d-c welding system in which a single phase current is superimposed upon the constant voltage or d-c background current. This system is used in conjunction with Mig and Tig welding applications.

Mig pulsed arc welding is a modified form of spray transfer, producing a controlled and periodic melting off of the droplets followed by their projection across the arc. It is accomplished using a welding machine normally consisting of a three-phase transformer rectifier type, which provides a constant d-c voltage output, together with a single phase half-wave rectifier which is superimposed on the d-c or background current.

Both transformer rectifiers are mounted in a single configuration with appropriate controls for adjustment of the background and pulsed currents. The pulsed current is applied for a brief duration at regular frequencies, and thus results in a lower heat output than with pure sprayed transfer, yet the heat output is greater than with dip transfer. This makes possible the welding of thinner sections than could be handled with spray transfer, without38 the danger of poor fusion in the root pass as sometimes occurs with dip transfer. There is a regular and even penetration, no spatter, and the welds are of high quality and good appearance.

To obtain these conditions of transfer, it is necessary to have two currents fed to the arc, ①a background current that keeps the gap ionized and maintains the arc, and ②the pulse current which is applied at 50 or 100 Hz and which melts off the wire tip into a droplet which then is projected across the arc. These two currents must be accurately determined, if satisfactory welding conditions are to be obtained.

Pulsed arc welding offers the advantages of welding at a lower mean welding current, controlling the size of metal droplets transferred and using lower average welding currents for a given wire size. The power level is between the spray transfer and the dip transfer settings and fills an operational gap between them.

Pulsed arc welding also is used in Tig applications, particularly in the welding of tubing in a fixed position where satisfactory penetration and weld face contours can be maintained. The pulsed arc agitates the molten weld metal and thus minimizes the porosity. Compared with a steady arc, the pulsing arc increases the penetration, with less heat input into the joint; however, welding speeds are reduced 20% to 40%.

Generally, the pulsation rate is adjustable between one and 100 pulses/sec. A faster pulsation rate in a frequency range from 1000 to 20000 pulses/sec. can also be used. Current pulsation starts at the beginning of the current upslope time, increases in amplitude of the wave at high and low values, continues to pulse during the welding current level and begins to decrease in amplitude at the start of the current down-slope diminishing to a final current level at the end of down-slope time. The time between pulses at high current level and the time at low current levels may be varied to suit the individual application.

Non-uniform penetration is caused by the use of a too slow pulse frequency. Roughness of the weld surface on the inside of the tube or pipe may be undesirable for nuclear or other applications of high volume flow.

3.3 Submerged Arc Welding Fundamentals of the process

3.3.1 Definition and general description

Submerged arc welding is defined by the American Welding Society as an arc welding process wherein coalescence is produced by heating with an arc or arcs between a bare metal electrode, or electrodes, and the work. The arc is shielded by a blanket of granular, fusible material on the work. Pressure is not used and filler metal is obtained from the electrode and sometimes from a supplementary welding rod. The fusible shielding material is known as the melt, flux or welding composi-tion; however, for purposes of uniformity this material will be referred to as flux throughout this chapter, although it performs functions in addition to those of a flux.

3.3.2 Principles of operation

In submerged arc welding, there is no visible evidence of the passage of current between the electrode and the workpiece. The end of the electrode and the welding zone are always surrounded and shielded by an envelope of molten flux on which is superimposed a layer of un-fused flux in a granular state. The electrode is not in contact with the workpiece; the current is carried across the gap through the fluid flux. Fluxes are specialty manufactured mineral compositions formulated so that, even when they are brought to the high temperature of the welding zone, appreciable a-mounts of gas are not evolved. In their usual finely divided, granular free-flowing state, they are laid either manually or automatically along the seam to be welded in advance of the electrode.

Since the end of the electrode and the welding zone are completely covered at all times during the actual welding operation, the weld is made without the sparks, spatter, smoke or flash commonly observed in other arc welding processes. No protective shields or helmets are necessary; safety glasses should be worn as routine protection for the eyes and may be tinted for protection against flash from adjacent arc welding operations. Since welding in general may produce fumes and gases hazardous to health, it is common practice to provide adequate ventilation, especially where submerged arc welding may be done in confined areas.

The flux is the basic feature of submerged arc welding and makes possible the special operating conditions that distinguish the process. The flux, when cold, is a nonconductor of electricity, but in the molten state it becomes a highly conductive medium. It is necessary, therefore, to pro-vide an initial conductive path for the welding current when the weld is started. This is sometimes accom-plished, particularly with a-c power, by placing a small wad of steel wool between the end of the welding electrode and the workpiece before the welding current is switched on. When weld-ing current flows through this momentary short circuit, the steel wool ignites and starts an arc which melts the surrounding flux. Another method commonly used is to strike an arc beneath the flux by momentarily touching the end of the electrode to the workpiece. In still another method of initiating the process, a high-voltage, high-frequency current is superimposed on the welding cur-rent in order to create an ionized path before the electrode touches the work. The heat produced by these meth-ods causes the surrounding flux to become molten, thus forming39 a conductive path kept molten by the continued flow of welding current. The upper, visible portion of the flux is not melted. It remains unchanged in appearance and properties, and it can be reused.

In its molten state, the flux provides exceptionally suitable conditions for unusually high current intensities, thus generating great quantities of heat. The insulating properties of the flux concentrate this intense heat into a relatively small welding zone, where the continuously fed weld-ing electrode and the base metal are rapidly fused. The deep penetration associated with this con-cen-tration of heat makes smaller welding grooves practicable, thus reducing the amount of pro-gression (welding speed) possible.

Furthermore, the flux protects the molten pool against the atmosphere by sealing it in an enve-lope of molten flux. Flux acts as a cleanser for the weld metal, modifies its chemical composition and influences the shape of the weld metal area.

Because of the properties of flux, submerged arc welds can be made over a wide range of welding currents, voltages and speeds, each of which can be controlled independently of the other. Each of these factors of itself affects to some degree the shape of the weld metal area, the weld metal chemistry and fluxing activity as well as the mechanical and metallurgical properties of the joint.

Clearly, even relatively thick joints may be completed by submerged arc welding in a single pass or by means of two heavy single passes, one on each side of the joint, or by conventional multi-pass methods.

In single-pass welds, a considerable amount of base metal is fused compared to the amount of filler metal fused. The base metal, therefore, may greatly influence the chemical and mechanical properties of the deposit, making it unnecessary to use electrodes of the same composition as the base metal for welding many of low-alloy steels.

Welds made in this manner, under the protective layer of flux, have unusually good ductility, impact strength, uniformity, density and corrosion resistance, as well as low nitrogen content. Generally, the weight of the flux melted is equal to 1 to 1.5 times the weight of the filler metal added. Mechanical properties at least equal to those of the base metal are consistently obtained.

Welds of uniformly high quality require good-quality, homogeneous base materials, free from rust, scale, moisture and other surface impurities. Special welding techniques and pass sequences are necessary when less homogeneous base metals, containing slag, laminations or other imperfections, are welded. Segregated sulfides in the base metal are particularly undesirable, since heavy sulfur banding or segregation contributes to cracking along the dendritic boundaries as the weld metal cools. The extent of such cracking can be minimized by the use of multi-pass welding.

The distinct dendritic structure seen in macro-etched cross sections of single-pass welds made by this process has sometimes been misinterpreted. Dendritic structure, as encountered in castings, is generally considered undesirable, and it has been assumed that it is equally undesirable in weld metal. Test data and service experience, however, have proved conclusively that these assumptions are not warranted and that the welds are satisfactory in the as-welded condition.

Moreover, it has definitely been established that the protection afforded by the flux against atmospheric contamination has much to do with the exceptional mechanical properties of the weld deposit.

The chemical composition and properties of the multi-pass weld depend to a far greater extent on the composition of the electrode, the activity of the flux and the welding conditions used. The influence of the base metal can be minimized by welding procedures that restrict the amount fused into the weld metal area.

Factors for consideration in the choice of a particular installation may be: use of alternating or direct current, use of single or multiple arcs, type of control, type of power source and special applications.

3.4 Plasma Arc Welding

Plasma arc welding is an arc welding process wherein coalescence is produced by heating with a constricted arc between an electrode and the workpiece (transferred arc) or the electrode and the constricting nozzle (non-transferred arc). The general characteristics and electrical circuit used for plasma arc welding are shown schematically in Figure 3.7. The arc plasma or orifice gas indicated in Figure 3.7 is supplied through the torch at a flow rate of 1 to 15 cfh. Suitable gases are argon, a mixture of argon and hydrogen, or argon and helium, depending on the application. The gas flowing through the arc constricting nozzle protects the electrode from contamination and provides the desired composition in the plasma jet.

Relatively low plasma gas flow rates are used to avoid turbulence and undesirable displacement of the molten metal in the weld puddle. Since the low gas flow rates are not adequate for shielding the puddle, supplementary shielding gas is provided through an outer gas cup. The type and flow rate of supplemental shielding gas are determined by the welding application. Typical arc and shielding gas flow rate are 4 and 35 cfh, respectively.

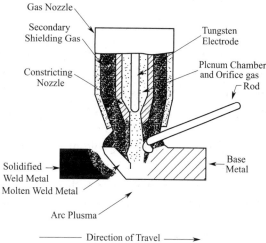

Figure 3.7 Transferred plasma arc process

3.4.1 Keyhole Action

ħ plasma arc welding, the term "keyhole" has been applied to a hole that is produced at the leading edge of the weld puddle where the plasma jet displaces the molten metal, allowing the arc to pass completely through the workpiece. As the weld progresses, surface tension causes the molten metal to flow in behind the keyhole to form the weld bead.

Key-holing can be obtained on most metals in the thickness range of 3/32 in. to 1/4 in. and is one of the chief differences between the plasma arc and gas tungsten-arc processes. Presence of the keyhole, which can be observed during welding, gives a positive indication of complete pene-tration.

3.4.2 Arc Shaping

The columnar nature of the constricted arc makes the plasma arc process to 44 variations in arc length. Since the unconstricted gas tungsten-arc has a conical shape, the area of heat input varies as the square of the arc length. A small change in arc length, therefore, causes a relatively large change in the unit area heat transfer rate. With the essentially cylindrical plasma jet, however, the area of heat input and intensity is virtually constant as arc length varies within normal limits.

3.4.3 Operating Data

Argon-hydrogen mixtures are used as the plasma and shielding gases for welding stainless steel. As in gas tungsten-arc welding, additions of hydrogen to argon produce a hotter arc and more effi-cient heat transfer to the workpiece. In this way higher welding speeds are obtained with a given arc current. However, higher percentages of hydrogen can be used with the plasma arc process than with gas tungsten-arc on a given material thickness and, therefore, a greater advantage can be real-ized from this technique. This ability to use greater percentages of hydrogen without inducing poro-sity may be associated with the keyhole process and the different solidification patterns which it produces.

Pure argon is used to weld reactive materials, which have a strong affinity for hydrogen, such as zirconium and titanium. Use of argon as the nozzle gas and CO_2 as the auxiliary shield has increased speeds on certain mild steel welding applications.

When making the second or cap pass on a joint requiring two passes, helium can be used for the plasma and shielding gases. The helium effluent does not have the momentum required to produce a keyhole, but this is not necessary on the cap pass.

3.4.4 Applications

Plasma arc welding has proved commercially important advantages in several specific areas of application. These include the welding of stainless steel tubing, making circumferential joints on copper-nickel and stainless steel pipe, and the welding of reactive metal compacts to form furnace electrodes. Development activities are under way on other promising applications including missile cases.

In general, any metal capable of being welded with the gas tungsten-arc process can also be welded with the plasma arc process. Advantages in either weld economics or reliability are obtained on metals and thicknesses which can be keyhole welded, with the exception of aluminum and mag-nesium. Development work is continuing with these two metals.

3.4.5 Summary

A plasma arc welding process has been developed that operates in the same field as gas tung-sten-arc welding and has advantage over it for some applications. Plasma arc welding can be used advantageously on all metals that would normally be gas tungsten-arc welded except aluminum and magnesium. In the thickness range where key-holing is obtained, plasma arc welding offers advantages over the gas tungsten-arc process in increased welding speed, uniform penetration, reduced joint preparation, reduced or eliminated filler metal requirements and less sensitivity to arc length variations.

Need for mechanical weld backing is eliminated when the key-holing plasma arc process is used, although gas backing is required to protect the weld underbead. Square butt joints are made in material up 45 1/4 in. thick with a single pass using the plasma arc process.

The plasma arc process has potential advantages on thin gage material and in other non-key-holing applications because of its relatively low sensitivity to changes in arc length and to joint mismatch.

Chapter 4　Other Welding Methods

4. 1　Resistance Welding

4. 1. 1　Introduction

The principle of resistance welding was discovered by the English physicist, James Joule, in 1856. In his experiments he buried a bundle of wire in charcoal and welded the wires by heating them with an electric current. This is believed to be the first application of heating by internal resistance for welding metal. It remained for Elihu Thompson to perfect the process and develop it for practical applications. In 1877 Thompson invented a small low-pressure resistance welding machine. Welding was accomplished with this machine by causing the internal resistance in the workpiece to generate the heat required to reach its plastic stage. For several years, little was done with this development, since it seemed to have little commercial value. Nevertheless, resistance welding was introduced commercially in the early 1880s as incandescent welding.

Resistance welding is a welding process that requires the application of both heat and pressure to achieve a sound joint. As shown in Figure 4. 1, there are a number of variants of the resistance welding process including spot, seam, projection and butt welding. It is an economical process ideally suited to producing large numbers of joints on a mass production basis.

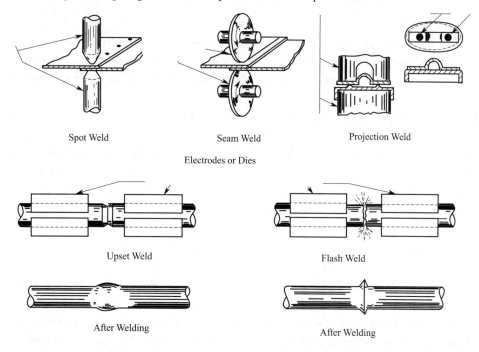

Figure 4. 1　Variants of resistance welding

Spot welding in particular has been used extensively in the automotive industry, albeit mostly for the joining of steel and in the aerospace industry for airframe components in aluminium alloys. Projection welding is generally used for welding items such as captive nuts onto plate. Seam welding is used in the production of thin sheet, leak-tight containers such as fuel tanks. Upset welding and flash welding, unlike spot and seam welding that require a lap joint, is capable of making butt welds. This is achieved by resistance heating the abutting faces and then forging them together.

4.1.2 Resistance Spot Welding (RSW)

The simplest form of the resistance welding process is resistance spot welding where the pressure is provided by clamping two or more overlapping sheets between two electrodes (Figure 4.2). A current is then passed between the electrodes, sufficient heat being generated at the interface by resistance to the flow of the current that melting occurs, a weld nugget is formed and an autogenous fusion weld is made between the plates.

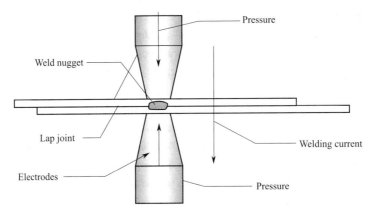

Figure 4.2 Principles of RSW

4.1.2.1 Heat sources

For resistance spot welding, the heat generated depends upon the current, the time the current is passed and the resistance at the interface. The resistance is a function of the resistivity and surface condition of the parent material, the size, shape and material of the electrodes and the pressure applied by the electrodes.

The general heat generation formula for resistance welding is:

$$H = I^2 R t \tag{4.1}$$

where "I" is the weld current through the workpieces, "R" is the electrical resistance (in ohms) of the workpieces, "t" is the weld time (in hertz, milliseconds or microseconds). The weld current (I) and duration of current (t) are controlled by the resistance welding power supply. The resistance of the workpieces (R) is a function of the weld force and the materials used.

The diagram (Figure 4.3) illustrates three contact and four bulk resistance values, which, combined, help determine the heat generated. Total resistance is the sum of the following:

CONTACT RESISTANCE ($R_c + 2R_{ew}$) is a function of the extent to which two surfaces mate intimately or come in contact. Contact resistance is an important factor in the first few milliseconds of a weld. The surfaces of metal are quite rough if they are examined on a molecular scale. When the metals are forced together with a relatively small amount of force, some of the peaks make contact. On those peaks where the contact pressure is sufficiently high, the oxide layer breaks, forming a limited number of metal-to-metal bridges. The weld current is distributed over a large area as

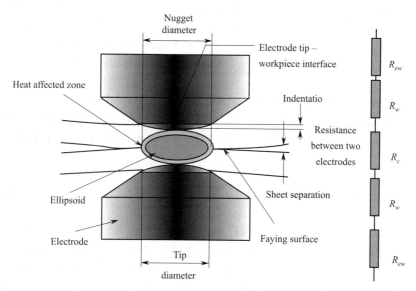

Figure 4. 3   Resistance of the RSW

it passes through the bulk metal. However, as it approaches the interface, the current is forced to flow through these metallic bridges. This "necking down" increases the current density, gener-a-ting enough heat to cause melting. As the first of these bridges melt and collapse, new peaks come into contact, forming new bridges and additional current paths. The resistance of the molten metal is higher than that of the new bridges so that the current flow transfers from bridge-to-bridge. This process continues until the entire interface is molten. When the current stops, the electrodes rapid-ly cool the molten metal, which solidifies forming a weld.

Factors Affecting Heat Generation (Q) :

① Surface condition causes inconsistent welds by inhibiting intimate contact at the weld joint. Preventive actions include pre-cleaning the workpieces.

② Electrode force. The proper and consistent application of force improves the mating of the materials increasing the current paths, reducing the interface resistance, and insuring that any ox-ide barriers between the workpieces are broken through.

BULK RESISTANCE ($2R_w$) is a function of temperature. All metals exhibit a Positive Tem-per-ature Coefficient (PTC) , which means that their bulk resistance increases with temperature. Bulk resistance becomes a factor in longer welds.

4. 1. 2. 2   Principles and parameters

Resistance spot welding is by far the most widely used variant of the resistance welding process. The basic principles of the technique are illustrated in Figure 4. 2. The weld nugget ex-tends through the sheets but without melting the surfaces of the outer plates. The main welding pa-rame-ters are current, pressure and time. The amplitude and duration of all force and heating pa-rameters can be defined in the "weld schedule. " It is recommended that when developing a weld-ing proce-dure the electrode sizes, the welding time and the welding force should be selected first and the welding current increased until the desired nugget size is achieved.

The welding force required by three phase frequency converter equipment is 2 to 5 times that of the single phase AC units and for three phase secondary rectified machines somewhere in the region of 0. 5 to 2 times. Excessive forging force will result in indentation of the sheets, increased distor-tion and sheet separation. Too low a forging force results in metal expulsion, surface burning because of poor contact, tip pickup or contamination and internal defects of porosity and cracking.

If a forging force is required to assist in consolidating the weld, particularly for the crack-sensitive alloys this should be in the region of 2. 5 to 3 times the welding force. Welding current for three phase frequency converter units should be some 30% higher than for the single phase AC units.

A controlled up-slope on the welding current, over two or three cycles, enables the electrodes to seat on the surface reducing metal expulsion and surface overheating. A downs-lope or current decay reduces the rate of solidification and assists in consolidation of the weld nugget if a post-weld forge is used.

4. 1. 2. 3 Electrodes

The bulk of the cost of a spot weld is the cost of dressing or replacing the electrode, the life being defined as the number of spot welds that can be made with a pair of electrodes while maintaining a minimum weld nugget diameter. Pick-up of alloys on to the tip and rapid wear are the two main reasons for the short life of spot welding electrodes. High welding currents, surface finish and electrode forces further assist in shortening the electrode life. It is not uncommon in very high-quality applications such as aerospace for the electrode to require cleaning after as few as 20 spot welds.

Electrode life may be extended by the use of replaceable caps on the electrode tips or, it is claimed, by the use of copper alloys with increased hardness which reduces mushrooming of the tip. Increases in hardness can be achieved by alloying with zirconium or cadmium-chromium and dispersion hardened with aluminium oxide. Of these the 1% Cd-Cu are used for the softer alloys with the harder 1% Cr-Cu or 21% Cr-Zr-Cu alloys for the welding of the cold-worked or age-hardened alloys.

The profile of the electrode tip is important with respect to both the tip life and weld quality. Tips may be conical, truncated conical, flat, domed or cylindrical. Of these types the truncated cone and the dome predominate. The most commonly recommended shape is the domed tip, the shape of which is more easily maintained in production than the truncated cone. Alignment is also less of an issue and is favoured particularly for portable equipment. The truncated cone tends to be used for commercial quality applications, mainly because electrode alignment is more critical and difficult to maintain consistently in production. Tip life, however, is markedly better, by a factor of two to three, than can be achieved with the domed electrode. Cone angles vary from $60°$ to $150°$ including an angle with a slight radius on the tip which aids in alignment and reduces marking of the sheet. The tip profile may be maintained by grinding, filing or by the use of abrasive cloth in a shaped former. While this dressing operation may be performed manually it is difficult to maintain the correct tip shape and electrode alignment. The use of automatic tip dressing tools or specially designed hand-held manual or pneumatic tip dressers is strongly recommended.

Efficient electrode cooling is also necessary to maintain tip life. Large diameter electrodes will provide a greater heat sink but efficient water cooling is imperative. The cooling channel should be carried as close to the tip as possible, a distance of between 12 and 20 mm being usual with water flow rates of 5-10 litres/min. Water inlet temperature should be in the region of 20℃ and the outlet temperature in the region of 30℃.

4. 1. 3 Projection Welding

Projection welding is a resistance welding process that produces coalescence by the heat obtained from the resistance to the flow of the welding current. The resulting welds are localized at predetermined points by projections, embossments, or intersections (Figure 4. 1).

4. 1. 3. 1　Projection Designs

By providing a projection on the surface of one of the workpieces, the current and force can be focused into the small area of the projection to produce heat at the desired weld location. The purpose of a projection is to localize the heat and pressure at a specific point on the joint.

The number and shape of the projections depend upon the requirements for joint strength. Circular or annular ring projections can be used to weld parts requiring either gas-tight or water-tight seals, or to obtain a larger area weld than button-type projections can provide.

The projection design determines the current density. The method of producing projections depends on the material in which they are to be produced. Projections in sheet metal parts are generally made by embossing, as opposed to projections formed in solid metal . pieces which are made by either machining or forging. In the case of stamped parts, projections are generally located on the edge of the stamping.

4. 1. 3. 2　Applications and Advantages

Projection welding is primarily used to join a stamped, forged, or machined part to another part. One or more projections are produced on the parts during the forming operations. Fasteners or mounting devices, such as bolts, nuts, pins, brackets, and handles, can be projection-welded to a sheet metal part. Projection welding is especially useful for producing several weld nuggets simul-taneously between two parts. Marking of one part can be minimized by placing the projections on the other part. The process is generally used for section thicknesses ranging from 0. 5 to 3. 2mm thick. Thinner sections require special welding machines capable of following the rapid collapse of the projections. Various carbon and alloy steels and some nickel alloys can be projection welded.

In general, projection welding can be used instead of spot welding to join small parts to each other and to larger parts. Selection of one method over another depends on the economics, advantages, and limitations of the two processes. The projection welding can extend electrode life by increasing the electrode contact area and decreasing the current density at the surface of the electrode. Projection welding is effective even if the weldments are thick.

4. 1. 4　Resistance Seam Welding（RSEW）

Resistance seam welding is a variation of spot welding in which a series of overlapping nuggets is produced to obtain a continuous, leak tight seam. One or both electrodes are generally wheels that rotate as the work passes between them. A seam weld can be produced with spot welding equipment but the operation will be much slower.

Seam welding uses a wheel-shaped electrode (Figure 4. 4) to make either a series of overlapping spot welds to form a continuously welded and leak tight seam or a number of spot welds spaced apart roll-spot welding. The requirements on electrodes and surface finish are the same as for spot welding. The shunt effect of the closely spaced nuggets and the short weld times mean that higher

Figure 4. 4　Typical resistance seam welding.

currents are necessary. Higher welding forces will be needed for harder alloys and lower values for softer alloys.

Pick-up on the electrode wheel can be a problem and may require the wheel to be cleaned after only one revolution. Mechanised cleaning systems that remove the contamination in-process by wire brushing or abrasive means have been successful in maintaining continuous production.

4.1.5 Upset Butt Welding

Upset butt welding is a resistance welding process that produces coalescence over the entire area of faying surfaces or progressively along a butt joint by the heat obtained from the resistance to the flow of welding current through the area where those surfaces are in contact. Pressure is applied before heating is started and is maintained throughout the heating period. The equipment used for upset welding is very similar to that used for flash welding. It can be used only if the parts to be welded are equal in cross-sectional area. The abutting surfaces must be very carefully prepared to provide for proper heating.

4.1.5.1　Principles and Variations

With this process, welding is essentially done in the solid state. The metal at the joint is resist-ance heated to a temperature where recrystallization can rapidly take place across the faying surfaces. A force is applied to the joint to bring the faying surfaces into intimate contact and then upset the metal. Upset hastens recrystallization at the interface and, at the same time, some metal is forced outward from this location. This tends to purge the joint of oxidized metal. The general arrangement for upset welding is shown in Figure 4.1. One clamping die is stationary and the other is movable to accomplish upset. Upset force is applied through the moveable clamping die or a mechanical backup, or both.

The contact resistance between the faying surfaces is a function of the smoothness and cleanliness of the surfaces and the contact pressure. This resistance varies inversely with the contact pressure, provided the other factors are constant. As the temperature at the joint increases, the contact resistance changes, but it finally becomes zero when the weld is formed. Upset welding differs from flash welding in that no flashing takes place at any time during the welding cycle. Generally, force and current are maintained throughout the entire welding cycle. The force is kept low at first to promote high initial contact resistance between the two parts. It is increased to a higher value to upset the joint when the welding temperature is reached. After the prescribed upset is accomplished, the welding current is turned off and the force is removed.

The upset process is generally used to join together two pieces of the same alloy and same cross-sectional geometry. In this case, heat balance should be uniform across the joint. If the parts to be welded are similar in composition and cross section but of unequal mass, the part of larger mass should project from the clamping die somewhat farther than the other part. With dissimilar metals, the one with higher electrical conductivity should extend farther from the clamp than the other. When upset welding large parts that do not make good contact with each other, it is sometimes advantageous to interrupt the welding current periodically to allow the heat to distribute evenly into the parts.

4.1.5.2　Applications

Upset welding is used in wire mills and in the manufacture of products made from wire. In wire mill applications, the process is used to join wire coils to each other to facilitate continuous processing. Upset welding is also used to fabricate a wide variety of products from bar, strip, and tubing stock. Wire and rod from 12.7 to 31.8 mm diameter can be upset welded.

Butt joints can be made that have about the same properties as the unwelded base metal. With proper procedures, welds made in wires are difficult to locate after they have passed through a subsequent drawing process. In many instances, the welds are then considered part of the continuous wire. Upset welds may be evaluated by tension testing. The tensile properties are compared to those of the base metal. Metallographic and dye penetrant inspection techniques are also used.

The difference from flash welding is that the parts are clamped in the welding machine and force is applied bringing them tightly together. High-amperage current is then passed through the joint, which heats the abutting surfaces. When they have been heated to a suitable forging tempera-ture an upsetting force is applied and the current is stopped. The high temperature of the work at the abutting surfaces plus the high pressure causes coalescence to take place. After cooling, the force is released and the weld is completed.

The pressure and current are applied throughout the weld cycle until the joint becomes plastic. The constant pressure (normally from an air cylinder) overcomes the softened area, producing the forging effect and subsequent welded joint. This is done without a change in current or pressure throughout the cycle. The true butt weld has no flash splatter. The final upset at the weld joint is usually smooth and symmetrical. Very little fagged expulsion of metal is evident.

4.1.6 Flash Butt Welding

Hash butt welding is a resistance welding process that produces a weld at the faying sugaces of a butt joint by a flashing action and by the application of pressure after heating is substantially completed. The flashing action, caused by the very high current densities at small contact points between the workpieces, forcibly expels the material from the joint as the workpieces are slowly moved togethel. The weld is completed by a rapid upsetting of the workpieces.

4.1.6.1 Principles and Parameters

Two parts to be joined are clamped in dies (electrodes) connected to the secondary of a resistance welding transformer. Voltage is applied as one part is advanced slowly toward the other. When contact occurs at surface irregularities, resistance heating occurs at these locations. High amperage causes rapid melting and vaporization of the metal at the points of contact, and then minute arcs form. This action is called "flashing". As the parts are moved together at a suitable rate, flashing continues until the faying surfaces are covered with molten metal and a short length of each part reaches forging temperature. A weld is then created by the application of an upset force to bring the molten faying surfaces in full contact and forge the parts together. Flashing voltage is terminated at the start of upset. The metal expelled from the interface is called "flash."

Figure 4.5 illustrates these basic steps in a flash welding. Additional steps such as preheat, dual voltage flashing, postheat, and trimming of the flash may be added as the application dictates. Flashing takes place between the faying surfaces as the movable part is advanced toward the stationary part. Heat is generated at the joint and the temperature of the parts increases with time. Flashing action (metal loss) increases with part temperature. A graph relating part motion with time is known as the flashing pattern. In most cases, a flashing pattern should show an initial period of constant velocity motion of one part toward the other to facilitate the start of flashing. This linear motion should then merge into an accelerating motion

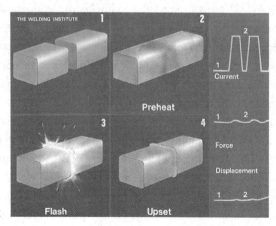

Figure 4.5   Principles of flash butt welding.

which should closely approximate a parabolic curve. This pattern of motion is known as "parabolic flashing." Upset occurs when a stable temperature distribution is achieved by flashing and the two parts are brought together rapidly. The movable part should be accelerated rapidly so that the molten metal on the flashing surfaces will be extruded before it can solidify in the joint. Motion should continue with sufficient force to upset the metal and weld the two pieces together. Upset current is sometimes applied as the joint is being upset to maintain temperature by resistance heating. This permits upset of the joint with lower force than would be required without it. Upset current is normally adjusted by electronic heat control on the basis of either experience or welding tests.

4.1.6.2　Applications

Many ferrous and nonferrous alloys can be flash welded. Typical metals are carbon and low alloy steels, stainless steels, aluminum alloys, nickel alloys. and copper alloys. Titanium alloys can be flash welded, but an inert gas shield to displace air from around the joint is necessary to minimize embrittlement. Dissimilar metals may be flash welded if their upsetting characteristics are similar. Some dissimilarity can be overcome with a difference in the initial extensions between the clamping dies, adjustment of flashing distance, and selection of welding variables. Typical examples are welding of aluminum to copper or a nickel alloy to steel.

The automotive industry uses wheel rims produced from flash welded rings that are formed from flat cold-rolled steel stock. The electrical industry uses motor and generator frames produced by flash welding plate and bar stock previously rolled into cylindrical form. Cylindrical transformer cases, circular flanges, and seals for power transformer cases are other examples. The aerospace industry uses flash welds in the manufacture of landing gear struts, control assemblies, hollow propeller blades, and rings for jet engines and rocket casings.

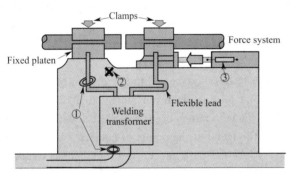

Figure 4.6　Schematic of a flash butt welding machine.

4.1.6.3　Machines

The basis of the flash welding machine is an AC transformer, the majority of production equipment being single phase machines. The electrodes or clamps are mounted on two rigid platens, at least one of which is movable and powered by a pneumatic or hydraulic system (Figure 4.6). The capacity of the machine is limited by the current require-ments of the joint and the upset pressure available. The power demanded of the transformer is based on the cross-sectional area of the faying faces as a critical current density is required. The varying electrical conductivity of the different alloys also has an effect on power requirements and the range of yield strengths place varying demands on the upset pressure mechanism.

For the welding of steel, copper alloys are generally used for the manufacture of the electrode clamps. For aluminium, however, steel, sometimes copper plated, has been found to give better results, conducting less heat away from the weld, providing a longer life and more positive clamping. By drawing the weld back through one of the clamps fitted with a knife edge it is also possible to shear off the upset as part of the removal process. A broach may be inserted into the bore of hollow components to remove any internal flash. To achieve a clean cut and to prevent smearing of the upset during removal the cutting edges must be kept sharp. The clamps are machined to match the outside shape of the components and are split to enable rapid insertion. They are also designed to clamp around 80% of the circumference and to be of a sufficient length that slippage does not occurduring upsetting.

4. 2　Friction Stir Welding

4. 2. 1　Introduction

Friction stir welding is a variation of friction welding that produces a weld between two butted workpieces by the friction heating and plastic material displacement caused by a high speed rotating tool that traverses along the weld joint.

Friction stir welding (FSW) was invented at The Welding Institute (TWI) of the United King-dom in 1991 as a solid-state joining technique and was initially applied to aluminum alloys. It has been used successfully in welding the 2000, 5000, and 6000 series of aluminum sheet alloys.

4. 2. 1. 1　Process Advantages

① The electromechanical machine tool equipment is energy efficient, requires very little main-tenance, and apart from welding tools and electric power, relies on no other consumable.

② The welding process requires neither filler metals nor weld pool shielding gas.

③ Special joint edge profiling is unnecessary.

④ Oxide removal immediately prior to welding is unnecessary.

⑤ The technique is ideally suited to automation.

⑥ If necessary, the welding operation can take place in all positions.

4. 2. 1. 2　Process Limitations

① The parts must be rigidly clamped against a backing bar to prevent weld metal breakout, if full penetrations are required.

② At the end of each weld run a hole is left where the tool pin is withdrawn. In many cases it may be necessary to fill the hole by an alternative process, such as friction taper plug welding.

③ Run-on/ run-off plates are necessary where continuous welds are required from one edge of a plate to the other.

④ Due to workpiece clamping and access requirements, applications where portable equip-ment could be used may be limited.

4. 2. 1. 3　Applications

Friction stir welding is considered to be the most significant development in metal joining in decades and, in addition, is a "green" technology due to its energy efficiency, environmental friendliness, and versatility. As compared to the conventional welding methods, FSW consumes considerably less energy, no consumables such as a cover gas or flux are used, and no harmful emissions are created during welding, thereby making the process environmentally friendly. Fur-ther, because FSW does not involve the use of filler metal and because there is no melting, any a-luminum alloy can be joined without concern for compatibility of composition or solidification cracking issues associated with fusion welding. Also, dissimilar aluminum alloys and composites can be joined with equal ease.

In contrast to traditional friction welding, which is a welding process limited to small axisym-metric parts that can be rotated and pushed against each other to form a joint, FSW can be applied to most geometric structural shapes and to various types of joints, such as butt, lap, T-butt, and fillet shapes. The most convenient joint configurations for FSW are butt and lap joints.

Friction stir welding has potential applications in major industries such as aerospace, aluminum production, automotive, construction, rail car manufacturing, refrigeration, shipbuilding, and storage tanks and pressure vessels.

For certain aluminum alloys, no shielding gas is required. The joining of aluminum alloys, especially those that are often difficult to weld, has been the initial target for developing and judging the performance of friction stir welding. As the technology for this process is developed, its use will be applied to other materials. It is anticipated that the number of applications will grow rapidly as fabricators learn the ease of application and property benefits attributable to FSW.

4. 2. 2 Principles

Friction stir welding is accomplished by rotating a nonconsumable probe and entering it into the abutting edges of the sheets to be welded. The frictional heat generated between the tool and the workpieces produces plastic deformation, then the tool is moved along the joint. The base material fills in behind the probe to complete the weld. No melting occurs during the operation, so the process is solid phase in nature.

4. 2. 2. 1 Forming of the weld

Two plates or sheets with the same thickness are placed on a backing plate and clamped firmly to prevent the abutting joint faces from being forced apart. The backing plate is required to resist the normal forces associated with FSW and the workpiece. During the initial tool plunge, the lateral forces are also fairly large, and extra care is required to ensure that plates in the butt configuration do not separate. To accomplish the weld, the rotating tool is plunged into the joint line and traversed along this line, while the shoulder of the tool is maintained in intimate contact with the plate surface. Tool position and penetration depth are maintained by either position control or control of the applied normal force.

In Figure 4. 7, the FSW tool rotates in the counterclockwise direction and travels into the page (or left to right). The advancing side is on the right, where the tool rotation direction is the same as the tool travel direction (opposite the direction of metal flow), and the retreating side is on the left, where the tool rotation is opposite the tool travel direction (parallel to the direction of metal flow). The tool serves three primary functions, that is, heating of the workpiece, movement of material to produce the joint, and containment of the hot metal beneath the tool shoulder. Heating is created within the workpiece both by friction between the rotating tool pin and shoulder and by severe plastic deformation of the work-piece. The localized heating sof-tens material around the pin and, combined with the tool rotation and translation, leads to movement of material from the front to the back of the pin, thus filling the hole in the tool wake as the tool moves forward. The tool shoulder restricts metal flow to a level equivalent to the shoulder position, that is,

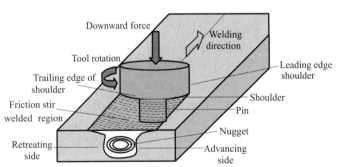

Figure 4. 7 Schematic of friction stir welding.

approximately to the initial workpiece top surface. As a result of the tool action and influence on the workpiece, when performed properly, a solid-state joint is produced, that is, no melting.

Because of various geometrical features on the tool, material movement around the pin can be complex, with gradients in strain, temperature, and strain rate. Accordingly, the resulting nugget zone microstructure reflects these different thermomechanical histories and is not homogeneous. In spite of the local microstructural inhomogeneity, one of the significant benefits of this solid-state welding technique is the fully recrystallized, equiaxed, fine grain microstructure created in the nug-get by the intense plastic deformation at elevated temperature. The fine grain microstructure produces excellent mechanical properties, fatigue properties, enhanced formability, and exceptional superplasticity.

4.2.2.2 Regions in the weld

In FSW, new terms are necessary to adequately describe the postweld microstructures. The first attempt at classifying friction stir welded microstructures was made by Threadgill. Figure 4.8 identifies the different micro structural zones existing after FSW, and a brief description of the different zones is presented. The system divides the weld zone into distinct regions, as follows:

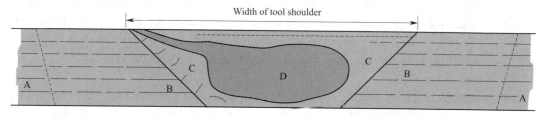

Figure 4.8   Regions in the transverse cross section of a friction stir welded material
A. parent metal; B. heat-affected zone; C. thermomechanically affected zone; D. weld nugget.

(1) Unaffected material or parent metal

This is material remote from the weld that has not been deformed and that, although it may have experienced a thermal cycle from the weld, is not affected by the heat in terms of micro structure or mechanical properties.

(2) Heat-affected zone

In this region, which lies closer to the weld-center, the material has experienced a thermal cycle that has modified the microstructure and/or the mechanical properties. However, there is no plastic deformation occurring in this area.

(3) Thermomechanically affected zone (TMAZ)

In this region, the FSW tool has plastically deformed the material, and the heat from the process will also have exerted some influence on the material. In the case of aluminum, it is possible to obtain significant plastic strain without recrystallization in this region, and there is generally a dis-tinct boundary between the recrystallized zone (weld nugget) and the deformed zones of the TMAZ.

(4) Weld nugget

The fully recrystallized area, sometimes called the stir zone, refers to the zone previously occupied by the tool pin. The term stir zone is commonly used in friction stir processing, where large volumes of material are processed.

4.2.3   Friction Stir Tool

Friction stir welding is not possible without the nonconsumable tool. The tool produces the thermomechanical deformation and workpiece frictional heating necessary for friction stirring. During the tool plunge, the rotating FSW tool is forced into the workpiece.

The friction stirring tool consists of a pin, or probe, and shoulder. Contact of the pin with the workpiece creates frictional and deformational heating and softens the workpiece material; contac-ting the shoulder to the workpiece increases the workpiece heating, expands the zone of softened material, and constrains the deformed material. Typically, the tool dwells (or undergoes only rotational motion) in one place to further increase the volume of deformed material. After the dwell period has passed, the tool begins the forward traverse along a predetermined path, creating a fine-grained recrystallized microstructure behind the tool. Forward motion of the tool produces loads parallel to the direction of travel, known as transverse load; normal load is the load required for the tool shoulder to remain in contact with the workpiece.

The initial aluminum FSW studies conducted at The Welding Institute (TWI) used a cylindrical threaded pin and concave shoulder tool machined from tool steel. Since that time, tools have advanced to complex asymmetric geometries and exotic tool materials to friction stir higher-temperature materials.

4. 2. 3. 1 Tool Shoulders

Tool shoulders are designed to produce heat (through friction and material deformation) to the surface and subsurface regions of the workpiece. The tool shoulder produces a majority of the deformational and frictional heating in thin sheet, while the pin produces a majority of the heating in thick workpieces. Also, the shoulder produces the downward forging action necessary for weld consolidation.

(1) Concave Shoulder

The first shoulder design was the concave shoulder, commonly referred to as the standard type shoulder, and is currently the most common shoulder design in friction stirring. Concave shoulders produce quality friction stir welds, and the simple design is easily machined. The shoulder concav-ity is produced by a small angle between the edge of the shoulder and the pin, between 6° and 10°. During the tool plunge, material displaced by the pin is fed into the cavity within the tool shoulder. This material serves as the start of a reservoir for the forging action of the shoulder. Forward movement of the tool forces new material into the cavity of the shoulder, pushing the existing material into the flow of the pin. Proper operation of this shoulder design requires tilting the tool 2° to 4° from the normal of the workpiece away from the direction of travel; this is necessary to maintain the material reservoir and to enable the trailing edge of the shoulder tool to produce a compressive forging force on the weld.

(2) Shoulder Features

The FSW tool shoulders can also contain features to increase the amount of material deformation produced by the shoulder, resulting in increased workpiece mixing and higher-quality friction stir welds. These features can consist of scrolls, ridges or knurling, grooves, and concentric circles (Figure 4. 9) and can be machined onto any tool shoulder profile (concave, flat, and con-vex). Currently, there are published examples of three types of shoulder features: scoops, concen-tric circles, and scrolls.

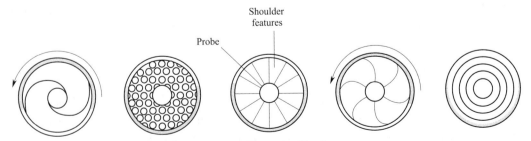

Figure 4. 9   Different shoulder features.

Scrolls are the most commonly observed shoulder feature. The typical scrolled shoulder tool consists of a flat surface with a spiral channel cut from the edge of the shoulder toward the center

(Figure 4.10). The channels direct deformed material from the edge of the shoulder to the pin, thus eliminating the need to tilt the tool. Removing the tool tilt simplified the friction stirring machine design and allowed for the production of complicated nonlinear weld patterns.

(3) Convex Shoulders

Friction stir tool shoulders can also have a convex profile. Early attempts at TWI to use a tool with a convex shoulder were unsuccessful, because the convex shape pushed material away from the pin. The only reported success with a smooth convex tool was with a 5 mm diameter shoulder tool that fric-tion stir welded 0. 4 mm sheet. Convex shoulder tools for thicker material were only realized with the addition of a scroll to the convex shape. The scrolls on the convex shoulders move material from the outside of the shoulder in toward the pin. The advantage of the convex shape is that the outer edge of the tool need not be engaged with the workpiece, so the shoulder can be engaged with the workpiece at any location along the convex surface. Thus, a sound weld is produced when any part of the scroll is engaged with the workpiece, moving material toward the pin. This shoulder design allows for a larger flexibility in the contact area between the shoulder and work-piece, improves the joint mismatch tolerance, in creases the ease of joining different-thickness workpieces, and improves the ability to weld complex curvatures. The profile of the convex shoulder can be either tapered (Figure 4.11) or curved (Figure 4.12).

Figure 4. 10   Scrolled shoulder.

Figure 4. 11   Curved convex shoulder.

Figure 4. 12   Tapered convex shoulder.

4. 2. 3. 2   Welding pin

Friction stirring pins produce deformational and frictional heating to the joint surfaces. The pin is designed to disrupt the faying, or contacting, surfaces of the workpiece, shear material in front of the tool, and move material behind the tool. In addition, the depth of deformation and tool travel speed are governed by the pin design.

(1) Round-Bottom Cylindrical Pin

The pin cited in the original FSW patent consists of a cylindrical threaded pin with a round bottom (Figure 4.13).

Threads are used to transport material from the shoulder down to the bottom of the pin; for example, a clockwise tool rotation requires lefthanded threads. A round or domed end to the pin tool reduces the tool wear upon plunging and improves the quality of the weld root directly underneath the bottom of the pin. The versatility of the cylindrical pin design is that the pin length and diameter can readily be altered to suit the user's needs.

(2) Flat-Bottom Cylindrical Pin

The flat-bottom pin design is currently the most commonly used pin design (Figure 4.14).

Figure 4. 13　Round-Bottom cylindrical pin.　　　　Figure 4. 14　Flat-Bottom cylindrical pin.

Changing from a round-bottom to a flat-bottom pin is attributed to a geometrical argument. The surface velocity of a rotating cylinder increases from zero at the center of the cylinder to a maximum value at the edge of the cylinder. The local surface velocity coupled with the friction coefficient between the pin and the metal dictates the deformation during friction stirring. The increased surface velocity at the bottom of the pin would increase the throwing power of the pin, or the ability of the pin to affect metal below the end of the pin. In addition, the flat-bottom pin is easier to machine, and the defects can be eliminated with correct tool parameters and sufficient forging load.

　(3)　Truncated Cone Pins

Cylindrical pins were found to be sufficient for aluminum plate up to 12 mm thick, but researchers wanted to friction stir weld thicker plates at faster travel speeds. A simple modification of a cylindrical pin is a truncated cone (Figure 4. 15). Truncated cone pins have lower transverse loads (when compared to a cylindrical pin), and the largest moment load on a truncated cone is at the base of the cone, where it is the strongest.

A variation of the truncated cone pin is the stepped spiral pin (Figure 4. 16), a design developed for high-temperature materials

Figure 4. 15　Truncated cone pins.　　　　Figure 4. 16　Stepped spiral pin.

　(4)　Whorl Pin

The next evolution in pin design is the Whorl pin developed by TWI. The Whorl pin reduces the displaced volume of a cylindrical pin of the same diameter by 60%. Reducing the displaced volume also decreases the traverse loads, which enables faster tool travel speeds. The key difference between the truncated cone pin and the Whorl pin is the design of the helical ridge on the pin surface. In the case of the Whorl pin, the helical ridge is more than an external thread, but the helical ridge acts as an auger, producing a clear downward movement. Variations of the Whorl pin include circular, oval, flattened, or reentrant pin cross sections (Figure 4. 17).

　(5)　MX Triflute Pin

The MX Triflute pin (TWI) is a further refinement of the Whorl pin (Figure 4. 18). In addition to the helical ridge, the MX Triflute pin contains three flutes cut into the helical ridge. The flutes reduce the displaced volume of a cylindrical pin by 70% and supply additional deformation at

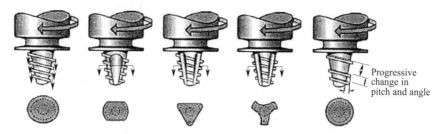

Figure 4. 17 Variations of the whorl pin.

the weld line. Additionally, the MX Triflute pin has a pin volume swept to pin volume ratio of 2. 6 to 1 (when welding 25 mm thick plate). An MX Triflute increased the tool travel speed by 2. 5 times over the previous tool design. In addition to welding thick-section copper, the MX Triflute has shown promise for thick-section aluminum alloys.

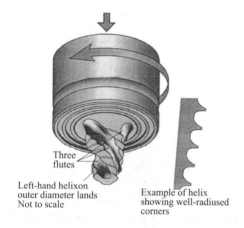

Figure 4. 18 MX triflute pin.

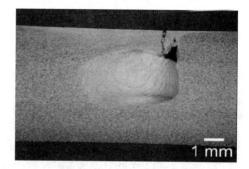

Figure 4. 19 Void imperfection.

4. 2. 4 Friction Stirring Imperfections

There are three common imperfections encountered in friction stirring: voids, joint line remnants, and root flaws (or incomplete root penetration). The presence of voids is easily detecta-ble by current nondestructive testing methods, but joint line remnants and root flaws can be quite difficult to find. These defects must be considered when designing an FSW tool for a given application.

4. 2. 4. 1 Voids

Voids are generally found on the advancing side of the weld, and they may or may not break through to the surface of the friction stir weld (Figure 4. 19). For a given tool design, void forma-tion is due to insufficient forging pressure, too high of welding speed, and insufficient workpiece clamping (too large of joint gap). Material deformed by the friction stir tool must be able to fill the void produced by a traversing pin. If the tool design is incorrect (i. e., pin diameter is too large for selected parameters) or the travel speed too fast, the deformed material will cool before the material can fully fill the region directly behind the tool. In addition, the shoulder is needed to apply suffi-cient heat generation to allow material flow around the tool; if insufficient heat is generated (through insufficient forging pressure or incorrect shoulder diameter), then material will not flow properly, and voids will form.

Figure 4. 20　Joint line remnant.

4. 2. 4. 2　Joint Line Remnant

A joint line remnant defect (also known as a kissing bond, lazy S, or entrapped oxide defect) is due to a semi-continuous layer of oxide through the weld nugget (Figure 4. 20). The semicontinuous layer of oxide was initially a continuous layer of oxide on the faying surfaces of the plates to be joined. Joint line remnants form because of insufficient cleaning of workpieces prior to welding or insufficient to incorrect tool location relative to the joint line, too fast of welding speed, or too large of tool shoulder diameter.

4. 2. 4. 3　Incomplete Root Penetration

There are several causes for incomplete root penetrations, including local variations in the plate thickness, poor alignment of tool relative to joint interface, and improper tool design. In the realm of tool design, incomplete root penetration occurs when the FSW pin is too distant from the support anvil. Thus, an undeformed region exists between the bottom of the tool and the bottom surface of the plate. When subjected to a bending stress, the friction stir weld will fail along the lack of pene-tration line.

4. 3　Laser Beam Welding

4. 3. 1　Introduction

Laser beam welding is a welding process that produces coalescence with the heat from a laser beam impinging on the joint. The process is used without a shielding gas and without the application of pressure.

The term laser is the abbreviation for "Light Amplification by Stimulated Emission of Radiation". Although the principle of the stimulated emission and the quantum mechanical fundamentals have already been postulated by Einstein in the beginning of the 20th century, the first laser, a ruby laser, was not implemented until 1960 in the Hughes Research Laboratories. Until then numerous tests on materials had to be carried out in order to gain a more precise knowledge about the atomic structure. The following years had been characterised by a fast development of the laser technology.

Already since the beginning of the Seventies and, increasingly since the Eighties when the first high performance lasers were available, CO_2 and solid state lasers have been used for production metal working. The focused, high power coherent monochromatic light beam used in laser beam welding causes the metal at the point of focus to vaporize, producing a deep penetrating column of vapor extending into the base metal.

4. 3. 1. 1　Process Advantages

Major advantages of laser beam welding include the following:

① Heat input is close to the minimum required to fuse the weld metal; thus, metallurgical effects in heat affected zones are reduced, and heat induced workpiece distortion is minimized.

② Single pass laser welding procedures have been qualified in materials of up to 32 mm thick, thus allowing the time to weld thick sections to be reduced and the need for filler wire to be eliminated.

③ No electrodes are required; welding is performed with freedom from electrode contamination, indentation, or damage from high resistance welding currents.

④ Laser beams are readily focused, aligned, and directed by optical elements. The laser can be located at a convenient distance from the workpiece. This permits welding in areas not easily accessible with other means of welding.

⑤ The workpiece can be located and hermetically welded in an enclosure that is evacuated or that contains a controlled atmosphere. No vacuum or X-ray shielding is required.

⑥ A wide variety of materials can be welded, including various combinations of different type materials. Welds in thin material and on small diameter wires are less susceptible to burn back than is the case with arc welding.

⑦ The laser can be readily mechanized for automated, high speed welding, including numeri-cal and computer control.

⑧ Laser welds are not influenced by the presence of magnetic fields, as are arc and electron beam welds; they also tend to follow the weld joint through to the root of the workpiece, even when the beam and joint are not perfectly aligned.

⑨ Aspect ratios (depth-to-width ratios) on the order of 10 : 1 are attainable when the weld is made by forming a cavity in the metal, as in keyhole welding.

4. 3. 1. 2   Process Limitations

Laser beam welding has certain limitations when compared to other welding methods, among which are the following:

① Joints must be accurately positioned laterally under the beam and at a controlled position with respect to the beam focal point.

② When weld surfaces must be forced together mechanically, the clamping mechanisms must ensure that the final position of the joint is accurately aligned with the impingement point.

③ The maximum joint thickness that can be laser beam welded is somewhat limited.

④ The high reflectivity and high thermal conductivity of some materials, such as aluminum and copper alloys, can affect their weldability with lasers.

⑤ Lasers tend to have a fairly low energy conversion efficiency, generally less than 10%.

⑥ As a consequence of the rapid solidification characteristic of LBW, some weld porosity and brittleness can be expected.

4. 3. 1. 3   Applications

The availability of more efficient laser beam sources opens up new application possibilities and makes the use of the laser also more attractive, Figure 4. 21.

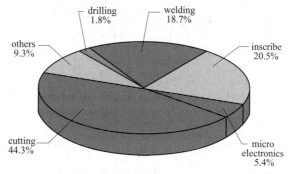

Figure 4. 21   Application of laser in manufacturing.

Yttrium aluminum garnet (YAG) lasers are used for spot and seam welding of thin materials. For welding thicker materials, multi-kilowatt carbon dioxide gas laser systems are available. Contin-uous power provides a high power laser with deep penetration welding capability. Laser beam weld-ing is a high speed process suited to automation, although it requires good joint fit up. The equip-ment is very sophisticated but is designed for use by welding operators who may not be skilled manual welders.

Laser beam welding is being used for an extensive variety of applications such as in the production of automotive transmissions and air conditioner clutch assemblies. In the latter applica-tion, laser welding permits the use of a design that could not otherwise be manufactured. The process is also being used in the production of relays and relay containers and for sealing electronic devices and heart pacemaker cases. Other applications include the continuous welding of aluminum tubing for thermal windows and for refrigerator doors. Successful laser welding applications in-clude welding transmission components (such as synchro gears, drive gears and clutch housings) for the auto industry. These annular and circumferential-type rotary welds need from 3 to 6 kW of beam power, depending on the weld speed being employed, and require penetrations which typi-cally do not exceed 3.2 mm. Materials welded are either carbon or alloy steels. In some cases, such as the gear teeth, they have been selectively hardened before welding.

4.3.2 Principles

4.3.2.1 Absorption of laser

Energy input into the workpiece is carried out over the absorption of the laser beam. The absorption coefficient is, apart from the surface quality, also dependent on the wave length and the material. The problem is that a large part of the radiation is reflected and that, for example, steel which is exposed to wave lengths of 10.6 μm reflects only 10% of the impinging radiation, Fig-ure 4.22. As copper is a highly reflective metal with also a good heat conductivity, it is frequently used as mirror material. Steel with treated surfaces reflect the laser beam to a degree of up to 95%.

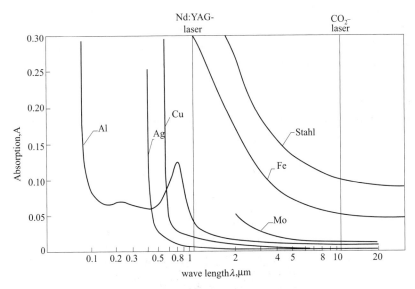

Figure 4.22 Wave length denpendent absorption of various materials.

Only a part of the beam energy from the resonator is used up for the actual welding process, Figure 4.23. Another part is absorbed by the optics in the beam manipulation system, another part is lost by reflection or transmission (beam penetration through the vapour cavity). Other parts flow over thermal conductance into the workpiece.

4. 3. 2. 2　Weld Processing Modes

As shown in Figure 4. 24, there are two distinctly different modes of energy transfer in laser welding which are commonly referred to as conduction mode welding and deep peneration welding (keyhole mode welding). It is the power density incident on the material surface, as well as the material prop-erties, which ultimately determine which mode is present for a given weld.

When metals are welded with a low intensity laser beam ($I \leqslant 10^5\,\mathrm{W/cm^2}$), just the workpiece surfaces and/or edges are melted and thus thermal conduction welding with a low penetration effect is possible. In conduction mode welding, the laser beam does not produce sufficient vaporization pressure to displace the weld pool, form a cavity, and allow the beam to emerge directly at the root of the

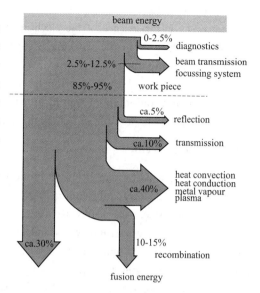

Figure 4. 23　Scheme of energy flow.

weld. Instead, the incident beam energy on the weld pool surface is transferred to the root of the weld solely by conductive and convective heat flow in the molten metal. For a given weld diameter, conduction limited welding has a maximum penetration value at which no further penetration can be obtained without creating a cavity. The maximum aspect ratio (pool depth divided by pool width) for conduction mode welding is between 0. 5 and 1. 0. Conduction mode welding can be obtained either with continuous wave lasers or with pulsed power lasers and with either low or high power. Selection of parameters and focusing optics that result in small vapor plumes and the absence of spatter are necessary to insure conduction mode welding.

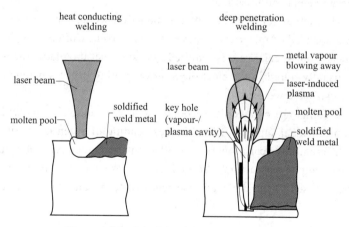

Figure 4. 24　Principle of laser beam welding.

Keyhole mode welding occurs when the power density of the beam is about $10^6\,\mathrm{W/cm^2}$ or greater. The material at the interaction point melts and vaporizes. The vapor recoil pressure, surface tension, and other phenomenon create a deep cavity. This cavity is a high pressure region surrounded by walls of molten metal. As the workpiece moves relative to the beam, the cavity is sustained, and the molten metal flows from the front edge of the cavity around the sides of the cavity in a direction opposite to the travel direction, and solidifies at the trailing edge forming a narrow fusion zone or weld.

However, in dependence of the electron density in the plasma and of the radiated beam intensity, plasma may detach from the workpiece surface and screen off the working zone. The plasma is heated to such a high degree that only a fraction of the beam radiation reaches the workpiece. This is the reason why, in deep peneration laser beam welding, gases are applied for plasma control. The gases' ionisation potential should be as high as possible, since also the formation of "shielding gas plasmas" is possible which again decreases the energy input.

4. 3. 3　Metals Welded

Laser beam welding can be used for joining most metals to themselves as well as dissimilar metals that are metallurgically compatible.

Low carbon steels are readily weldable, but when the carbon content exceeds 0. 25% martensitic transformation may cause brittle welds and cracking. Pulsed welding helps minimize the tendency for cracking. Fully killed or semi-killed steels are preferable, especially for structural applications, because welds in rimmed steel may have voids. Steels having high amounts of sulfur and phosphorus may be subject to hot cracking during welding. Also, porosity may occur in free machining steels containing sulfur, sele-nium, cadmium, or lead.

Most of the 300 series stainless steels, with the exception of free machining Types 303 and 303Se and stabilized Types 321 and 347, are readily weldable. Welds made in some of the 400 series stainless steels can be brittle and may require post weld annealing. Many heat resistant nickel and iron based alloys are being welded successfully with laser welding. Titanium alloys and other refractory alloys can be welded in this way, but an inert atmosphere is always required to prevent oxidation.

Copper and brass are often welded to themselves and other materials with specialized joint designs used for conduction welding. Aluminum and its weldable alloys can be joined for partial penetration assembly welds and are commonly joined by pulsed conduction welds for hermetically sealed electronic packages. Joint designs must retain aluminum in tension.

Refractory metals such as tungsten are often conduction welded in electronic assemblies, but require higher power than other materials. Nickel-plated Kovar is often used in sealing welds for electronic components, but special care is required to ensure that the plating does not contain phosphorous, which is usually found in the electroless nickel plating process commonly used for Kovar parts that are to be resistance welded.

Dissimilar metal joints are commonly encountered in conduction welds where the twisting of conductors forms a mechanical support that minimizes bending of potentially brittle joints. Dissimilar metals having different physical properties (reflectivity, conductivity and melting points) are often joined in the welding of conductors. Special techniques such as adding extra turns of one material to the joint as opposed to the other may be required to balance the melting characteristics of the materials.

4. 3. 4　Machines

In the field of production metal working, and particularly in welding, especially CO_2 and Nd: YAG lasers are applied for their high power outputs. At present, the development of diode lasers is so far advanced that their sporadic use in the field of material processing is also possible. The industrial standard powers for CO_2 lasers are, nowadays, approximately $5 \sim 20kW$, lasers with powers of up to 40kW are available. In the field of solid state lasers average output powers of up to 4kW are nowadays obtainable.

4.3.4.1 CO₂ laser

In the case of the CO_2 laser, where the resonator is filled with a N_2-CO_2-He gas mixture, pumping is carried out over the vibrational excitation of nitrogen molecules which again, with thrusts of the second type, transfer their vibrational energy to the carbon dioxide. During the transition to the lower energy level, CO_2 molecules emit a radiation with a wavelength of 10.6 μm. The helium atoms, finally, lead the CO_2 molecules back to their energy level.

The efficiency of up to 15%, which is achievable with CO_2 high performance lasers, is, in comparison with other laser systems, relatively high. The high dissipation component is the heat which must be dis-charged from the resonator. This is achieved by means of the constant gas mixture circulation and cooling by heat exchangers.

In dependence of the type of gas transport, laser systems are classified into longitudinal-flow and trans-verse-flow laser systems, Figures 4.25 and 4.26. With transverse-flow laser systems of a compact design can the multiple folding ability of the beam reach higher output powers than those achievable with longitudinal-flow systems, the beam quality, however, is worse.

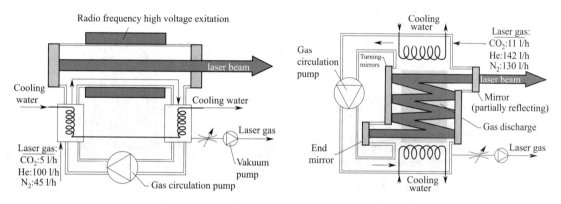

Figure 4.25   Axial flow CO_2 laser.　　　　Figure 4.26   Cross flow CO_2 laser.

4.3.4.2 YAG laser

In the case of solid state laser, the normally cylindrical rod serves only the purpose to pick up the laser active ions, Figure 4.27. The excitation is, for the most part, carried out using flash or arc lamps, which for the optimal utilisation of the excitation energy are arranged as a double ellipsoid; the rod is positioned in their common focal point. The achieved efficiency is below 4%. In the meantime, also diode-pumped solid state lasers have been introduced to the market. The possi-

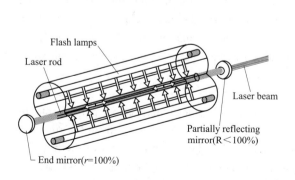

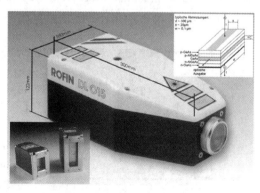

Figure 4.27   YAG laser.　　　　　　　　Figure 4.28   Diode laser.

bility to guide the solid state laser beam over flexible fibre optics makes these systems destined for the robot application, whereas the CO_2 laser application is restricted, as its necessary complex mirror systems may cause radiation losses.

4.3.4.3 Diode lasers

The semiconductor or diode lasers are characterised by their mechanical robustness, high efficiency and compact design, Figure 4.28. High performance diode lasers allow the welding of metals, although no deep penetration effect is achieved. In material processing they are therefore particularly suitable for welding thin sheets.

4.3.5 Parameters and Technology

4.3.5.1 Penetration depths

Penetration depths in dependence of the beam power and welding speed which are achievable in laser beam welding are depicted in Figure 4.29. Further relevant influential factors are, among others, the material (thermal conductivity), the design of the resonator (beam quality), the focal position and the applied optics (focal length; focus diameter).

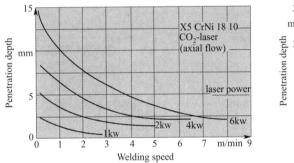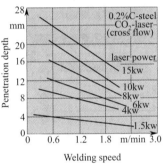

Figure 4.29 Penertation depth.

4.3.5.2 Cooling rate

The high cooling rate during laser beam welding leads, when transforming steel materials are used, to significantly increased hardness values in comparison with other welding methods. These are a sign for the increased strength at a lower toughness and they are particularly critical in circumstances of dynamic loads.

The small beam diameter demands the very precise manipulation and positioning of the workpiece or of the beam and an exact weld preparation. Otherwise, as result, lack of fusion, sagged welds or concave root surfaces are possible weld defects. Caused by the high cooling rate and, in connection with this, the insufficient degassing of the molten metal, pore formation may occur during laser beam welding of thick plates or while carrying out welding-in works.

4.3.5.3 Weld speed

Too low a weld speed may cause pore formation when the molten metal picks up gases from the root side (Figure 4.30). The high carbon content of the transforming steel materials is, due to the high cooling rate, to be considered a critical influential factor where contents of C>0.22% may be stipulated as the limiting reference

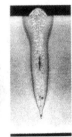

V_w=0.7m/min $\quad$ V_w=0.9m/min $\quad$ V_w=1.5m/min

Figure 4.30 Porosity.

value. Aluminium and copper properties cause problems during energy input and process stability. Highly reactive materials demand, also during laser beam welding, sufficient gas shielding beyond the solidification of the weld seam.

4. 3. 5. 4　Filler wire

The application of laser beam welding may be extended by process variants. Laser beam welding with filler wire offers the following advantages:

① Influence on the mechanic technological properties of the weld and fusion zone over the metallurgical composition of the filler wire.

② Reduction of the demands on the accuracy of the weld preparation in regard to edge misalignment, edge preparation and beam misalignment, due to larger molten pools.

③ "Filling" of non-ideal, for example, V-shaped groove geometries

④ A realisation of a defined weld reinforcement on the beam entry and beam exit side.

4. 4　Electron Beam Welding

4. 4. 1　Introduction

Electron beam welding is a welding process that produces coalescence with a concentrated beam, composed primarily of high velocity electrons, impinging on the joint.

4. 4. 1. 1　Applications

In general, metals and alloys that can be fusion welded by other welding processes can also be joined by electron beam welding. The weldability of a particular alloy or combination of alloys will depend on the metallurgical characteristics of that alloy or combination, in addition to the part configurations, joint design, process variation, and selection of welding procedure. Considering these variables, the electron beam process can be used to weld steels, stainless steels, aluminum alloys, titanium and zirconium, the refractory metals, and dissimilar metals.

Electron beam welding is primarily used for two different types of applications: high precision and high production. High precision requires a high-purity environment to avoid contamination by oxygen or nitrogen, or both, and with minimum heat effects and maximum reproducibility. These types of applications are mainly in the nuclear, aircraft, aerospace, and electronic industries. Typical products include nuclear fuel elements, special alloy jet engine components, pressure vessels for rocket propulsion systems, and hermetically sealed vacuum devices.

High production applications take advantage of the low heat input and the high reproducibility and reliability of electron beam welding if a high purity environment is not required. These relaxed conditions permit welding of components in the semifinished or finished condition, using both medium and nonvacuum equipment. Typical examples are gears, frames, steering columns, and transmission and drive train parts for automobiles; thin-wall tubing; bandsaw and hacksaw blades, and other bimetal strip products. The major application of nonvacuum electron beam welding is in high-volume production of parts, the size or composition of which preclude effective welding in a vacuum. The automotive industry employs nonvacuum EB welding for many applications. Manufacturers of welded tubing also use nonvacuum EB welding.

4. 4. 1. 2　Advantages

Electron beam welding has unique performance capabilities. The high quality environment, high power densities, and outstanding control solve a wide range of joining problems. The following are advantages of electron beam welding:

① EBW is efficient because it directly converts electrical energy into beam output energy.

② Electron beam weldments exhibit a high depth to width ratio. The resulting narrow weld zone has low distortion, and fewer thermal effects.

③ A high purity environment minimizes contamination of the metal by oxygen and nitrogen.

④ Rapid travel speeds are possible because of the high melting rates.

⑤ The beam of electrons can be magnetically deflected to produce various shaped welds, to improve weld quality, or increase penetration.

⑥ Dissimilar metals and metals with high thermal conductivity can be welded.

4.4.1.3 Limitations

Some of the limitations of electron beam welding are:

① Capital costs are substantially higher than those of arc welding equipment.

② Preparation for welds with high depth-to-width ratio requires precision machining of the joint edges, exacting joint alignment, and good fit-up.

③ The rapid solidification rates achieved can cause cracking in highly constrained, low ferrite stainless steel.

④ For high and medium vacuum welding, work chamber size must be large enough to accommodate the assembly operation.

⑤ Because the electron beam is deflected by magnetic fields, nonmagnetic or properly de-gaussed metals should be used for tooling and fixturing close to the beam path.

⑥ With all modes of EBW, radiation shielding must be maintained to ensure that there is no exposure of personnel to the X-rays generated by EB welding.

4.4.2 Principles

When the high velocity electrons impinge on a joint, their kinetic energy is converted into heat. The density of energy (or heat) is so great that vaporization of the metal (or ceramic) usually occurs, creating a cavity called a keyhole. This keyhole allows exceptionally deep penetration, for a relatively narrow width. The vapor cavity is surrounded by a liquid shell which closes behind the beam to produce a liquid pool by capillary action. The weld and joint are formed on solidification. A vacuum is required to prevent scattering and dispersion of the beam. This vacuum provides shiel-ding to the molten weld pool and surrounding base metal.

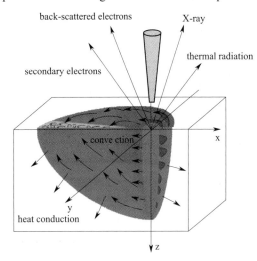

Figure 4.31　Energy transformations inside workpiece.

4.4.2.1 Energy conversion

The energy conversion in the workpiece, which is schematically shown in Figure 4.31, indicates that the kinetic energy of the highly accelerated electrons is, at the operational point, not only converted into the heat necessary for welding, but is also released by heat radiation and heat dissipation. Furthermore, a part of the incident electrons (primary electrons) is subject to backscatter and by secondary processes the secondary electrons are emitted from the workpiece thus generating X-rays.

4.4.2.2 Deep penetration

The impact of the electrons, which are tightly focussed into a corpuscular beam, onto the workpiece surface stops the electrons; their penetration depth into the workpiece is very low, just a few μm. Most of the kinetic energy is released in the form of heat. The high energy density at the impact point causes the metal to evaporate thus allowing the following electrons a deeper penetration. This finally leads to a metal vapour cavity which is surrounded by a shell of fluid metal, covering the

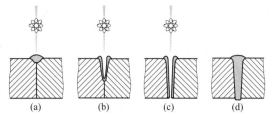

Figure 4. 32　Principle of deep penetration welding.

entire weld depth, Figure 4. 32. This deep weld effect allows penetration depths into steel materials of up to 300mm, when modern high vacuum-high voltage machines are used.

The diameter of the cavity corresponds approximately with the beam diameter. By a relative motion in the direction of the weld groove between workpiece and electron beam the cavity penetrates through the material, Figure 4. 33. At the front side of the cavity new material is molten which, to some extent, evaporates, but for the most part flows around the cavity and rapidly solid-ifies at the backside. In order to maintain the welding cavity open, the vapour pressure must press the molten metal round the vapour column against the cavity walls, by counteracting its hydrostatic pressure and the surface tension.

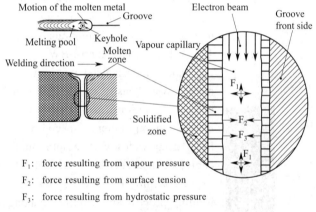

F_1: force resulting from vapour pressure

F_2: force resulting from surface tension

F_3: force resulting from hydrostatic pressure

Figure 4. 33　Condition in capillary.

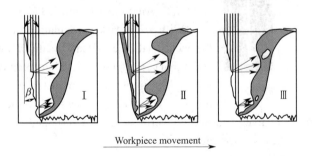

Figure 4. 34　Model of shrinkage cavity formation.

4. 4. 2. 3　Stability of cavity

However, the equilibrium of forces in cavity is unstable. The transient pressure and temperature conditions inside the cavity as well as their respective, momentary diameters are subject to dynamic changes. Under the influence of the resulting, dynamically changing geometry of the vapour cavity and with an unfavourable selection of the welding parameters, metal fume bubbles may be included which on cooling turn into shrinkholes, Figure 4. 34. The unstable pressure exposes the molten backside of the vapour cavity to strong and irregular changes in shape (case Ⅱ). Pressure variations interfere with the regular flow at the cavity backside, act upon the molten metal and, in the most unfavourable case, press the unevenly distributed molten metal into different zones of the molten cavity backside, thus forming the so called vapour pockets. The cavities are not always filling with molten metal, they collapse sporadically and remain as hollow spaces after solidi-fication (case Ⅲ). The angle β (case Ⅰ) increases with the rising weld speed and this is defined as a turbulent process. Flaws such as a constantly open vapour cavity and subsequent continuous weld solidification could be avoided by selection of job suitable welding parameter combination and in particular of beam oscillation characteristics, it has to be seen to a constantly of the molten metal, in order to avoid the abovementioned defects. Customary beam oscillation types are: circular, sine, double parabola or triangular functions.

4. 4. 3　Variations

While during the beam generation, the vacuum ($p = 10^{-5}$ mbar) for the insulation of the beam generation compartment and the prevention of cathode oxidation is imperative, the possible working pressures inside the vacuum chamber vary between a high vacuum ($p = 10^{-4}$ mbar) and atmos-pheric pressure. A collision of the electrodes with the residual gas molecules and the scattering of the electron beam which is connected to this is, naturally, lowest in high vacuum.

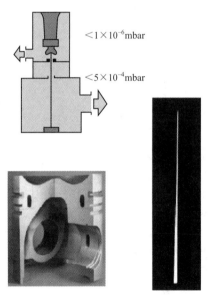

$<1 \times 10^{-6}$ mbar

$<5 \times 10^{-4}$ mbar

Figure 4. 35　EBW in high vacuum.

4. 4. 3. 1　High vacuum EBW

The beam diameter is minimal in high vacuum and the beam power density is maximum in high vacuum, Figure 4. 35. The reasons for the application of a high vacuum u-nit are, among others, special demands on the weld (narrow, deep welds with a minimum energy input) or the choice of the materials to be welded (materials with a high oxygen affinity). The application of the electron beam welding process also entails advantages as far as the structural design of the components is concerned.

4. 4. 3. 2　Medium vacuum EBW

With a low risk of oxidation and reduced demands on the welds, the so-called "medium vacuum units" ($p = 10^{-2}$ mbar) are applied. This is mainly because of economic considerations, as, for instance, the reduction of cycle times, Figure 4. 36. Areas of application are in the automo-tive industry (pistons, valves, torque converters, gear parts) and also in the metalworking industry (fittings, gauge heads, accumulators).

4. 4. 3. 3　Non vacuum EBW

Under extreme demands on the welding time, reduced requirements to the weld geometry, distortion and in case of full material compatibility with air or shielding gas, out-of-vacuum weld-ing units are applied, Figure 4. 37. Their advantages are the continuous welding time and/or short cycle times. Areas of application are in the metal-working industry (precision tubes, bimetal strips) and in the automotive industry (converters, pinion cages, socket joints and module hold-ers).

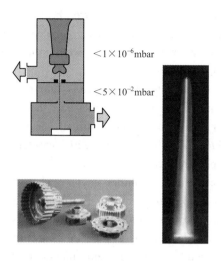

Figure 4.36   EBW in medium vacuum.

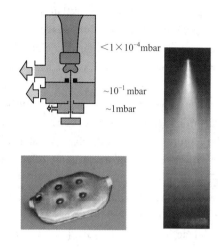

Figure 4.37   Atmospheric welding (NV-EBW).

4.4.4   Equipment

As shown in Figure 4.38, high vacuum, medium vacuum, and nonvacuum EBW equipment employs an electron beam gudcolumn assembly, one or more vacuum pumping systems, and a power supply. High and medium vacuum equipment operates with the work in an evacuated welding chamber. Although nonvacuum work does not need to be placed in a chamber, a vacuum environ-ment is necessary for the electron beam gun column.

All three basic modes can be performed using so called highvoltage equipment, i. e., equipment using gun columns with beam accelerating voltages greater than 60 kV. Nonvacuum electron beam welding performed directly in air requires beam accelerating voltages greater than 150 kV. High vacuum and medium vacuum welding can also be performed with so called low voltage equipment (equipment with gun columns that employ beam accelerating voltages of 60 kV and lower).

Because high voltage gun columns are generally fairly large, they are usually mounted on the exterior of the welding chamber, and are either fixed in position or provided with a limited amount of tilting or translational motion, or both. Low voltage gun columns are usually

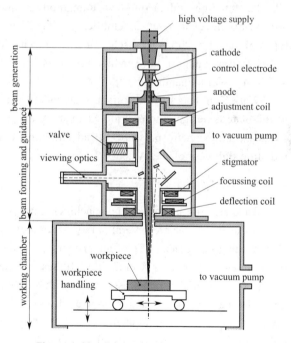

Figure 4.38   Schematic of an EBW machine.

small. Some units are "fixed" externally. Others are internally mounted "mobile" units capable of being moved about, with up to five axes of combined translational motion.

4.4.4.1   Electron Beam Guns.

Basically, an electron beam welding gun functions in much the same manner as a TV picture tube. The primary difference is that a TV picture tube uses a low intensity electron beam to continuously scan the surface of a luminescent screen, and thereby produces a picture. An electron beam welding gun uses a high intensity electron beam to continuously bombard a weld joint, which converts that energy to the level of heat input need to make a fusion weld.

An electron beam gun generates, accelerates, and collimates the electrons into a directed beam. The gun components can logically be divided into two categories: ①elements that generate free electrons (the emitter portion), and ② a rod- or disc-type filament indirectly heated by an auxiliary source, such as electron bombardment or induction heating. The specific emitter design chosen will affect the characteristics of the final beam spot produced on the work.

In both of these cases, the beam of electrons is created in a similar manner. The electron beam welding gun typically contains some type of thermionic electron emitter (normally referred to as the gun "cathode" or "filament"), and an anode. Various supplementary devices, such as focus and deflection coils, are also provided to focus and deflect this beam. In EBW, the total beam genera-ting system (gun and electron optics) is called the electron beam gun/column assembly, or simply the electron beam gun column.

4. 4. 4. 2   Power Supplies

The electron gun power source used for an electron beam welding machine is an assembly of at least one main power supply and one or more auxiliary power supplies. It produces high voltage power for the gun arid auxiliary power for the emitter and beam control.

4. 4. 4. 3   Vacuum Pumping Systems

Vacuum pumping systems are required to evacuate the electron beam gun chamber, the work chamber for high and medium vacuum modes, and the orifice assembly used on the beam exit portion of the gudcolumn assemblies for medium vacuum and nonvacuum welding. Two basic types of vacuum pumps are used: one is a mechanical piston or vane-type, and the other is an oil diffusion type pump used to reduce the pressure.

4. 4. 4. 4   Work Chambers

Work chambers of low voltage systems are usually made of carbon steel plate. The thickness of the plate is designed to provide adequate X-ray protection and the structural strength necessary to withstand atmospheric pressure. Lead shielding may be required in certain areas to ensure total radiation tightness of the system.

4. 4. 5   Safety

Since electron beam welding machines employ a high energy beam of electrons, the process requires users to observe several safety precautions not normally necessary with other types of fusion welding equipment. The four primary potential dangers associated with electron beam equipment are electric shock, X-radiation, fumes and gases, and damaging visible radiation. In addition to the potential dangers associated with welding specific materials, such as beryllium, there may also be a potential danger associated with collateral materials (solvents, greases and others) used in operating the equipment. Precautionary measures should be taken to assure that all required safety procedures are strictly observed.

Chapter 5　Welding Metallurgy

5.1　Chemical Reactions in Welding

5.1.1　Overview

5.1.1.1　Effect of Nitrogen, Oxygen, and Hydrogen

Nitrogen (N_2), oxygen (O_2), and hydrogen (H_2) gases can dissolve in the weld metal during welding. These elements usually come from air, the consumables such as the shielding gas and flux, or the workpiece such as the moist or dirt on its surface. Nitrogen, oxygen, and hydrogen can affect the soundness of the resultant weld significantly. Some examples of the effect of these gases are summarized in Table 5.1

Table 5.1　Effect of nitrogen, oxygen, and hydrogen on weld soundness

	Nitrogen	Oxygen	Hydrogen
Steels	Increases strength but reduces toughness	Reduces toughness but improves it if acicular ferrite is promoted	Induces hydrogen cracking
Austenitic or duplex stainless steels	Reduces ferrite and promotes solidification cracking		
Aluminum		Forms oxide films that can be trapped as inclusions	Forms gas porosity and reduces both strength and ductility
Titanium	Increases strength but reduces ductility	Increases strength but reduces ductility	

Table 5.2　Protection techniques in common welding processes

Protection Technique	Fusion Welding Process	Protection Technique	Fusion Welding Process
Gas	Gas tungsten arc, gas metal arc, plasma arc	Gas and slag	Shielded metal arc,fluxcored arc
		Vacuum	Electron beam
Slag	Submerged arc,electroslag	Self-protection	Self-shielded arc

5.1.1.2　Techniques for Protection from Air

As described in Chapter 1, various techniques can be used to protect the weld pool during fusion welding. These techniques are summarized in Table 5.2. Figure 5.1 shows the oxygen and nitrogen levels in the weld expected from several different arc welding processes. As will be explained below, techniques provide different degrees of weld metal protection.

(1) GTAW and GMAW

GTAW (Gas Tungsten Arc Welding) is the cleanest arc welding process because of the use of inert shielding gases (Ar or He) and a short, stable arc. Gas shielding through the torch is sufficient for welding most materials. However, as shown in Figure 5.2, additional gas shielding to protect the solidified but still hot weld is often provided both behind the torch and under the weld of highly reactive metals such as titanium. Welding can also be conducted inside a special gas-filled box. Although also very clean, GMAW (Gas Metal Arc Welding) is not as clean as GTAW due to the less stable arc associated with the use of consumable electrodes. Furthermore, the greater arc length in GMAW reduces the protective effects of the shielding gas. CO_2 (Carbon dioxide) is sometimes employed as shielding gas in GMAW. Under the high temperature of the arc, The CO_2 is favored to decompose into CO and O, potentially increasing the weld oxygen level.

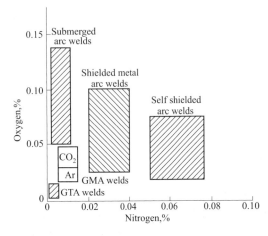

Figure 5. 1 Oxygen and nitrogen levels expected from several arc welding processes.

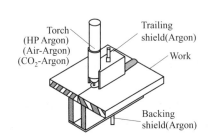

Figure 5. 2 Gas-tungsten arc welding of titanium with additional gas shielding.

(2) SMAW

The flow of gas in SMAW (Shielded Metal Arc Welding) is not as well directed toward the weld pool as the flow of inert gas in GTAW or GMAW. Consequently, the protection afforded the weld metal is less effective, resulting in higher weld oxygen and nitrogen levels.

(3) SAW

The weld oxygen level in SAW (Submerged Arc Weld) can vary significantly, depending on the composition of the flux; the very high oxygen levels associated with acidic fluxes containing large percentages of SiO_2, according to Eagar, are the result of SiO_2 decomposition. This is consistent with the large increase in the weld metal silicon content when acidic fluxes are used. If atmospheric contamination were the reason for the weld metal oxygen content, the nitrogen content would also have been high.

5. 1. 2 Gas-Metal Reactions

The gas-metal reactions here refer to chemical reactions that take place at the interface between the gas phase and the liquid metal. They include the dissolution of nitrogen, oxygen, and hydrogen in liquid metal and the evolution of carbon monoxide.

5. 1. 2. 1 Thermodynamics of Reactions

In steelmaking, exposure of molten steel to molecular nitrogen, N_2, can result in dissolution of nitrogen atoms in the molten steel, that is,

$$\frac{1}{2}N_2(g) = \underline{N} \tag{5.1}$$

where the underlining bar denotes dissolution in molten metal. From thermodynamics, the equilibri-um concentration of dissolved nitrogen, $[\underline{N}]$, at any given temperature T can be determined from the following relationship:

$$\ln K_N^d = \ln\left(\frac{[\underline{N}]}{\sqrt{p_{N_2}}}\right) = \frac{-\Delta G^\circ}{RT} \tag{5.2}$$

where K_N^d is the equilibrium constant for reaction (5.1) based on dissolution from a diatomic gas N_2, p_{N_2} the partial pressure (in atmospheres) of N_2 above the molten metal, ΔG° the standard free energy of formation (in calories per mole), and R the gas constant 1.987cal/ (K · mol). Table 5.3 shows the values of ΔG° for several chemical reactions involving nitrogen, oxygen, and hydrogen. From Equation (5.2), the well-known Sievert law for the dissolution of a diatomic gas in molten metal can be written as

$$[\underline{N}] = K_N^d \sqrt{p_{N_2}} \tag{5.3}$$

In arc welding, however, a portion of the N_2 molecules can dissociate (or even ionize) under the high temperature of the arc plasma. The atomic N so produce can dissolve in the molten metal as follows:

$$N = \underline{N} \tag{5.4}$$

$$\ln K_N^m = \ln\left(\frac{[\underline{N}]}{p_N}\right) = \frac{-\Delta G^\circ}{RT} \tag{5.5}$$

where K_N^m is the equilibrium constant for Equation (5.4) based on dissolution from a monatomic gas N and p_N the partial pressure (in atmospheres) of N above the molten metal.

It is interesting to compare dissolution of nitrogen in molten steel from molecular nitrogen to that from atomic nitrogen. Consider an arbitrary temperature of 1600℃ for molten steel for the purpose of discussion. Based on the free energy of reaction ΔG° shown in Table 5.3, for molecular nitrogen a pressure of $p_{N_2} = 1$atm is required in order to have $[\underline{N}] = 0.045$ wt %. For atomic nitrogen, however, only a pressure of $p_N = 2 \times 10^{-7}$ atm is required to dissolve the same amount of nitrogen in molten steel.

Table 5.3　Free Energy of Reactions Involving Nitrogen, Oxygen, and Hydrogen

Gas	Reaction	Free Energy of Reaction, ΔG°(cal/mol)	Reference
Nitrogen	$\frac{1}{2}N_2(g) = N(g)$	86596.0 − 15.659T(K)	6
		−85736.0 + 21.405T	
	$N(g) = \underline{N}(wt\%$ in steel$)$	860.0 + 5.71T	7
	$\frac{1}{2}N_2(g) = \underline{N}(wt\%$ in steel$)$		
Oxygen	$\frac{1}{2}O_2(g) = O(g)$	60064 − 15.735T	6
		−88064 + 15.045T	
	$O(g) = \underline{O}(wt\%$ in steel$)$	−28000 − 0.69T	8
	$\frac{1}{2}O_2(g) = \underline{O}(wt\%$ in steel$)$		
Hydrogen	$\frac{1}{2}H_2(g) = H(g)$	53500.0 − 14.40T	9
		−44780.0 + 3.38T	9
	$H(g) = \underline{H}(ppm$ in steel$)$	8720.0 − 11.02T	8
	$\frac{1}{2}H_2(g) = \underline{H}(ppm$ in steel$)$		

Similarly, for the dissolution of oxygen and hydrogen from O_2 (g) and H_2 (g),

$$\frac{1}{2}O_2(g) = \underline{O} \tag{5.6}$$

$$\frac{1}{2}H_2(g) = \underline{H} \tag{5.7}$$

However, as in the case of nitrogen, a portion of the O_2 and H_2 molecules can dissociate (or even ionize) under the high temperature of the arc plasma. The atomic O and H so produced can dissolve in the molten metal as follows:

$$\text{O}=\underline{\text{O}} \tag{5.8}$$

$$\text{H}=\underline{\text{H}} \tag{5.9}$$

DebRoy and David showed, in Figure 5.3, the dissolution of mono-atomic, rather than diatomic, nitrogen and hydrogen dominates in molten iron. As they pointed out, several investigators have concluded that the species concentration in the weld metal can be significantly higher than those calculated from dissolution of diatomic molecules. Dissociation of such to neutral atoms and ions in the arc leads to enhanced dissolution in the molten metal.

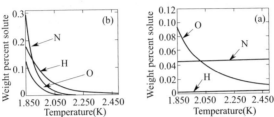

Figure 5.3   Equilibrium concentration of nitrogen, oxygen, and hydrogen in liquid iron as a function of temperature: (a) N_2 (g) with $p_{N_2} = 1$ atm, O_2 (g) with $p_{O_2} = 10^{-9}$ atm, H_2 (g) with $p_{H_2} = 1$ atm; (b) N (g) with $p_N = 10^{-6}$ atm, O (g) with $p_O = 10^{-8}$ atm, H (g) with $p_H = 5 \times 10^{-2}$ atm.

In the case of hydrogen, the calculated results are consistent with the earlier ones of Gedeon and Eagar shown in Figure 5.4. The calculation is based on a dissociation temperature of 2500℃, 0.01atm hydrogen added to the argon shielding gas, and the pool surface temperature distribution measured by Krause. As shown, the majority of hydrogen absorption appears to take place around the outer edge of the weld pool, and monatomic hydrogen absorption dominates the contribution to the hydrogen content. This contradicts predictions based on Sievert's law that the maximum absorption occurs near the center of the pool surface where the temperature is highest. However, as they pointed out, the dissolution process alone does not determine the hydrogen content in the resultant weld metal. Rejection of the dissolved hydrogen atoms by the solidification front and diffusion of the hydrogen atoms from the weld pool must also be considered. It is interesting to note that Hooijmans and Den Ouden suggested that a considerable amount of hydrogen absorbed by the liquid metal during welding leaves the weld metal immediately after the extinction of the arc.

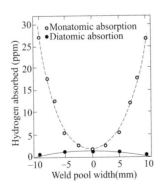

Figure 5.4   Equilibrium concentration of hydrogen as a function of weld pool location.

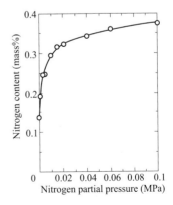

Figure 5.5   Effect of nitrogen partial pressure in Ar-N_2 shielding gas on nitrogen content in welds of duplex stainless steel.

5. 1. 2. 2　Nitrogen

For metals that neither dissolve nor react with nitrogen, such as copper and nickel, nitrogen can be used as the shielding gas during welding. On the other hand, for metals that either dissolve nitrogen or form nitrides (or both) , such as Fe, Ti, Mn, and Cr, the protection of the weld metal from nitrogen should be considered.

(1)　Sources of Nitrogen

The presence of nitrogen in the welding zone is usually a result of improper protection against air. However, nitrogen is sometimes added purposely to the inert shielding gas. Figure 5. 5 shows the weld nitrogen content of a duplex stainless steel as a function of the nitrogen partial pressure in the Ar-N_2 shielding gas. Nitrogen is an austenite stabilizer for austenitic and duplex stainless steels. Increasing the weld metal nitrogen content can decrease the ferrite content and increase the risk of solidification cracking.

(2)　Effect of Nitrogen

The presence of nitrogen in the weld metal can significantly affect its mechanical properties. Figure 5. 6 shows the needlelike structure of iron nitride (Fe_4N) in a ferrite matrix. The sharp ends of such a brittle nitride act as ideal sites for crack initiation. As shown in Figure 5. 7, the ductility and the impact toughness of the weld metal decrease with increasing weld metal nitrogen. Figure 5. 8 shows that nitrogen can decrease the ductility of Ti welds.

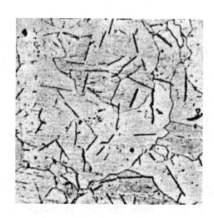

Figure 5. 6　Iron nitride in a
ferrite matrix.

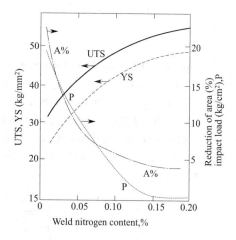

Figure 5. 7　Effect of nitrogen on the room
temperature mechanical properties of mild steel welds.

(3)　Protection against Nitrogen

In the self-shielded arc welding process, strong nitride formers (such as Ti, Al, Si, and Zr) are often added to the filler wire. The nitrides formed enter the slag and nitrogen in the weld metal is thus reduced. As already shown in Figure 5. 8, however, the nitrogen contents of self-shielded arc welds can still be rather high, and other arc welding processes such as GTAW, GMAW, or SAW should be used if weld nitrogen contamination is to be minimized.

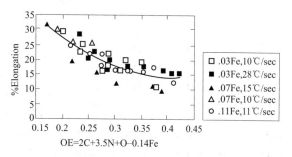

Figure 5. 8　Effect of oxygen equivalence
(OE) on ductility of titanium welds.

73

5. 1. 2. 3 Oxygen

(1) Sources of Oxygen

Oxygen in the weld metal can come from the air, the use of excess oxygen in oxyfuel weld-ing, and the use of oxygen or CO_2 containing shielding gases. It can also come from the decomposition of oxides (especially SiO_2 and MnO and FeO) in the flux and from the slag-metal reactions in the weld pool, which will be discussed subsequently.

In GMAW of steels the addition of oxygen or carbon dioxide to argon (e. g., Ar-2% O_2) helps stabilize the arc, reduce spatter, and prevent the filler metal from drawing away from (or not flowing out to) the fusion line. Carbon dioxide is widely used as a shielding gas in FCAW, the advantages being low cost, high welding speed, and good weld penetration. Baune et al. pointed out that CO_2 can decompose under the high temperature of the welding arc as follows:

$$CO_2(g) = CO(g) + \frac{1}{2}O_2(g) \tag{5.10}$$

$$CO(g) = C(g) + \frac{1}{2}O_2(g) \tag{5.11}$$

(2) Effect of Oxygen

Oxygen can oxidize the carbon and other alloying elements in the liquid metal, modifying their prevailing role, depressing hardenability, and producing inclusions. The oxidation of carbon is as follows:

$$\underline{C} + \underline{O} = CO(g) \tag{5.12}$$

The oxidation of other alloying elements, which will be discussed subsequently in slag-metal reactions, forms oxides that either go into the slag or remain in the liquid metal and become inclusion particles in the resultant weld metal.

Table 5. 4 shows the effect of gas composition in oxyacetylene welding of mild steel on the weld metal composition and properties. When too much oxygen is used, the weld metal has a high oxygen level but low carbon level. On the other hand, when too much acetylene is used, the weld metal has a low oxygen level but high carbon level (the flame becomes carburizing). In either case, the weld mechanical properties are poor. When the oxygen-acetylene ratio is close to 1, both the impact toughness and strength (proportional to hardness) are reasonably good.

If oxidation results in excessive inclusion formation in the weld metal or significant loss of alloying elements to the slag, the mechanical properties of the weld metal can deteriorate. Figure 5. 9 shows that the strength, toughness, and ductility of mild steel welds can all decrease with increasing oxygen contamination. In some cases, however, fine inclusion particles can act as nucleation sites for acicu-lar ferrite to form and improve weld metal toughness.

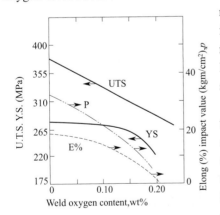

Figure 5. 9 Effect of the oxygen content on the mechanical properties of mild steel welds.

For aluminum and magnesium alloys, the formation of insoluble oxide films on the weld pool surface during welding can cause incomplete fusion. Heavy oxide films prevent a keyhole from being established properly in conventional PAW of aluminum, and more advanced DC variable-polarity PAW has to be used. In the latter, oxide films are cleaned during the electrode-positive part of the current cycle.

Table 5. 4　Effect of Oxygen-Acetylene Ratio on Weld Metal
Composition and Properties of Mild Steel

	Before	$a = O_2/C_2H_2 > 1$				$a \leqslant 1$	
		$a = 1.14$	$a = 1.33$	$a = 2$	$a = 2.37$	$a = 1$	$a = 0.82$
C	0.155	0.054	0.054	0.058	0.048	0.15	1.56
Mn	0.56	0.38	0.265	0.29	0.18	0.29	0.375
Si	0.03						
S	0.030						
P	0.018						
O	—	0.04	0.07	0.09	—	0.02	0.01
N	—	0.015	0.023	0.030	—	0.012	0.023
Impact value,kg/cm²	—	5.5	1.40	1.50	1.30	6.9	2.3
Hardness,HB	—	130	132	115	100	140	320
Grain size	—	6	5	4	4	4	5

Bracarense and Liu discovered in SMAW that the metal transfer droplet size can increase gradually during welding, resulting in increasing Mn and Si transfer to the weld pool and hence increasing weld metal hardness along the weld length, as shown in Figure 5. 10. As the electrode is heated up more and more during welding, the droplet size increases gradually (becomes more globular). This reduces the surface area (per unit volume) for oxygen to react with Mn and Si and hence improves the efficiency of Mn and Si transfer to the weld pool.

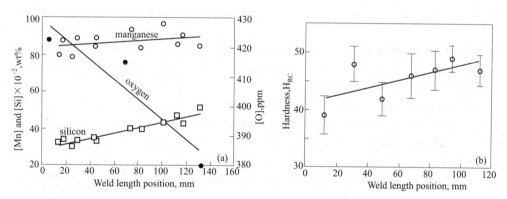

Figure 5. 10　Variations of weld metal along the length of a weld made with an E7018 electrode:
(a) composition; (b) hardness.

5. 1. 2. 4　Hydrogen

(1) Steels

The presence of hydrogen during the welding of high-strength steels can cause hydrogen cracking.

① Sources of Hydrogen　Hydrogen in the welding zone can come from several different sources: the combustion products in oxyfuel welding; decomposition products of cellulose-type electrode coverings in SMAW; moisture or grease on the surface of the workpiece or electrode; and moisture in the flux, electrode coverings, or shielding gas.

As mentioned previously in Chapter 1, in SMAW high-cellulose electrodes contain much cellulose, $(C_6H_{10}O_5)_x$, in the electrode covering. The covering decomposes upon heating during welding and produces a gaseous shield rich in H_2, for instance, 41% H_2, 40% CO, 16% H_2O, and 3% CO_2 in the case of E6010 electrodes. On the other hand, low-hydrogen electrodes contain much $CaCO_3$ in the electrode covering. The covering decomposes during welding and produces a gaseous shield low in H_2, for example, 77% CO, 19% CO_2, 2% H_2, and 2% H_2O in the case of E6015 electrodes. As such, to reduce weld metal hydrogen, low-hydrogen electrodes should be used.

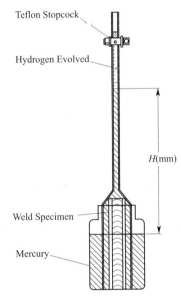

Figure 5.11 Mercury method for measuring diffusible hydrogen in welds.

② Measuring Hydrogen Content Various methods have been developed for measuring the hydrogen content in the weld metal of steels. The mercury method and the gas chromatography method are often used. Figure 5.11 shows the mercury method. A small test specimen (13 × 25 × 127mm, or 1/2 × 1 × 5in.) is welded in a copper fixture. The welded test specimen is then immersed in mercury contained in a eudiometer tube. As hydrogen diffuses out of the welded test specimen, the mercury level in the eudiometer tube continues to drop. From the final mercury level, H (in millimeters) , the amount of hydrogen that diffuses out of the specimen, that is, the so-called diffusible hydrogen, can be measured. This method, however, can take days because of the slow diffusion of hydrogen at room temperature. In the gas chromatography method, the specimen is transferred to a leak-tight chamber after welding, which can be heated to accelerate the hydrogen evolution from the specimen. After that, the cham-ber can be connected to a gas chromatograph analyzer to measure the total amount of hydrogen present. The advanta-ges are that it can separate other gases present and measure only hydrogen and it takes hours instead of days. One disadvantage is the relatively high cost of the equipment.

Newer methods have also been developed. Albert et al. developed a new sensor for detecting hydrogen. The sensor is a conducting polymer film coated with Pd on one side to be exposed to a hydrogen-containing gas and the other side to air. The current going through the sensor is directionally proportional to the hydrogen content in the gas. Figure 5.12 shows the hydrogen contents measured by the new sensor as well as gas chromatography (GC) . These are gas-tungsten arc welds of a 0.5Cr-0.5Mo steel made with Ar-H_2 as the shielding gas. Smith et al. developed a new hydrogen sensor that generates results in less than 1h and allows analysis to be done on the actual welded structure. The sensor is a thin porous film of tungsten oxide, which changes color upon reacting with hydrogen.

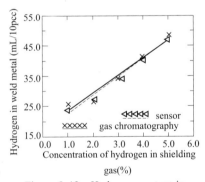

Figure 5.12 Hydrogen content in gas-tungsten arc welds of 0.5Cr-0.5Mo steel as a function of volume percent of hydrogen in Ar-H_2 shielding gas.

③ Hydrogen Reduction Methods The weld hydrogen content can be reduced in several ways. First, avoid hydrogen-containing shielding gases, including the use of hydrocarbon fuel gases, cellulose-type electrode coverings, and hydrogen-containing inert gases. Second, dry the electrode covering and flux to remove moisture and clean the filler wire and workpiece to remove grease. Figure 5.13 shows the effect of the electrode baking temperature on the weld metal hydrogen content. Third, adjust the composition of the consumables if feasible. Figure 5.14 shows that CO_2 in the shielding gas helps reduce hydrogen in the weld metal, possibly because of reaction between the two gases. Increasing the CaF_2 content in the electrode covering or the flux has been reported to reduce the weld hydrogen content. This reduction in hydrogen has been ascribed to the reaction between hydrogen and CaF_2. Fourth, as shown in Figure 5. 15, use postweld heating to help hydrogen diffuse out of the weld.

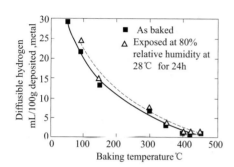

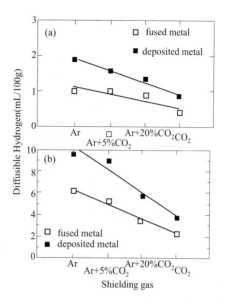

Figure 5. 13   Effect of electrode baking temperatureon weld metal diffusible hydrogen levels.

Figure 5. 14   Effect of shielding gases on weld metal hydrogen content: (a) GMAW;   (b) FCAW.

(2) Aluminum

Hydrogen can cause porosity in aluminum welds. The oxide films on the surface of the work-piece or electrode can absorb moisture from the air and introduce hydrogen into molten aluminum during welding. Grease on the surface of the workpiece or electrode and moisture in shielding gas can also be the sources of hydrogen. Figure 5. 16 shows the solubility of hydrogen in aluminum. Since the solubility of hydrogen is much higher in liquid aluminum than in solid aluminum, hydrogen is rejected into the weld pool by the advancing solid-liquid interface. Consequently, hydrogen porosity is often observed in aluminum welds. Devletian and Wood have reviewed the factors affecting porosity in aluminum welds.

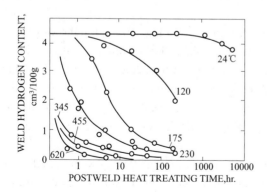

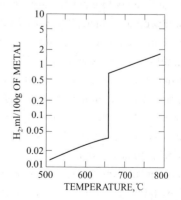

Figure 5. 15   Effect of postweld heating on the weld metal hydrogen content of mild steel.

Figure 5. 16   Solubility of hydrogen in aluminum.

① Effect of Hydrogen Porosity   As shown in Figure 5. 17, excessive hydrogen porosity can severely reduce both the strength and ductility of aluminum welds. It has also been reported to reduce the fatigue resistance of aluminum welds.

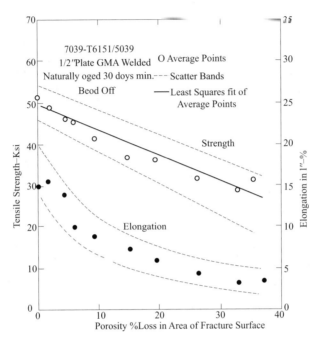

Figure 5. 17   Effect of porosity on tensile properties of aluminum welds.

② Reducing Hydrogen Porosity   To reduce hydrogen porosity, the surface of Al-Li alloys has been scrapped, milled, or even thermovacuum degassed to remove hydrogen present in the form of hydrides or hydrated oxides. Similarly, Freon (CCl_2F_2) has been added to the shielding gas to reduce hydrogen in aluminum welds. The weld pool has been magnetically stirred to help hydrogen bubbles escape and thus reduce hydrogen porosity. Keyhole plasma arc welding, with variable-polarity direct current, has been used to reduce hydrogen porosity in aluminum welds. The cleaning action of the DCEP cycle helps remove hydrated oxides and hydrides. The keyhole, on the other hand, helps eliminate entrapment of oxides and foreign materials in the weld, by allo-wing contami-nants to enter the arc stream instead of being trapped in the weld. Consequently, the welds produced are practically porosity free.

Consider the reduction of severe gas porosity in the welding of a high strength light weight Al-5Mg-2Li alloy. The presence of Li in the alloy promotes the formation of lithium hydride during heat treatment as well as the hydration of the surface oxide at room temperature. Surface cleaning and thermovacuum treatment before welding, which help reduce the hydrogen content of the work-piece surface, have been reported to reduce the porosity level of the weld metal. Reduction in po-rosity has also been achieved by using an alternating magnetic field to stir the weld pool and by u-sing variable-polarity keyhole PAW.

Consider also the reduction of severe gas porosity in the welding of PM (powder metallurgy) parts of Al-8.0Fe-1.7Ni alloy. Oxidation and subsequent hydration of the aluminum powder during and after powder production by air atomization result in a high surface moisture content. When the powder is consolidated into PM parts, the moisture is trapped inside the parts. Because of the dif-fi-culty in removing the moisture from deep inside the work-piece, thermovacuum treatments at temperatures as high as 595℃ have been found necessary. Unfortunately, the use of such a high temperature causes unacceptable degradation in the base-metal strength. Therefore, atomization and consolidation techniques that minimize powder oxidation and hydration are required for producing porosity-free welds.

(3) Copper

Hydrogen can also cause problems in copper welding. It can react with oxygen to form steam, thus causing porosity in the weld metal. It can also diffuse to the HAZ and react with oxygen to form steam along the grain boundaries. This can cause microfissuring in the HAZ. These problems can be minimized if deoxidized copper is used for welding.

5. 1. 3　Slag-Metal Reactions

5. 1. 3. 1　Thermochemical Reactions

The thermochemical slag-metal reactions here refer to thermochemical reactions that take place at the interface between the molten slag and the liquid metal. Examples of such reactions are decomposition of metal oxides in the flux, oxidation of alloying elements in the liquid metal by the oxygen dissolved in the liquid metal, and desulfurization of the weld metal.

(1) Decomposition of Flux

In studying SAW, Chai and Eagar suggested that in the high-temperature environment near the welding plasma, all oxides are susceptible to decomposition and produce oxygen. It was found that the stability of metal oxides during welding decreases in the following order: (i) CaO, (ii) K_2O, (iii) Na_2O and TiO_2, (iv) Al_2O_3, (v) MgO, and (vi) SiO_2 and MnO (FeO was not included but can be expected to be rather unstable, too). For instance, SiO_2 and MnO can decompose as follows:

$$(SiO_2)\!\!=\!\!=\!\!SiO(g)+\frac{1}{2}O_2(g) \tag{5. 13}$$

$$(MnO)\!\!=\!\!=\!\!Mn(g)+\frac{1}{2}O_2(g) \tag{5. 14}$$

It was concluded that in fluxes of low FeO content ($<10\%$ FeO), SiO_2 and MnO are the primary sources of oxygen contamination and the stability of metal oxides in welding is not directly related to their thermodynamic stability. It was also concluded that CaF_2 reduces the oxidizing potential of welding fluxes due to dilution of the reactive oxides by CaF_2 rather than to reactivity of the CaF_2 itself and significant losses of Mn may occur by evaporation from the weld pool due to the high vapor pressure of Mn.

(2) Oxidation by Oxygen in Metal

$$\underline{Mn}+\underline{O}\!\!=\!\!=\!\!(MnO) \tag{5. 15}$$

$$\underline{Si}+2\underline{O}\!\!=\!\!=\!(SiO_2) \tag{5. 16}$$

$$\underline{Ti}+2\underline{O}\!\!=\!\!=\!\!(TiO_2) \tag{5. 17}$$

$$2\underline{Al}+3\underline{O}\!\!=\!\!=\!(Al_2O_3) \tag{5. 18}$$

(3) Desulfurization of Liquid Metal

$$\underline{S}+(CaO)\!\!=\!\!=\!\!(CaS)+\underline{O} \tag{5. 19}$$

5. 1. 3. 2　Effect of Flux on Weld Metal

Composition Burck et al. welded 4340 steel by SAW with manganese silicate fluxes, keeping SiO_2 constant at 40wt % and adding CaF_2, CaO, and FeO separately at the expense of MnO. Figure 5. 18 shows the effect of such additions on the extent of oxygen transfer from the flux to the weld metal, expressed in D (weld metal oxygen). A positive D quantity means transfer of an element (oxygen in this case) from the flux to the weld metal, while a negative D quantity means loss of the element from the weld metal to the flux. The FeO additions, at the expense of MnO, increase the extent of oxygen transfer to the weld metal. This is because FeO is less stable than MnO and thus decomposes and produces oxygen in the arc more easily than MnO. The CaO additions at the expense of MnO decrease the extent of oxygen transfer to the weld metal because CaO is more stable than MnO. The CaF_2 additions at the expense of MnO also decrease the extent of oxygen transfer to the weld metal but more significantly. It is worth noting that Chai and Eagar reported previously that CaF_2 reduces oxygen transfer by acting as a diluent rather than an active species.

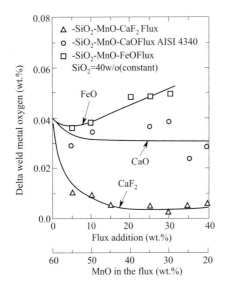

Figure 5. 18　Effect of flux additions to manganese silicate flux on extent of oxygen transfer to the weld metal in submerged arc welding of 4340 steel.

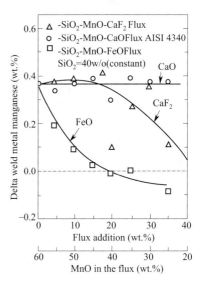

Figure 5. 19　Effect of flux additions to manganese silicate flux on extent of manganese transfer to the weld metal in submerged arc welding of 4340 steel.

Figure 5. 19 shows the effect of flux additions on the manganese change of the weld metal. It is surprising that the CaO additions at the expense of MnO do not decrease the extent of manganese transfer from the flux to the weld metal. From the steelmaking data shown in Figure 5. 20, it appears that the CaO additions do not reduce the activity of MnO, as indi-cated by the dots along the constant MnO activity of about 0. 30. The additions of FeO and CaF_2 at the expense of MnO decrease the extent of manganese transfer from the flux to the weld metal, as expected. Beyond 20% FeO, D (weld metal manganese) becomes nega-tive, namely, Mn is lost from the weld metal to the slag. This is likely to be caused by the oxidation of Mn by the oxygen introduced into the liquid metal from FeO, namely, $Mn + O = (MnO)$. The flux additions also af-

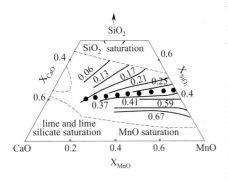

Figure 5. 20　Activity of MnO in CaO-MnO-SiO$_2$ melts at 1500℃.

fect the extents of loss of allo-ying elements such as Cr, Mo, and Ni. Therefore, the flux composition can affect the weld metal composition and hence mechanical properties rather significantly.

The loss of alloying elements can be made up by the addition of ferroalloy powder (e. g., Fe-50% Si and Fe-80% Mn) to SAW fluxes or SMAW electrode coverings. In doing so, the alloying element recovery, that is, the percentage of the element transferred across the arc and into the weld metal, should be considered. The recovery varies significantly from element to element. In SMAW, for example, it can be about 100% for Ni and Cr, 75% for Mn, 70% for Nb, 45% for Si, and 5% for Ti.

5. 1. 3. 3 Types of Fluxes, Basicity Index, and Weld Metal Properties

The use of proper welding fluxes during fusion welding helps control the composition of the weld metal as well as protect it from air. Welding fluxes can be categorized into the following three groups according to the types of main constituents:

(a) Halide-type fluxes: for example, CaF_2-NaF, CaF_2-$BaCl_2$-NaF, KC1-NaCl-Na_3AlF_6, and BaF_2-MgF_2-CaF_2-LiF.

(b) Halide-oxide-type fluxes: for example, CaF_2-CaO-Al_2O_3, CaF_2-CaO-SiO_2, CaF_2-CaO-Al_2O_3-SiO_2, and CaF_2-CaO-MgO-Al_2O_3.

(c) Oxide-type fluxes: for example, MnO-SiO_2, FeO-MnO-SiO_2, and CaO-TiO_2-SiO_2.

The halide-type fluxes are oxygen free and are used for welding titanium and aluminum alloys. The halide-oxide-type fluxes, which are slightly oxidizing, are often used for welding high-alloy steels. The oxide-type fluxes, which are mostly oxidizing, are often used for welding low-carbon or low-alloy steels. When oxide-type fluxes are used for welding a reactive metal such as titanium, the weld metal can be contaminated with oxygen.

The oxides in a welding flux can be roughly categorized into the following three groups:

(a) Acidic oxides, in the order of decreasing acidity: SiO_2, TiO_2, P_2O_5, V_2O_5.

(b) Basic oxides, in the order of decreasing basicity: K_2O, Na_2O, CaO, MgO, BaO, MnO, FeO, PbO, Cu_2O, NiO.

(c) Amphoteric oxides: Al_2O_3, Fe_2O_3, Cr_2O_3, V_2O_3, ZnO.

Oxides that are donors of free oxide ions, O^{2-}, are considered as basic oxides, CaO being the most well known example. Oxides that are acceptors of O_2 are considered as acidic oxides, SiO_2 being the most well known example.

Oxides that are neutral are considered as amphoteric oxides.

5. 1. 3. 4 Basicity Index

The concept of the basicity index (BI) was adopted in steelmaking to explain the ability of the slag to remove sulfur from the molten steel. It was later broadened to indicate the flux oxidation capability. The BI of a flux (especially an oxide-type one) can be defined in the following general form:

$$BI = \frac{\Sigma(\% \text{basic oxides})}{\Sigma(\% \text{nonbasic oxides})} \tag{5.20}$$

The concept of the BI was applied to welding. Tuliani et al. used the following well-known formula for the fluxes in SAW:

$$BI = \frac{CaF_2 + CaO + MgO + BaO + SrO + Na_2O + K_2O + Li_2O + 0.5(MnO + FeO)}{SiO_2 + 0.5(Al_2O_3 + TiO_2 + ZiO_2)} \tag{5.21}$$

where components are in weight fractions. Using the above expression, the flux is regarded as acidic when BI<1, as neutral when 1.0<BI<1.2, and as basic when BI>1.2. The formula correlates well with the oxygen content in submerged arc welds.

Eagar and Chai, however, modified Equation (3.21) by considering CaF_2 as neutral rather than basic and omitting the CaF_2 term. As shown in Figure 5.21, the formula correlates well with the oxygen content in submerged arc weld. The oxygen content decreases as the basicity index increases up to about 1.25 and reaches a constant value around 250 ppm at larger basicity values.

Baune et al. modified Equation (5.21) for FCAW electrodes by using the composition of the solidified slag after welding rather than the composition of the flux before welding. Furthermore, mole fraction was used rather than weight fraction, and FeO was replaced by Fe_2O_3. The composition of the solidified slag was thought to provide more information about the extent of the slag-metal reactions during welding than the composition of the flux before welding. The Fe_2O_3 was thought to be the iron oxide that forms in a welding slag. As shown in Figure 5.22, the weld oxygen content correlates well with the new basicity index.

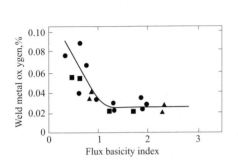

Figure 5.21 Weld metal oxygen content in steel as a function of flux basicity in submerged arc welding.

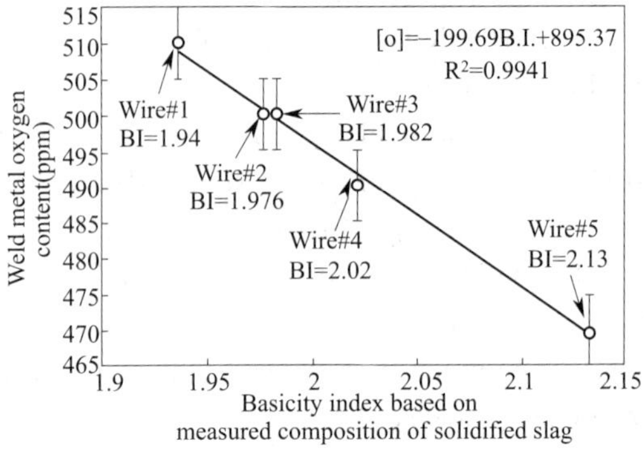

Figure 5.22 Weld metal oxygen content in steel as a function of flux basicity in flux-core arc welding.

Oxide inclusions in steel welds can affect the formation of acicular ferrite, which improves the weld metal toughness. It has been reported that acicular ferrite forms in the range of about 200–500 ppm oxygen. This will be discussed later in Chapter 9.

For SAW of high-strength, low-alloy steels with the CaF_2-CaO-SiO_2 flux system, Dallam et al. used the following simple formula for the basicity index:

$$BI = \frac{CaO}{SiO_2} \tag{5.22}$$

Figure 5.23 shows the effect of the basicity index on sulfur transfer. As the basicity index increases from 0 to 5, Dsulfur becomes increasingly negative, namely, more undesirable sulfur is transferred from the weld metal to the slag (desulfurization). This is because CaO is a strong desulfurizer, as shown previously by Equation (5.19).

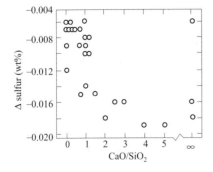

Figure 5.23 Desulfurization of high-strength, low-alloy steel welds as a function of basicity index CaO/SiO_2 of CaF_2-CaO-SiO_2 type flux.

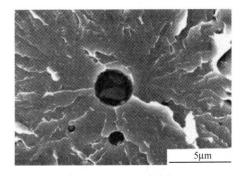

Figure 5.24 Fracture initiation at an inclusion in flux-cored arc weld of high-strength, low-alloy steel.

Excessive weld metal oxygen and hence oxide inclusions can deteriorate weld metal mechanical properties. As shown in Figure 5. 24, some inclusion particles can act as a fracture initiation site. Besides oxide inclusions, oxygen in the weld pool can also react with carbon to form CO gas during solidification. As shown in Figure 5. 25, this can result in gas porosity in steel welds. The addition of deoxidizers such as Al, Ti, Si, and Mn in the filler metal helps reduce the amount of porosity. Figure 5. 26 shows that the toughness of the weld metal decreases with increasing oxygen content. However, if the content of the acicular ferrite in the weld metal increases with the weld oxygen content, the weld metal toughness may in fact increase (Chapter 9).

Figure 5. 25 Wormhole porosity in weld metal.

Figure 5. 26 Relationship between the toughness at 20℃ and the oxygen content of steel welds.

Basic fluxes, however, can have some drawbacks. They are often found to have a greater tendency to absorb moisture, which can result in hydrogen embrittlement unless they are dried before welding. The slag detachability may not be very good in a fully basic flux. This makes slag removal more difficult, especially in multiple-pass or narrow-groove welding. In the case of FCAW, basic fluxes have also been observed to generate unstable arcs.

5. 1. 3. 5 Electrochemical Reactions

Kim et al. studied the effect of electrochemical reactions on the weld metal composition in SAW, and significant composition differences were observed when the electrode polarity was varied in DC welding. The following anodic oxidation reactions were proposed:

$$M(\text{metal}) + nO^{2-}(\text{slag}) = MO_n(\text{slag}) + 2ne^- \tag{5.23}$$

$$O^{2-}(\text{slag}) = O(\text{metal}) + 2e^- \tag{5.24}$$

These reactions occur at the electrode tip-slag interface in the electrode-positive polarity or the weld pool-slag interface in the electrode-negative polarity. Therefore, oxidation losses of alloying elements and pickup of oxygen are expected at the anode.

The following cathodic reduction reactions were also proposed:

$$M^{2+}(\text{slag}) + 2e^- = M(\text{metal}) \tag{5.25}$$

$$Si^{4+}(\text{slag}) + 4e^- = Si(\text{metal}) \tag{5.26}$$

$$O(\text{metal}) + 2e^- = O^{2-}(\text{slag}) \tag{5.27}$$

The first two reactions are the reduction of metallic cations from the slag, and the third reaction is the removal (refining) of oxygen from the metal. These reactions occur at the electrode tip-slag interface in the electrode-negative polarity or the weld pool-slag interface in the electrode-positive polarity. The current density is much higher at the electrode tip-slag interface than at the weld pool-slag interface. Therefore, reactions at the electrode tip may exert a greater influence on the weld metal composition than those at the weld pool.

A carbon steel containing 0. 18% C, 1. 25% Mn, and 0. 05% Si was submerged arc welded with a low-carbon steel wire of 0. 06% C, 1. 38% Mn, and 0. 05% Si and a flux of 11. 2% SiO_2, 18. 14% Al_2O_3, 33. 2% MgO, 25. 3% CaF_2, 6. 9% CaO, and 1. 2% MnO. Figure 5. 27 shows

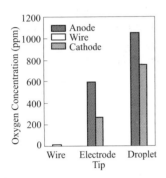

Figure 5. 27   Oxygen contents of the welding wire, melted electrode tips, and detached droplets for both electrode-positive and electrode-negative polarities.

the oxygen contents of the melted electrode tips and the detached droplets for both polarities, the 20ppm oxygen content of the wire being included as a reference. A significant oxygen pickup in the electrode tips is evident for both polarities, suggesting that the excess oxygen came from decomposition of oxide components in the flux and the surrounding atmosphere. The anodic electrode tip has about twice as much oxygen as the cathodic electrode tip, suggesting the significant effect of electrochemical reactions. The difference in the oxygen content is due to oxygen pickup at the anode and oxygen removal (refining) at the cathode. In either polarity the detached droplets contain more oxygen than the melted electrode tip. This suggests that the electrochemical reactions cease after the droplets separate from the electrode tips, but the droplets pick up more oxygen from decomposed oxides while falling through the arc plasma. The higher oxygen content in the droplets separated from the anodic electrode tip is due to the higher oxygen content of the melted anodic electrode tip.

Figure 5. 28 shows the silicon change in the weld pool for both polarities. Since there is plenty of oxygen from the decomposition of oxides, loss of silicon from the weld pool due to the thermochemical reaction $Si + 2O \Longrightarrow (SiO_2)$ is likely. But the silicon loss is recovered by the cathodic reduction $(Si^{4+}) + 4e^- \Longrightarrow Si$ and worsened by the anodic oxidation $Si + 2(O^{2-}) \Longrightarrow (SiO_2) + 4e^-$. Consequently, the silicon loss is more significant at the anode than at the cathode.

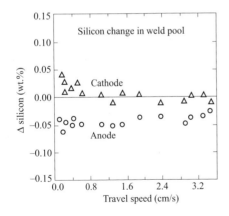

Figure 5. 28   Gain or loss of weld metal silicon due to reactions in weld pool for electrode-positive and electrode-negative polarities as a function of welding speed.

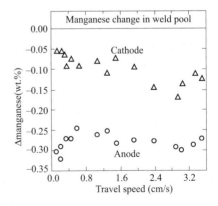

Figure 5. 29   Loss of weld metal manganese due to reactions in weld pool for electrode-positive and electrode-negative polarities as a function of welding speed.

Figure 5. 29 shows the manganese change in the weld pool for both polarities. The manganese loss from the weld pool to the slag is significant in both cases. This is because manganese is the richest alloying element in the weld pool (judging from the compositions of the workpiece and the filler metal) and MnO is among the poorest oxides in the flux. As such, the thermochemical reaction $Mn+O ==$ (MnO) can shift to the right easily and cause much manganese loss. Since manga-nese is known to have a high vapor pressure, evaporation from the liquid can be another reason for much manganese loss. However, the manganese loss is partially recovered by the cathodic re-duc-tion $(Mn^{2+})+2e^- ==Mn$ and worsened by the anodic oxidation $Mn+(O^{2-})==(MnO)+2e^-$. Consequently, the manganese loss is more significant at the anode than at the cathode.

5. 2 Weld Metal Solidification

5. 2. 1 Epitaxial Growth at Fusion Boundary

5. 2. 1. 1 Nucleation Theory

Figure 5. 30 shows the nucleation of a crystal from a liquid on a flat substrate with which the liquid is in contact. The parameters γ_{LC}, γ_{LS}, and γ_{CS} are the surface energies of the liquid-crystal interface, liquid-substrate interface, and crystal-substrate interface, respectively. According to Turnbull, the energy barrier ΔG for the crystal to nucleate on the substrate is

$$\Delta G = \frac{4\pi\gamma_{LC}^3 T_m^2}{3(\Delta H_m \Delta T)^2}(2-3\cos\theta+\cos^3\theta) \tag{5. 28}$$

where T_m is the equilibrium melting temperature, ΔH_m the latent heat of melting, ΔT the under-cooling below T_m, and q the contact angle. If the liquid wets the substrate completely, the contact angle q is zero and so is ΔG. This means that the crystal can nucleate on the substrate without having to overcome any energy barrier re-quired for nucleation. The energy barrier can be significant if no substrate is available or if the liquid does not wet the sub-strate completely.

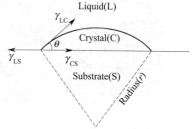

In fusion welding the existing base-metal grains at the fu-sion line act as the substrate for nucleation. Since the liquid metal of the weld pool is in intimate contact with these

Figure 5. 30 Spherical cap of a crystal nucleated on a planar substrate from a liquid.

substrate grains and wets them completely $(q=0)$, crystals nucleate from the liquid metal upon the substrate grains without difficulties. When welding without a filler metal (autogenous welding), nucleation occurs by arranging atoms from the liquid metal upon the substrate grains without altering their existing crystallographic orientations. Such a growth initiation process, shown schematically in Figure 5. 31, is called epitaxial growth or epitaxial nucle-ation. The arrow in each grain indicates its $<100>$ direction. For materials with a face-centered-cubic (fcc) or body-centered-cubic (bcc) crystal structure, the trunks of columnar dendrites (or cells) grow in the $<100>$ direction. As shown, each grain grows without changing its $<100>$ direction.

5. 2. 1. 2 Epitaxial Growth in Welding

Savage et al. first discovered epitaxial growth in fusion welding. By using the Laue x-ray back-reflection technique, they confirmed the continuity of crystallographic orientation across the fusion boundary. Savage and Hrubec also studied epitaxial growth by using a transparent organic material (camphene) as the workpiece, as shown in Figure 5. 32. Three grains are visible in the base metal at the fusion line. All dendrites growing from each grain point in one direction, and this direction varies from one grain to another. From the welds shown in Figure 5. 33 epitaxial growth at the fusion line is evident.

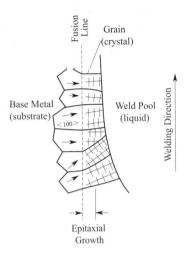

Figure 5. 31　Epitaxial growth of weld metal near fusion line.

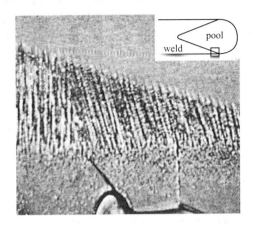

Figure 5. 32　Epitaxial growth during the "welding" of camphene in the area indicated by the square.

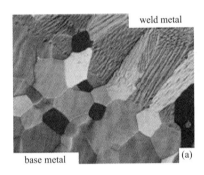

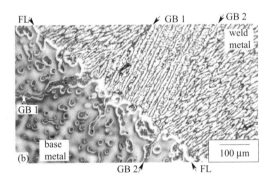

Figure 5. 33　Epitaxial growth. (a) Near the fusion boundary of electron beam weld of C103 alloy (b) Near the fusion boundary of as-cast Al-4. 5Cu welded with 4043 filler (Al-5Si).

Epitaxial growth can also occur when the workpiece is a material of more than one phase. Elmer et al. observed epitaxial growth in electron beam welding of an austenitic stainless steel consisting of both austenite and ferrite. As shown in Figure 5. 34, both austenite (A) and ferrite (F) grow epitaxially at the fusion line (dotted line) from the base metal to the weld metal (resolidified zone).

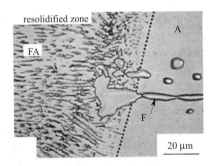

Figure 5. 34　Epitaxial growth of austenite (A) and ferrite (F) from the fusion line of an austenitic stainless steel containing both phases.

5. 2. 2　Nonepitaxial Growth at Fusion Boundary

When welding with a filler metal (or joining two different materials), the weld metal composition is different from the base metal composition, and the weld metal crystal structure can differ from the base metal crystal structure. When this occurs, epitaxial growth is no longer possible and new grains will have to nucleate at the fusion boundary.

Nelson et al. Welded a type 409 ferritic stainless steel of the bcc structure with a Monel (70Ni-30Cu) filler metal of the fcc structure and produced a fcc weld metal. Figure 5. 35 shows the fusion boundary microstructure. They proposed that, when the base metal and the weld metal exhibit two different crystal structures at the solidification temperature, nuclea-tion of solid weld metal occurs on heterogeneous sites on the partially melted base metal at the fusion boundary. The fusion boundary exhibits random misorientations between base metal grains and weld metal grains as a result of heterogeneous nucleation at the pool boundary. The weld metal grains may or may not follow special orientation relationships with the base metal grains they are in contact with, namely, orient themselves so that certain atomic planes are parallel to specific planes and directions in the base-metal grains.

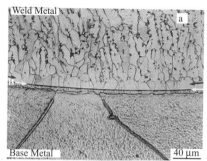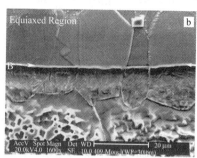

Figure 5. 35   Fusion boundary microstructure in 409 ferritic stainless steel (bcc) welded with Monel filler wire (fcc): (a) optical micrograph; (b) scanning electron micrograph. White arrows: fusion boundary; dark arrows: new grains nucleated along fusion boundary.

5. 2. 3   Competitive Growth in Bulk Fusion Zone

As described in the previous section, the grain structure near the fusion line of a weld is dominated either by epitaxial growth when the base metal and the weld metal have the same crystal structure or by nucleation of new grains when they have different crystal structures. Away from the fusion line, however, the grain structure is domina-ted by a different mechanism known as competitive growth. During weld metal solidification grains tend to grow in the di-rection perpendicular to pool boundary because this is the direc-tion of the maximum temperature gradient and hence maximum heat extraction. However, columnar dendrites or cells within each grain tend to grow in the easy-growth direction. Table 5. 5 shows the easy-growth directions in several materials and, as shown, it is$<100>$for both fcc and bcc materials. There-fore, during solidification grains with their easy-growth direc-tion essentially perpendicular to the pool boundary will grow more easily and crowd out those less favorably oriented grains, as shown schematically in Figure 5. 36. This mechanism of competitive growth dominates the grain structure of the bulk weld metal.

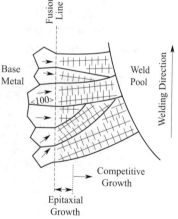

Figure 5. 36   Competitive growth in bulk fusion zone.

Table 5. 5   Easy-Growth Directions

Crystal Structure	Easy-Growth Direction	Examples
Face-centered-cubic(fcc)	$<100>$	Aluminum alloys,austenitic stainless steels
Body-centered-cubic(bcc)	$<100>$	Carbon steels,ferritic stainless steels
Hexagonal-close-packed(hcp)	$<10\bar{1}0>$	Titanium,magnesium
Body-centered-tetragonal(bct)	$<110>$	Tin

5. 2. 4　Effect of Welding Parameters on Grain Structure

The weld pool becomes teardrop shaped at high welding speeds and elliptical at low welding speeds. Since the trailing pool boundary of a teardrop-shaped weld pool is essentially straight, the columnar grains are also essentially straight in order to grow perpendicular to the pool boundary, as shown schematically in Figure 5. 37 (a). On the other hand, since the trailing boundary of an elliptical weld pool is curved, the columnar grains are also curved in order to grow perpendicular to the pool boundary, as shown in Figure 5. 37 (b). Figure 5. 38 shows the gas-tungsten arc welds of high-purity (99. 96%) aluminum made by Arata et al. . At the welding speed of 1000mm/min straight columnar grains point toward the centerline, while at 250mm/min curved columnar grains point in the welding direction.

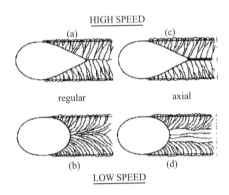

Figure 5. 37　Effect of welding speed on columnar -grain structure in weld metal: (a), (b)regular structure; (c), (d)with axial grains.

Axial grains can also exist in the fusion zone. Axial grains can initiate from the fusion boundary at the starting point of the weld and continue along the length of the weld, blocking the columnar grains growing inward from the fusion lines. Like other columnar grains, these axial grains also tend to grow perpendicular to the weld pool boundary. With a teardrop-shaped pool, only a short section of the trailing pool boundary can be perpendicular to the axial direction, and the region of axial grains is thus rather narrow, as shown in Figure 5. 37 (c). With an elliptical weld pool, however, a significantly longer section of the trailing pool boundary can be perpendicular to the axial direction, and the region of axial grains can thus be significantly wider, as shown in Figure 5. 37 (d). Figure 5. 38 and Figure 5. 39 shows aluminum welds with these two types of grain structure. Axial grains have been reported in aluminum alloys, austenitic stainless steels, and iridium alloys.

Figure 5. 38　Gas-tungsten arc welds of 99. 96% aluminum:
(a)　1000mm/min welding speed;　(b)　250 mm/min welding speed.

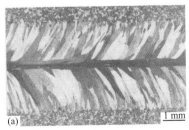
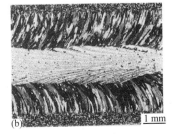

Figure 5. 39　Axial grains in GTAW: (a)　1100 aluminum at 12. 7mm/s welding speed;
(b)　2014 aluminum at 3. 6mm/s welding speed.

5. 2. 5　Weld Metal Nucleation Mechanisms

The mechanisms of nucleation of grains in the weld metal will be discussed in the present section. In order to help understand these mechanisms, the microstructure of the material around the weld pool will be discussed first.

Figure 5. 40 shows a 2219 aluminum (essentially Al-6. 3% Cu) weld pool quenched with ice water during GTAW. The S + L region around the weld pool consists of two parts [Figure 5. 40 (a)]: the partially melted material (clear) associated with the leading portion of the pool boundary and the mushy zone (shaded) associated with the trailing portion. Area 1 [Figure 5. 40 (b)] covers a small portion of the partially melted material. Area 2 [Figure 5. 40 (c)] covers a small portion of the mushy zone as well as the partially melted material.

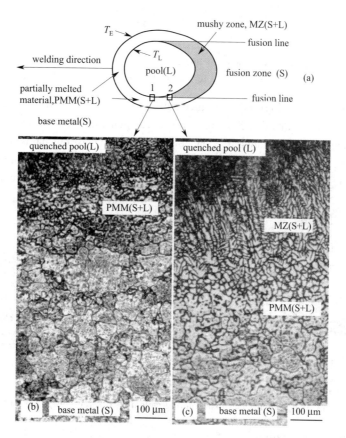

Figure 5. 40　Weld pool of 2219 aluminum quenched during GTAW:
(a) overall view; (b) microstructure at position 1; (c) microstructure at position 2.

Based on Figure 5. 40, the microstructure around the weld pool boundary of an alloy is shown schematically in Figure 5. 41, along with thermal cycles at the weld centerline and at the fusion line and a phase diagram. The eutectic type phase diagram is common among aluminum alloys. As shown, the mushy zone behind the trailing portion of the pool boundary consists of solid dendrites (S) and the interdendritic liquid (L). The partially melted material around the leading portion of the pool boundary, on the other hand, consists of solid grains (S) that are partially melted and the intergranular liquid (L).

In summary, there is a region of solid-liquid mixture surrounding the weld pool of an alloy.

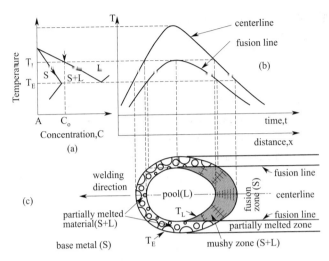

Figure 5. 41   Microstructure around the weld pool boundary:
(a) phase diagram; (b) thermal cycles; (c) microstructure of solid plus liquid around weld pool.

Figure 5. 42 (a) shows three possible mechanisms for new grains to nucleate during welding: dendrite fragmentation, grain detachment, and heterogeneous nucleation. Figure 5. 42 (b) shows the fourth nucleation mechanism, surface nucleation. These mechanisms, which have been well docu-mented in metal casting, will be described briefly below. The techniques for producing new grains in the weld metal by these mechanisms will be discussed in a subsequent section.

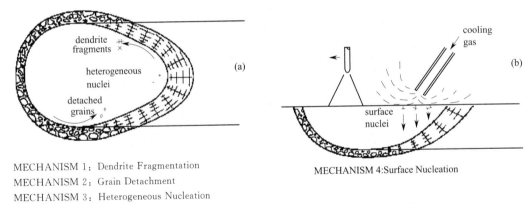

MECHANISM 1: Dendrite Fragmentation
MECHANISM 2: Grain Detachment
MECHANISM 3: Heterogeneous Nucleation

MECHANISM 4:Surface Nucleation

Figure 5. 42   Nucleation mechanisms during welding: (a) top view; (b) side view.

5. 2. 5. 1   Dendrite Fragmentation

Weld pool convection can in principle cause fragmentation of dendrite tips in the mushy zone, as illustrated in Figure 5. 42 (a). These dendrite fragments are carried into the bulk weld pool and act as nuclei for new grains to form if they survive the weld pool temperature. It is interesting to note that this mechanism has been referred to frequently as the grain refining mecha-nism for weld metals without proof.

5. 2. 5. 2   Grain Detachment

Weld pool convection can also cause partially melted grains to detach themselves from the sol-id-liquid mixture surrounding the weld pool, as shown in Figure 5. 42 (a). Like dendrite frag-ments, these partially melted grains, if they survive in the weld pool, can act as nuclei for the formation of new grains in the weld metal.

5. 2. 5. 3　Heterogeneous Nucleation

Foreign particles present in the weld pool upon which atoms in the liquid metal can be arranged in a crystalline form can act as heterogeneous nuclei. Figure 5. 43 depicts heterogeneous nucleation and the growth of new grains in the weld metal. Figure 5. 44 (a) shows two (dark) heterogeneous nuclei at the centers of two equiaxed grains in an autogenous gas-tungsten arc weld of a 6061 aluminum containing 0. 043% tita-nium. Energy dispersive spec-trometry (EDS) analysis, shown in Figure 5. 44 (b), indicates that these nuclei are rich in tita-nium (boron is

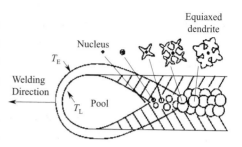

Figure 5. 43　Heterogeneous nucleation and formation of equiaxed grains in weld metal.

too light to be detected by EDS). A scanning electron microscopy (SEM) image of a nucleus is shown in Figure 5. 44 (c). The morphology of the nucleus is similar to that of the agglomerated TiB_2 particles, shown in Figure 5. 44 (d), in an Al-5% Ti-0. 2% B grain refiner for ingot casting of aluminum alloys. This suggests that the TiB_2 particles in the weld metal are likely to be from the Al-Ti-B grain refiner in aluminum ingot casting. Figure 5. 45 shows a heterogeneous nucleus of TiN at the center of an equiaxed grain in a GTA weld of a ferritic stainless steel.

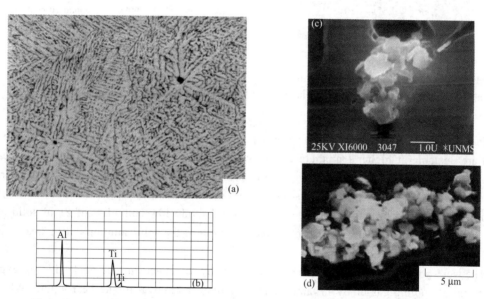

Figure 5. 44　Heterogeneous nuclei in GTAW of 6061 aluminum: (a) optical micrograph; (b) EDS analysis; (c) SEM image; (d) SEM image of TiB_2 particles in a grain refiner for aluminum casting.

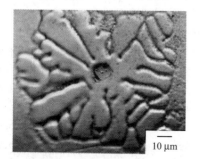

Figure 5. 45　TiN particle as heterogeneous nucleus in GTAW of ferritic stainless steel.

As mentioned previously, Nelson et al. have ob-served nucleation of solid weld metal on heterogeneous sites on the partially melted base metal at the fusion boundary when the weld metal and the base metal differ in crystal structure. Gutierrez and Lippold have also studied the for-mation of the nondendritic equiaxed zone in a narrow region of the weld metal adjacent to the fusion boundary of 2195 a-luminum (essentially Al-4Cu-1Li). Figure 5. 46 shows an example of the equiaxed zone in a 2195 weld made with a 2319 (essen-tially Al-6. 3Cu) filler metal. The width of the equiaxed zone was found to increase with increasing Zr and Li contents in the alloy. They proposed that near the pool boundary the cooler liquid is not mixed with the warmer bulk weld pool. Consequently, near the pool boundary heterogeneous nuclei such as Al_3Zr and Al_3 (Li_xZr_{1-x}) , which are originally present as dispersoids in the base metal, are able to survive and form the nondendritic equiaxed zone, as illustrated in Figure 5. 47. By using a Gleeble thermal simulator, Kou strivas and Lippold found that the equiaxed zone could be formed by heating in the temperature range of approximately 630-640℃ and at temperatures above 640℃ the normal epitaxial growth occurred. This is consistent with the proposed mechanism in the sense that the heterogeneous nuclei can only survive near the cooler pool boundary and not in the warmer bulk weld pool.

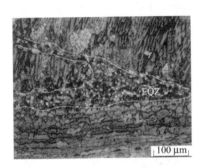

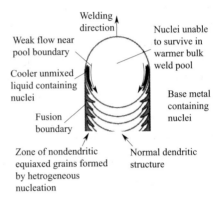

Figure 5. 46　Nondendritic equiaxed zone
in narrow region adjacent to fusion boundary
of 2195 Al-Cu-Li alloy.

Figure 5. 47　Mechanism for formation of
nondendritic equiaxed zone in Al-Cu-Li
weld according to Gutierrez and Lippold.

In the metal casting process the metal is superheated during melting before it is cast. Since the nuclei are unstable at higher temperatures, they dissolve in the superheated liquid in the casting process. As such, there is no equiaxed zone in the weld of an as-cast alloy 2195. However, the equiaxed zone occurs again if the as-cast alloy 2195 is solution heat treated first and then welded. Gutierrez and Lippold proposed that because of the relatively low solubility of Zr in solid aluminum, Al_3Zr and Al_3 (Li_xZr_{1-x}) particles precipitate out of the solid solution during heat treating.

5. 2. 5. 4　Surface Nucleation

The weld pool surface can be undercooled thermally to induce surface nucleation by exposure to a stream of cooling gas or by instantaneous reduction or removal of the heat input. When this occurs, solid nuclei can form at the weld pool surface, as illustrated in Figure 5. 42 (b). These solid nuclei then grow into new grains as they shower down from the weld pool surface due to their higher density than the surrounding liquid metal.

5. 2. 5. 5　Effect of Welding Parameters on Heterogeneous Nucleation

Before leaving this section, an important point should be made about the effect of welding par-ameters on heterogeneous nucleation. Kato et al., Arata et al., Ganaha et al., and Kou and Le observed in commercial aluminum alloys that the formation of equiaxed grains is enhanced by higher heat inputs and welding speeds. As shown in Figure 5. 48, equiaxed grains can form a band along the centerline of the weld and block off columnar grains as the heat input and welding speed are increased. Kou and Le showed in Figure 5. 49 that, as the heat input and the welding speed are increased, the temperature gradient (G) at the end of the weld pool is reduced. Furthermore, as the welding speed is increased, the solidification rate of the weld metal (R) is also in-

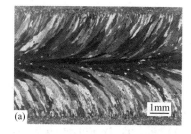 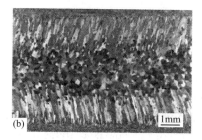

Figure 5. 48   Effect of welding parameters on grain structure in GTAW of 6061 aluminum:
(a) 70A×11V heat input and 5. 1 mm/s welding speed;
(b) 120A×11V heat input and 12. 7 mm/s welding speed.

creased. As illustrated in Figure 5. 50, the ratio G/R should be decreased and the constitutional supercooling in front of the advancing solid-liquid interface should, therefore, be increased. Kato et al. and Arata et al. proposed that the transition to an equiaxed grain structure is due to the existence of a sufficiently long constitutionally undercooled zone in the weld pool. Ganaha et al., however, indicated that the transition is not due to constitu-tional supercooling alone. In fact, it was observed that significant amounts of equiaxed grains formed only in those alloys containing around or more than 0. 01wt% Ti or

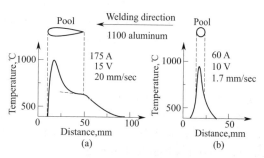

Figure 5. 49   Effect of welding parameters on temperature gradient at weld pool end of 1100 aluminum: (a) higher welding speed and heat input; (b) lower welding speed and heat input.

0. 10wt% Zr. Furthermore, tiny second-phase particles rich in titanium and/or zirconium (possibly $Ti_x Zr_y C$ compounds) existed at the dendrite centers of the equiaxed grains. Consequently, it was proposed that equiaxed grains in the fusion zone form by heterogeneous nucleation aided by constitutional supercooling. The observation of Ganaha et al. was confirmed by Kou and Le. The effect of welding parameters on grain refining in aluminum welds was discussed by Kou and Le.

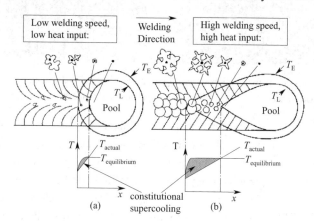

Figure 5. 50   Effect of welding parameters on heterogeneous nucleation:
(a) low constitutional supercooling at low welding speed and heat input; (b) heterogeneous nucleation aided by high constitutional supercooling at high welding speed and heat input.

5.2.6　Grain Structure Control

The weld metal grain structure can affect its mechanical properties significantly. Arata et al. tensile tested aluminum welds in the welding direction. The weld metal ductility of 99. 96% aluminum dropped greatly when the columnar grains pointed to the weld centerline [Figure 5 38 (a)], that is, when the grains became nearly normal to the tensile axis. Also, the weld metal tensile strength of 5052 aluminum increased as the amount of equiaxed grains increased.

The formation of fine equiaxed grains in the fusion zone has two main advantages. First, fine grains help reduce the susceptibility of the weld metal to solidification cracking during welding. Second, fine grains can improve the mechanical properties of the weld, such as the ductility and fracture toughness in the case of steels and stainless steels. Therefore, much effort has been made to try to grain refine the weld fusion zone. This includes the application of grain refining techniques that were originally developed for casting. Described below are several techniques that have been used to control the weld metal grain structure.

5.2.6.1　Inoculation

This technique has been used extensively in metal casting. It involves the addition of nucleating agents or inoculants to the liquid metal to be solidified. As a result of inoculation, heterogeneous nucleation is promoted and the liquid metal solidifies with very fine equiaxed grains. In the work by Davies and Garland, inoculant powders of titanium carbide and ferrotitanium- titanium carbide mixtures were fed into the weld pool during the submerged arc welding of a mild steel and very fine grains were obtained. Similarly, Heintze and McPherson grain refined submerged arc welds of C-Mn and stainless steels with titanium. Figure 5. 51 shows the effect of inoculation on the grain structure of the weld fusion zone of the C-Mn steel. It is interesting to note that Petersen has grain refined Cr-Ni iron base alloys with aluminum nitride and reported a significant increase in the ductility of the resultant welds, as shown in Figure 5. 52.

 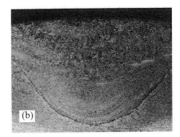

Figure 5. 51　Effect of inoculation on grain structure in submerged arc welds of C-Mn steel
(magnification 6×) : (a) without inoculation; (b) inoculation with titanium.

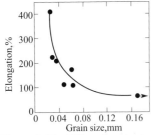

Figure 5. 52　Effect of grain size on weld metal ductility of a Cr-Ni iron base alloy at 925℃.

Pearce and Kerr, Matsuda et al., Yunjia et al., and Sundaresan et al. grain refined aluminum welds by using Ti and Zr as inoculants. Yunjia et al. showed the presence of $TiAl_3$ particles at the origins of equiaxed grains in Ti microalloyed 1100 aluminum welds. Figure 5. 53 shows grain refining in a 2090 Al-Li-Cu alloy gas-tungsten arc welded with a 2319 Al-Cu filler inoculated with 0. 38% Ti.

5.2.6.2　External Excitation

Different dynamic grain refining techniques, such as liquid pool stirring, mold oscillation, and ultrasonic vibration of the liquid metal, have been employed in metal casting, and recently simi-

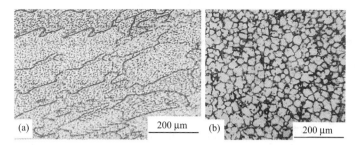

Figure 5. 53　Effect of inoculation on grain structure in GTAW of 2090 Al-Li-Cu alloy:
(a) 2319 Al-Cu filler metal;　(b) 2319 Al-Cu filler metal inoculated with 0. 38% Ti.

lar tech-niques,　including weld pool stirring,　arc oscillation,　and arc pulsation,　have been ap-plied to fusion welding.

(1) Weld Pool Stirring

Weld pool stirring can be achieved by electromagnetic stirring,　as shown in Figure 5. 54,　by applying an alterna-ting magnetic field parallel to the welding electrode. Matsuda et al. and Pearce and Kerr increased the degree of grain re-finement in aluminum alloys containing small amounts of tita-nium by electromagnetic pool stirring. Pearce and Kerr sug-gested that the increased grain refinement was due to hetero-geneous nucleation,　rather than to dendrite fragmentation. This is because in GTAW,　unlike ingot casting,　the liquid pool and the mushy zone are rather small,　and it is therefore difficult for the liquid metal in the pool to penetrate and break away dendrites,　which are so short and so densely packed together.

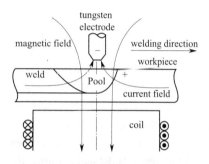

Figure 5. 54　Schematic sketch showing application of external magnetic field during autogenous GTAW.

Stirring of the weld pool tends to lower the weld pool temperature,　thus helping heterogeneous nuclei survive.　Figure 5. 55 shows the increased grain refinement by weld pool stirring in an Al-2. 5wt% Mg al-loy containing 0. 11wt% Ti. As shown in Figure 5. 56,　Villafuerte and Kerr grainer fined a weld of 409 ferritic stainless steel containing 0. 32% Ti by the same technique. The higher the Ti content,　the more effective grain refining was. Titanium-rich particles were found at the origin of equiaxed grains,　sugges-ting heterogeneous nucleation as the grain refining mechanism.

Pearce and Kerr also found that by applying weld pool stirring,　the partially melted grains along the leading portion of the pool boundary,　if they are only loosely held together,　could be swept by the liquid metal into the weld pool,　where they served as nuclei. Significant amounts of equiaxed grains were so produced in gas-tungsten arc welds of a 7004 aluminum alloy containing very little Ti.

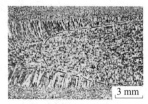
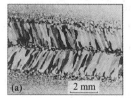
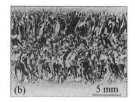

Figure 5. 55　Widening of equiaxed zone in GTAW of alloy Al-2. 5Mg-0. 011 Ti by magnetic stirring (at dotted line)

Figure 5. 56　Effect of electromagnetic pool stirring on grain structure in GTAW of 409 ferritic stainless steel: (a) without stirring; (b) with stirring.

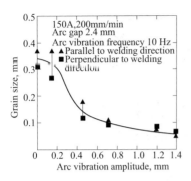

Figure 5. 57　Effect of arc vibration
amplitude on grain size in Al-2. 5Mg welds.

(2)　Arc Oscillation

Arc oscillation, on the other hand, can be produced by magnetically oscillating the arc column using a single- or multipole magnetic probe or by mechanically vibrating the welding torch. Davies and Garland produced grain refining in gas-tungsten arc welds of Al-2. 5wt% Mg alloy by torch vibration. Resistance to weld solidification cracking was improved in these welds. Figure 5. 57 shows the effect of the vibration amplitude on the grain size. Dendrite fragmentation was proposed as the grain refining mechanism. It is, however, suspected that heterogeneous nucleation could have been the real mechanism, judging from the fact that the Al-2. 5wt% Mg used actually contained about 015wt% Ti. Venkataraman et al. obtained grain refining in the electroslag welds of steels by electrode vibration and enhanced electromagnetic stir-ring of the weld pool and improved their toughness and resistance to centerline cracking. Dendrite fragmentation was also considered as the mechanism for grain refining.

Sharir et al. obtained grain refinement in gas-tungsten arc welds of pure tantalum sheets by arc oscillation. Due to the high melting point of pure tantalum (about 3000℃) , the surface heat loss due to radiation was rather significant. As a result, the liquid metal was cooled down rapidly and was in fact undercooled below its melting point when the heat source was deflected away during oscillated arc welding. This caused surface nucleation and resulted in grain refinement.

Sundaresan and Janaki Ram grain refined Ti alloys by magnetic arc oscillation and improved the weld metal tensile ductility. No specific grain refining mechanism was identified.

(3)　Arc Pulsation

Arc pulsation can be obtained by pulsating the welding current. Sharir et al. also obtained grain refinement in gas-tungsten arc welds of pure tantalum sheets by arc pulsation. The liquid metal was undercooled when the heat input was suddenly reduced during the low-current cycle of pulsed arc welding. This caused surface nucleation and resulted in grain refinement.

Figure 5. 58 shows grain refining in a pulsed arc weld of a 6061 aluminum alloy containing 004wt% Ti. Heterogeneous nucleation, aided by thermal undercooling resulting from the high cooling rate produced by the relatively high welding speed used and arc pulsation, could have been responsible for the grain refinement in the weld.

Figure 5. 58　Equiaxed grains in
pulsed arc weld of 6061 aluminum.

5. 2. 6. 3　Stimulated Surface Nucleation

Stimulated surface nucleation was originally used by Southin to obtain grain refinement in ingot casting. A stream of cool argon gas was directed on the free surface of molten metal to cause thermal undercooling and induce surface nucleation. Small solidification nuclei formed at the free surface and showered down into the bulk liquid metal. These nuclei then grew and became small equiaxed grains. This technique was used to produce grain refining in Al-2. 5Mg welds by Davies and Garland and in Ti alloys by Well.

5. 2. 6. 4　Manipulation of Columnar Grains

Kou and Le manipulated the orientation of columnar grains in aluminum welds by low-frequency arc oscillation. Figure 5.59 (a) shows a 2014 aluminum weld made with 1Hz transverse arc oscillation, that is, with arc oscillating normal to the welding direction. Similarly, Figure 5.59 (b) shows a 5052 aluminum weld made with 1 Hz circular arc oscillation. In both cases, columnar grains grew perpendicular to the trailing portion of the weld pool, and the weld pool in turn followed the path of the moving oscillating arc.

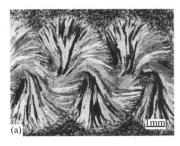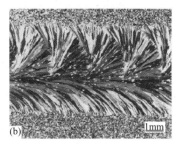

Figure 5.59 Grain structures in oscillated arc welds of aluminum alloys.
(a) For alloy 2014 with transverse arc oscillation; (b) For alloy 5052 with circular arc oscillation.

As will be discussed later, periodic changes in grain orientation, especially that produced by transverse arc oscillation at low frequencies, can reduce solidification cracking and improve both the strength and ductility of the weld metal.

5.2.6.5 Gravity

Aidun and Dean gas-tungsten arc welded 2195 aluminum under the high gravity produced by a centrifuge welding system and eliminated the narrow band of nondendritic equiaxed grains along the fusion boundary. As shown in Figure 5.60, the band disappeared when gravity was increased from 1 g to 10 g. It was suggested that buoyancy convection enhanced by high gravity caused Al_3Zr and Al_3 (Li_xZr_{1-x}) nuclei near the pool boundary to be swept into the bulk pool and completely dissolved, thus eliminating formation of equiaxed grains by heterogeneous nucleation.

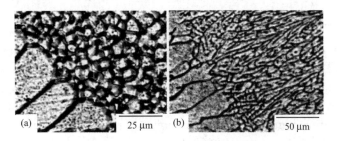

Figure 5.60 Effect of gravity on grain structure in GTAW of 2090 Al-Li-Cu alloy:
(a) 1g; (b) 10g and with equiaxed zone (EQZ) near the fusion boundary eliminated.

5.3 The Microstructure and Properties of Heat-affected Zone

When C-Mn or low-alloy steels are welded, the resulting joint consists of four distinct regions, namely, the deposited weld metal, the phase transformation (visible) heat-affected zone (HAZ), the subcritical (non-visible) HAZ, and the unaffected parent materials. Because of the engineering design is based usually on the last of these four, it is important that the properties of the HAZ, which will be very different from those of the parent material, are adequate for the intended use of the structure. This part will discuss the main effects of weld thermal cycle on the HAZ properties, such as the microstructures, hardness, the cracks and the mechanical properties.

5.3.1 Welding Thermal Cycle

During arc welding, mass heat conducts with the deposit metal to the weld pool quickly. The base metal in the vicinity of the weld is subjected to complex thermal cycle in which all temperatures from the melting range down to mare warming are involved. In general, the heating and cooling rates of the weld thermal cycle are very high, and the heated metal is subjected to plastic tensile strain during cooling. Figure 5.61 shows a typical welding thermal cycle curve. The area affected by the welding thermal cycle named heat-affected zone (HAZ), which is in general a thin band around the weld beam. It is not surprising therefore that the metallurgical effects of the weld thermal cycle are complex and may in some instance result in an unfavorable change in the properties of the HAZ of a weld joint.

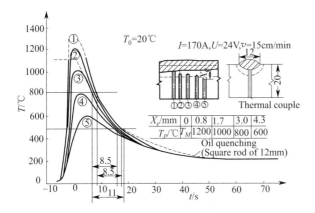

Figure 5.61 typical welding thermal cycle profile
for a low-alloy steel weld joint.

Figure 5.62 The microstructure
of weld HAZ.

5.3.2 The Microstructure Changes in the HAZ

In general, the HAZ may be divided into two regions: the high temperature region (phase trans-formation HAZ, visible) in which major changes such as grain growth take place, and the lower temperature region (subcritical HAZ, non-visible) in which secondary effects such as precipitation may occur. For the C-Mn and low-alloyed steel, the phase transformed HAZ can be further divided to a coarsened grain region which bordered on the fusion line of the weld, and a fine grain region, which bordered on the unaffected parent metal. The peak temperature, the residence time and the cooling rate are the three main factors which affect the microstructures in the HAZ mainly. Figure 5.62 is a typical photomicrograph of weld HAZ.

5.3.2.1 Effects of the Peak Temperature and Residence Time on Microstructure

In the coarsened grain region the final grain size for any given alloys will depend mainly on the peak temperature to which it is exposed and the time of heating and cooling (the *residence time*). In the case of steel it is found that for isothermal heating the final mean grain size d_t is given by

$$d_t^n = kt + d_0^n \qquad (5.29)$$

where k is a constant, t is time and d_0 is the initial grain size. If the exponent n and the constant k are determined by isothermal heating, the grain growth in the HAZ may be estimated by a stepwise calculation.

However, it will generally be sufficient to note that the final grain size will increase with increasing peak temperature and increasing residence time. In fact, the maximum peak temperature is the melting point and it is the grain size at the fusion boundary in which we are mainly interested, since this determines the grain size in the weld metal. The only significant variable therefore is re-si-dence time. The residence time for three-dimensional heat flow may be obtained from the charts developed by Christensen *et al*, as shown in Figure 5. 63. These results show that residence time is roughly proportional to the parameter q/v (the heat input rate). Thus, welding processes having characteristically high values of q/v, such as electroslag and high-current submerged arc welding would be expected to generate coarse grain in the HAZ and in the weld metal. And this is indeed the case. For carbon and ferritic alloy steel, we are referring here to the austenitic grain size.

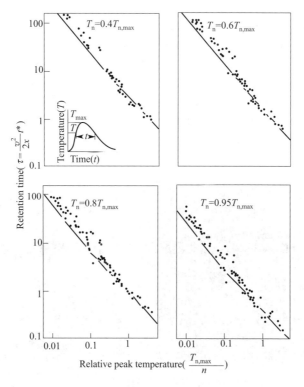

Figure 5. 63　Time spent in various ranges below the peak
temperature: from T_n (max) to T_n.

If the metal that is subject to the weld thermal cycle has previously been hardened by cold work, then grain growth may be preceded by recrystallisation which, in turn, results in soften-ing. Copper and aluminum are typical of metals that can acquire a useful increase in mechanical proper-ties by cold reduction and fusion welding will usually destroy the effect of cold word in the HAZ. Similarly, alloys that are hardened by precipitation will usually be softened by fusion welding.

To prevent the grain growth in the HAZ, there are two ways in which the residence time can be reduced: firstly, by using a process that generates two-dimensional rather than three-dimension-al heat flow (residence times for two-dimensional heat flow are about half those for three-dimen-sional flow), and secondly by decreasing the heat input rate q/v.

Electron beam and laser welding have these characteristics and it is one of the advantages of such process that they minimize the metallurgical disturbance in the HAZ.

5. 3. 2. 2　Effects of the Cooling Rate on Microstructure

The cooling rate associated with the weld nugget depends on the total heat in the molten weld metal and the mass and temperature of the welded part. For any process the volume of molten metal will depend upon the heat input and the efficiency of utilizing this heat in producing molten metal. Most of the electric welding processes with suitable techniques utilize 40-70% of the input to produce molten metal. However, oxy-fuel (gas) welding processes may have an efficiency as low as 10 or 20%.

For a given welding method, the cooling rates depend mainly on three variables: the rate of heat input, the base metal temperature before welding, and the section thickness and joint geometry. High inputs and preheating favor slow cooling, while heavy sections encourage fast cooling rate. The first tow factors can be used in welding to control the cooling, whether the process is arc, gas, or resistance.

Besides the peak temperature and residence time, the cooling rate affects the microstructure of HAZ, too. A comparison of the microstructures in two HAZs, one produced by a high heat input and slow cooling and the other by a low heat input and fast cooling, both in an arc welded 3/4 inch thick 0. 25% carbon steel, is presented in Figure 5. 64. In the left micrograph (a), the slowly cooled, coarse-grained, HAZ contains only pearlite and ferrite. In the right micrograph (b), the rapid cooled HAZ shows a considerable amount of light-etching martensite in the coarse grains. Here cooling has been so fast that formation of the high temperature decomposition products has been partly suppressed.

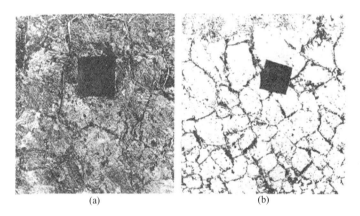

(a)   (b)

Figure 5. 64　Microstructure of coarse grains in HAZ of 0. 25% carbon steel.
(a) high heat input, slowly cooled;　(b) low heat input, rapidly cooled (100).

5. 3. 2. 3　Precipitation and Embrittlement in the HAZ

In addition to grain growth, which may in itself cause embrittlement, there are a number of metallurgical changes that result from the weld thermal cycle and that may alter the properties of the parent metal. Also, the HAZ may be permeated by hydrogen. Hydrogen does not appear to have any significant effect on the properties of austenitic chromium-nickel steel or non-ferrous metals other than copper. Ferritic steel is embrittled to a greater or lesser degree by hydrogen, and copper, if it is not deoxidized, may be severely embrittled by the reaction of hydrogen with residual oxygen to form steam. The steam precipitates at grain boundaries and generates fissures.

Ferritic alloy steels may be embrittled by the formation of unfavorable transformation products, by carbide precipitation, by grain boundary segregation (temper brittleness) and by strain ageing. Austenitic chromium-nickel steels may embrittle at elevated temperature due to a strain ageing mechanism during postweld heat treatment or in service.

A number of alloys may be embrittled within a specific temperature range, causing ductility dip cracking. These include fully austenitic chromium-nickel steels, some nickel-base alloys and some cu-pronickels. Figure 5. 65 shows a plot of ductility against temperature for a number of cupronickels, which indicates that for nickel contents of 18% and higher the ductility falls sharply to a minimum at about 1000K. Above and below the ductility trough, fracture is by microvoid coalescence; in the trough itself the fractures are intergranular. Such intergran-ular failure is normally attributed to segregation of impurity atoms (S or P in the case of austenitic Cr-Ni steel) to the grain boundary. In the case of the cupronickel tests illustrated in figure 5. 65, high puri-ty material was used and the segregating element could have been nickel itself.

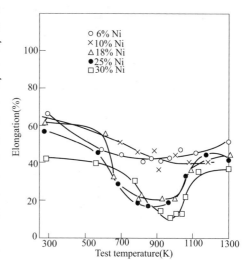

Figure 5. 65   Ductility test results for binary copper-nickel alloys.

Ductility dip cracking occurs in multi-pass welding with a susceptible weld deposit composition. Cracks occur in weld metal below the finishing pass due to tensile straining in the susceptible temperature range (possibly during the heating phase of the weld thermal cycle). Such cracks may not be detected by surface crack detection methods, but would show up in destructive testing, particularly side bend tests. Changes in welding procedure, by modifying the thermal cycle, may eliminate the cracking and in some instances the steps used to avoid solidification cracking may be effective: in the case of austenitic Cr-Ni steel, for example, by reducing S and P, increasing manganese, and adding special deoxidants such as calcium or zirconium.

5. 3. 3   Hardness Distribution in the HAZ

The weld metal and the HAZ base metal may receive from the surrounding cold base metal a quench that ranges from that of relatively slow air cooling to fast water quenching. Therefore, the weld metal and the HAZ base metal may contain soft, almost fully hardened, or mixed soft and hard structures.

5. 3. 3. 1   Effect of Composition on the Hardness Distribution in the HAZ

To study the effect of composition of steel on the HAZ hardness, three typical steels, that is, mild steel, Ducol steel, and Ni-Cr steel are selected. Two parts of the parent materials were welded together by manual welding process with the same electrode. After welding, the joint was cut off from center and polished the cross section. Then, the hardness was measured. Figure 5. 66 showed the hardness distribution results. Firstly, it was shown that the Vickers hardness in weld metal in the center of the weld is about 165 in case of mild steel plate, about 200 in case of Ducol steel plate, and about 300 in case of Ni-Cr steel. Secondly, according to the Figure 5. 66, a hardness peak exists which is strikingly higher than in the other part and this tendency becomes more remarkable in order of middle steel, Ducol steel and Ni-Cr steel, in other words, this tendency becomes more remarkable with an increase in the ability to harden by quenching. As we know, the weld metal microstructures are ferritic and pealite for the mild steel, ferrite, troostite, and martensite for the Ducol steel, and all martensite for the Ni-Cr steel, respectively. Table 5. 6 listed the maximum hardness of the welding HAZ for the three metals. The stronger the quenching tendency, the higher the hardness of the welding HAZ is.

Table 5. 6   Max. hardness of welding HAZ and kinds of steel

Kinds of steel	Max.hardness(Vickers)
Mild steel	170
Ducol steel	305
Ni-Cr steel	535

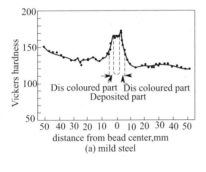

(a) mild steel

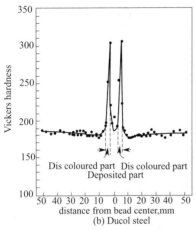

(b) Ducol steel

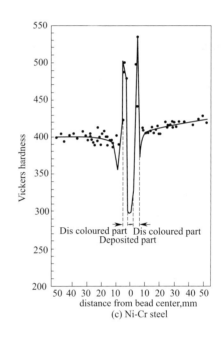

(c) Ni-Cr steel

Figure 5. 66   Hardness distribution in the neighborhood of bead on various kinds of steel.

However, for the same kind of steel, the structural constituents of the HAZ depend on the cooling rate of the portion from the high temperature to which it is exposed by welding, that is, the maximum hardness also changes with this rate. For example, the maximum hardness increases with an increase in the direction perpendicular to the bead is small. Figure 5. 67 gives an example which shows the relation between the thickness of the plate and the maximum hardness of HAZ in the case of the Ducol steel plate deposited with manual welding.

When other conditions are equal, the greater the maximum hardness of welding HAZ, the *occurrence frequency of cracks* in the neighborhood will be the higher generally, as shown in Figure 5. 68. Accordingly, also about Ducol steel, if plate thickness is larger, cracks may occur in the neighborhood of the hardened part. In the case of Ni-Cr steel, even if it has been preheated, the maximum hardness is markedly great and occurring frequency of cracks in the neighborhood of the hardened part is strikingly high, so long as due attention is not paid to the welding rod and the welding process to be used.

5. 3. 3. 2   Effect of Welding Methods on the Hardness Distribution in the HAZ

(1)   Manual Arc Welding Process

Using the ilmenite type coated rod (JIS D 4301) of 3. 2~6. 0mm diameter and adopting

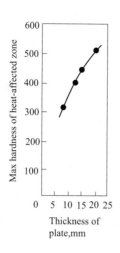

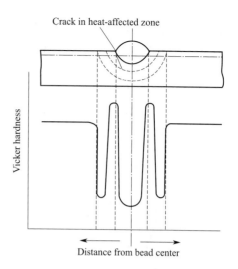

Figure 5. 67　Effect of plate thickness on
the max. hardness of HAZ.

Figure 5. 68　Position of HAZ crack and
hardness distribution.

alternate current from flat position, the welding was executed in three layers on the surface side in one layer on the back side. After welding, the central part was cut off in the direction perpendicular to the bead and after grinding and polishing, the Vickers hardness distribution on the straight line were shown in Figure 5. 69. The hardness of the HAZ is slightly higher than the weld and parent metal.

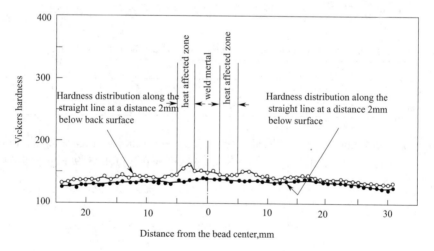

Figure 5. 69　Hardness distribution in the neighborhood of bead
(Mild steel joint by manual arc welding process).

Submerged Arc Welding Process. A kind of mild steel (JIS SS 41) have the following composition and dimensions used in the experiment was shown in Table 5. 7. Figure 5. 70 shows the other welding parameters.

Figure 5. 71 shows the hardness distribution of a joint welded with the submerged arc welding process. The hardness profile indicated that the hardness in the HAZ is higher than that of the parent metal but lower than the weld nugget slightly, which is different from the manual arc welding process. Higher heat input and much lower cool rate are the typical characters of the submerged arc welding process, which are the main reason for such a hardness distribution results.

Table 5.7 The composition and dimensions of the weld experiment

items	C	Mn	Si	P	S
Composition(wt%)	0. 16	0. 55	0. 24	0. 013	0. 019
Wire(wt%)	0. 13	1. 95	0. 03	—	—
Dimensions(mm)	16. 0(thickness)	400(width)		900(length)	
Weld parameters	Current:AC 1250A	Voltage:36V		Rate:420mm/min	

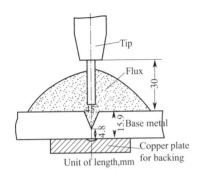

Figure 5. 70　Submerged arc welding process and butt welding with Y-groove.

Figure 5. 71　Hardness distribution in the neighborhood of bead (mild steel joint by submerged arc welding process, along the straight line at a distance of 2mm below surface).

(2) Narrow Gap One Side Welding Process (NOW)

A kind of mild steel of 25mm thickness (JIS SS 41) was used in the present welding experiment. The composition of the parent metal and flux cored wire used in the experiment was shown in Table 5. 8.

Table 5.8 The composition of parent metal and the flux cored wire

Items	C	Si	Mn	P	S	Cu	Ti
Parent metal	0. 03	0. 75	1. 70	0. 01	0. 015	0. 15	0. 15
Flux cored wire	0. 05	0. 70	1. 74	0. 007	0. 016	0. 08	0. 10

Figure 5. 72 shows the hardness distribution of the weld joint and Figure 5. 73 shows the principle of NOW process. The welding conditions are given in the Table 5. 9. Figure 5. 74 shows the positions of hardness measurement.

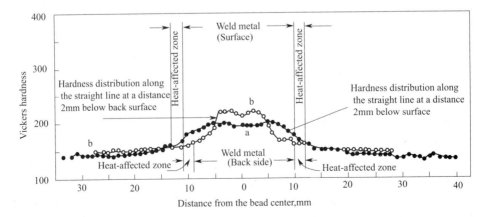

Figure 5. 72　Hardness distributions on the neighborhood of bead (Mild steel joint by NOW process)

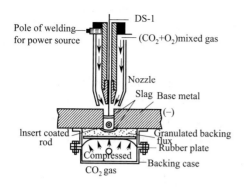

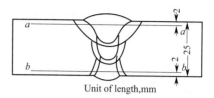

Figure 5. 73　Principle of Narrow gap One side Welding Process (NOW process).

Figure 5. 74　Positions of hardness distribution measurement.

Table 5. 9　Conditions of welding

Item		1st layer	2nd layer	3rd layer
Current,A		340	350	430
Voltage,V		31	33	36
Proceeding rate of bead,cm/min		18	23	24
Hight of tip,mm		8	12	20
Root gap,mm	1st layer	7. 8	7. 4	—
	2nd layer	7. 8	7. 0	6. 3
	3rd layer	7. 9	6. 9	6. 1
	4th layer	7. 9	6. 95	6. 1
	5th layer	7. 8	7. 3	6. 7

The hardness distribution of a NOW joint is similar to that of a submerged arc welding process, that is, the hardness of HAZ is higher than the parent metal but lower than the weld nugget. Furthermore, the hardness profile is different between the top side (line a) and bottom side (line b). The hardness of the bottom side weld nugget is higher than the top side. Such a hardness distribution also was decided by the heat input and the cooling rate.

5. 3. 4　Welding Cracks in the HAZ

Welding cracks are often found in the HAZ of "air hardenable" alloy steel. Though these cracks are of various types, they are sometimes called by the name of hardened zone cracks or by some other names. There is no doubt that the formation of the martensite in the welding HAZ is an indispensable condition for the appearance of hardened zone cracks in the air hardenable alloy steel, such as the Ni-Cr-Mo steel. When an intensively "air hardenable" steel is used in welding crack tests, it always causes an almost entirely martensitic HAZ in welding, even when the welding parameters are varied to some extent. Therefore, such a kind of steel is favorable in welding cracking tests for the clarification of the causes other than the martensite formation. Accordingly, an "air hardenable" Ni-Cr-Mo steel, of which the chemical composition is given in Table 5. 10, was chosen as specimens in the following cracks tests.

Table 5. 10　Chemical composition of Ni-Cr-Mo steel

Elements	C	Si	Mn	P	S	Cu	Ni	Cr	Mo
Content(wt%)	0. 45	0. 25	0. 47	0. 016	0. 007	0. 10	2. 80	1. 23	0. 27

Many small plate specimens, approximately 80mm square, with various thicknesses (i. e. ,35, 30,25,20,15,10, 5 and 3mm) were produced by slicing laterally 80mm square forged billets. These specimens were kept at 870℃ for 10min. and hardened by cooling in air before welding. A single bead with a length 50mm was deposited on the center of the plate surface by using several welding parameters, as shown in Figure 5. 75.

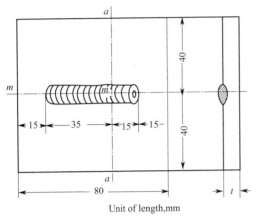

Unit of length,mm

Figure 5. 75 Detail of the specimen.

Welding was accomplished by the coated electrode arc welding method and the argon arc welding method, respectively. In coated rod arc welding, three types of coated rod, of which the core diameter is 4. 0mm, namely, ilmenite type mild steel coated rods, low hydrogen type mild steel coated rods and 18-8 austenitic steel type coated rods were used. Welding current used was AC 140amp. The time required for welding each bead to a length 50mm was 15～20s.

In argon arc welding, the core rods of ilmenite type mild steel coated rods were used as filler rods. Direct current (DC) was adopted, connecting the electrode to the negative pole, and tungsten electrodes were employed. In order to obtain almost the same quantity of weld metal and nearly the same penetration as in the case of coated rod arc welding, higher welding currents were used in argon arc welding. That is, welding currents, 300, 280, 250 and 200amp. were used for the specimens with thickness 25 to 35mm, 15 to 20mm, 5 to 10mm and 3mm, respectively. The filler rods with a diameter of 4mm were used for the specimens thicker than 15mm, and those with a diameter of 3. 2mm were used for the others. The rate of argon flow was 15cfh. Before operation, the coated rods were dried at 100℃ and 300℃ for the ilmenite type and other type rods, respectively.

When over twenty four hours elapsed after welding, all specimens were cut in transverse direction (a-a in Figure 5. 75) and longitudinal direction (m-m in Figure 5. 75). Four types of cracks, namely, toe, underbead, transverse and longitudinal cracks, were observed macroscopically and microscopically in these sections, which had been polished and etched with 5% Nital, as schemati-cally illustrated in Figure 5. 76. Though transverse cracks are more often observed on the surface of specimens before cutting, their existence was confirmed in the sections. The results of the cracking tests are summarized in Table 5. 11.

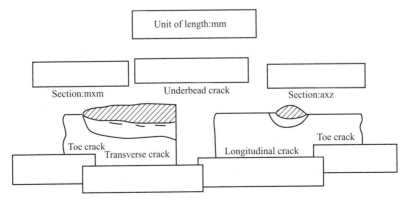

Figure 5. 76 Four types of cracks

Toe cracks have different aspects from underbead cracks. They occur in nearly all the specimens welded with the ilmenite type coated rod, low hydrogen type coated rod. And mold steel filler rod under the shield of argon. But they are observed in only one of the 14 specimens welded with the austenitic steel type coated rods.

From these results, it may be concluded that ferritic steel type weld metal is prone to cause toe cracks, but austenitic steel type weld metal causes hardly any toe crack regardless of the differences in welding procedures.

Taking a glance at Table 5. 11, one may feel that transverse cracks occur in the same degree in all welding procedures. But analyzing the results in detail, it will be understood that transverse cracks are less likely to occur in the specimens welded with the austenitic steel type coated rod than in other specimens. Meanwhile, there are no longitudinal cracks on the specimens welded with the austenitic steel type rods, but in other specimens they are observed on some measure.

Table 5. 11　Summary of the HAZ cracks in Ni-Cr-Mo steel welded by four procedures

Specimen thickness, mm	Hardened zone cracks in specimens							
	Are welded with ilmenite type mild steel coated rods				Are welded with low hydrogen type mild steel coated rods			
	Underbead crack	Toe crack	Transverse crack	Longitudinal crack	Underbead crack	Toe crack	Transverse crack	Longitudinal crack
35	occur	occur	occur(2)*	occur	none	occur	occur(1)*	none
	occur	occur	occur(3)	occur	slightly	occur	occur(3)	occur
30	occur	none	occur(1)	none	none	occur	occur(4)	none
	occur	occur	occur(4)	occur	none	occur	occur(3)	none
25	occur	occur	occur(3)	none	none	occur	occur(2)	none
	occur	occur	occur(5)	occur	none	occur	occur(3)"	none
20	occur	occur	none	none	slightly	occur	occur(1)	none
	occur	occur	occur(2)	none	none	occur	none	none
15	occur	occur	occur(1)	none	none	occur	occur(1)	none
	occur	occur	occur(2)	none	none	occur	occur(1)	occur
10	occur	occur	occur(1)	none	none	occur	occur(1)	none
	occur	occur	occur(1)	occur	none	occur	none	none
5	occur	occur	none	none	none	none	none	none
	slightly	occur	none	none	none	occur	none	none
3	slightly	occur	none	none	/	/	/	/
	slightly	occur	none	none	/	/	/	/

Specimen thickness, mm	Hardened zone cracks in specimens							
	Argon are welded with mild steel filler rods				Are welded with austenitic steel type coate rods			
	Underbead crack	Toe crack	Transverse crack	Longitudinal crack	Underbead crack	Toe crack	Transverse crack	Longitudinal crack
35	none	occur	occur(3)*	occur	none	none	occur(1)*	none
	none	occur	none	none	none	none	occur(1)	none
30	none	occur	occur(2)	occur	none	none	occur(1)	none
	none	occur	occur(2)	none	none	none	occur(1)	none
25	none	none	occur(1)	occur	none	none	occur(1)	none
	none	occur	occur(3)	"	none	none	none	none
20	none	none	occur(1)	none	none	none	none	none
	none	occur	occur(3)	occur	none	none	occur(1)	none
15	none	occur	occur(1)	none	none	none	occur(1)	none
	none	occur	occur(1)	none	none	none	occur(2)	none
10	none	occur	occur(1)	none	none	none	none	none
	none	occur	none	none	none	none	none	none
5	none	occur	none	none	none	none	none	none
	none	occur	none	none	none	occur	none	none
3	none	occur	none	none	/	/	/	/
	none	occur	none	none	/	/	/	/

Remark:　——* The number in parentheses indicates the number of transverse cracks occurring in one specimen.

Many investigators have published the results showing that hydrogen plays an important part in causing hardened zone cracks in an air hardenable alloy steel. At present the hydrogen theory seems to be well established, but it is doubtful whether hydrogen plays a leading role in causing all types of hardened zone cracks. Unfortunately, there are few investigators who have identified the types of cracking in studying the causes of hardened zone cracks.

The weld metal resulting form the ilmenite type coated rods used in the present investigation contains about 23cc of the so-called diffusible hydrogen in 100grams of weld metal, immediately after welding, and the weld metal from the low hydrogen type electrode contains about 3cc. In argon arc welding, the content of diffusible in the weld metal is supposed to be very low, as hydrogen source is almost nonexistent. As for austenitic steel type coated rods, the hydrogen content of the weld metal may be low from the beginning, as their coating is of low hydrogen type. Moreover, the weld metal is of austenitic structure even at room temperature and can dissolve much more hydrogen than ferritic weld metal. Therefore, the quantity of hydrogen which diffuses into the welding HAZ is supposed to be very small.

The theory that hydrogen plays an important role in causing underbead cracking, can explain satisfactorily one of the results of this investigation which shows that underbead cracking occurs almost only in the use of ilmenite type coated rods.

Judging from the results of this investigation, however, it is unreasonable to think that hydrogen is one of the main factors causing toe cracks, transverse cracks and longitudinal cracks. Ferritic weld metal causes cracks other than underbead cracks more easily than austenitic steel type weld metal, regardless of their hydrogen contents. Particularly, the fact that these cracks easily occur even in the case of argon arc welding with the mild steel filler rods, may give a strong support to the view that hydrogen does not play an important part in the occurrence of hardened zone cracks other than underbead crack.

Chapter 6   Weldability of Material

6. 1   Weldability of Material and Testing Method

6. 1. 1   Weldability of Material

A component consisting of metallic material is considered to be weldable by a given process when metallic continuity can be obtained by welding using a suitable welding procedure. At the same time, the welds shall comply with the requirements specified in regard to both their metallurgical and mechanical properties and their influence on the construction of which they form a part. Weldability is governed by three factors, namely material, design and production (see Figure 6. 1).

Each of these factors is associated with different properties:

(a) Metallurgical weldability: material properties

These are influenced primarily by production and to a minor extent by the design.

(b) Constructional weldability: design properties

These are influenced primarily by the material and to a minor extent by production.

(c) Operative weldability: production properties

These are influenced primarily by the design and to minor extent by the material.

Each of these sets of properties depends (like the weldability of a component) on material, design and production, but the importance of the influencing factors differs for each.

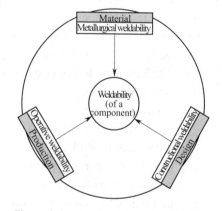

Figure 6. 1   Representation of weldability.

(1) Metallurgical weldability

A material possesses Metallurgical Weldability if, in the course of the procedure adopted, the chemical, metallurgical and physical properties inherent in the material allow a weld to be made which satisfies the requirements of the application. The less the factors governed by the material have to be taken into account when determining the welding procedure for a given construction, the better is the Metallurgical Weldability of a material within a material group.

Factors which influence metallurgical weldability include the following:

(a) Chemical composition, critical for, e. g.

——tendency to brittle fracture;

——tendency to ageing;

——tendency to hardening;

——tendency to hot cracking;

——behaviour of the molten pool;

——vaporization temperature;

——melting range.

(b) Metallurgical properties governed by production methods, e. g. method of steelmaking and deoxidation, hot and cold working, heat treatment, critical for

——segregations;

——inclusions;

——anisotropy;

——grain size;

——formation of crystalline structure.

(c) Physical properties, e. g.

——expansion behaviour;

——thermal conductivity;

——melting point;

——mechanical strength and toughness.

(2) Constructional weldability

Constructional weldability exists in a construction if, using the material concerned, the component remains capable of functioning under the envisaged operating conditions by virtue of its design. The less the factors governed by the design have to be taken into account when selecting the material for a specific welding procedure, the greater is the constructional weldability of a specific structure or component.

Factors which influence constructional weldability include the following:

(a) Design of the construction, e. g.

——distribution of forces in the component;

——arrangement of welds;

——workpiece thickness;

——notch effect;

——differences in stiffness.

(b) Conditions regarding loading, e. g.

——type and magnitude of stresses in the component;

——dimensional extent of stresses;

——speed of stressing;

——temperatures;

——corrosion.

(3) Operative weldability

Operative weldability exists for a welding procedure if the welds envisaged for a particular construction can be made properly under the chosen conditions of production. The less the factors governed by the welding procedure have to be taken into account in designing a construction for a specific material, the better is the operative weldability of a procedure intended for a specific structure or component.

Factors which influence operative weldability include the following:

(a) Preparation for welding, e. g.

——type of joint;

——shape of joint.

(b) Welding procedure (s) , including:

——welding process (es) ;

——types of filler materials/welding consumables;

——welding parameters;

——welding sequence;

——preheating;

——welding position (s) ;

——precautions taken with respect to unfavorable weather conditions.

(c) Pre-and post-treatment, e. g.

——post weld heat treatment;

——mechanical treatment (e. g. grinding, machining, peening) ;

——chemical treatment (e. g. pickling).

During manufacture, the requested chemical composition (e. g. by alloying) and metallurgical properties (e. g. type of teeming) of the steel are obtained. Another modification of the material behavior takes place during subsequent treatment, where the raw material is rolled to processible semi-finished goods, e. g. like strips, plates, bars, profiles, etc. With the rolling process, material-typical transformation processes, hardening and precipitation processes are used to adjust an optimised material characteristics.

A survey from quality point of view about the influence of the most important alloy elements to some mechanical and metallurgical properties is shown in Table 6. 1.

Table 6. 2 depicts the decisive importance of the carbon content to suitability of fusion welding of mild steels. A guide number of flawless fusion weldability is a carbon content of $C < 0.22\%$, with higher C contents, there is a danger of hardening, and welding becomes only possible by observing special precautions (e. g. pre-and post-weld heat treatment).

Table 6. 1　Influence of alloy elements on some steel properties

	C	Si	Mn	P	S	O	Cr	Ni	Al
Tensile strength	+	+	+	+	(−)	+	+	+	+
Hardness	+	+	+	+		+	+	+	
Charpy-v-toughness	−	−	+	−	−	−	(−)	++	
Hot cracking				−	++				
Creep resistance	+(−400℃)	(+)		(+)	(−)		+	+	
Critical cooling rate	−	−	−				−	−	
Formation of segregations	+	++	++	++	+				
Formation of incluations		+With Mn	+With Mn S		+	+With Al			+

Table 6. 2　Fusion weldability of unalloyed quality steels

Material	C-content(%)(Melt analysis)	Fusion weldability
S185(St33)[EN10025]	Unlimited(up to 0. 30)	Not guaranteed,hower mostly no problem with low C-content
S250GT(St34),S235JR(St37) S275JR(St42)[EN10025]	up to 0. 21	Up to 0. 22%C:good weldable(exception:plate thickness< 0. 5mm,special order conditions),as long as content of impurities(P,S etc)not too high
L235GT(St35),L275GT(St55) [steels for tubing EN 10208]	up to 0. 17	
P235GH(H Ⅰ), P265GH (H Ⅱ), P235GH(HⅢ)	up to 0. 22	
[steels for pressure vessel construction EN10028]	up to 0. 18(up to 0. 24)	
C10(C 10),C15(C 15),C22(C22) [case hardening and tempering steels EN10083]		
S355J0(St52)	Up to 0. 22 and higher contents of Mn and Si	Weldable

Material	C-content(%)(Melt analysis)	Fusion weldability
E295(St50)steels for mechanical engineering	Unlimited about 0. 30	Restricted weldability with electric arc methods, no gas welding of thin plates
E355(St60),C35(C 35)	About 0. 40	Weldable with special electrodes and mostly pre-and post-welding heat treatment
E360(St70),C45(C 45)	About 0. 50	Very restricted weldability in spite of special measures

6. 1. 2　Weldability Evaluation and Test Method

6. 1. 2. 1　Indirect Evaluation

(1) Carbon Equivalent Value (CEV)

Objective: to evaluate cold crack sensitivity of the low alloy steel.

(a) Recommended by the International Institute of Welding (IIW)
$$CE=C+Mn/6+(NI+Cu)/15+(CR+Mo+V)/5(\%)$$

Applicable Object: the low-alloyed high-tensile steel without quenched and tempered of medium or high strength $(\sigma_b=500\text{-}900MPa)$.

In respect to $\delta<20mm$ steel:

When $CE<0.4\%$, the hardenability of the steel is not high, and the weldability is good, then the weld preheating is not needed.

When $CE=0.4\%\text{-}0.6\%$, the steel tends to harden, then the weld preheating is needed, with the preheating temperature of $70\text{-}200℃$.

When $CE>0.6\%$, the steel has a high tendency of hardenability as well as the bad weldability.

The smaller the carbon equivalent, the better the weldability

(b) Recommended by the Japanese Industrial Standards (JIS) and the Welding Engineering Standard (WES)
$$C_{eq}=C+Mn/6+Si/24+Ni/40+Cr/5+Mo/4+V/14(\%)$$

Applicable Object: the low-alloyed hardened and tempered steel $(\sigma_b=500-1000MPa)$

Composition Requirements: $C\leqslant0.2\%$; $w_{Si}\leqslant0.55\%$; $w_{Mn}\leqslant1.5\%$; $w_{Cu}\leqslant2.5\%$; $w_{Ni}\leqslant2.5\%$; $w_{Cr}\leqslant1.25\%$; $w_{Mo}\leqslant0.7\%$; $w_V\leqslant0.1\%$; $w_B\leqslant0.006\%$.

In respect to $\delta<20mm$ steel, when SMAW heat input is at 17 KJ/cm, the rough preheating range is:

When $\sigma_b=500MPa$, $C_{eq}=0.46\%$, preheating is not needed

When $\sigma_b=600MPa$, $C_{eq}=0.52\%$, preheating temperature is $75℃$

When $\sigma_b=700MPa$, $C_{eq}=0.52\%$, preheating temperature is $100℃$

When $\sigma_b=800MPa$, $C_{eq}=0.62\%$, preheating temperature is $150℃$

(c) Recommended by the American Welding Society (AWS)
$$C_{eq}=C+Mn/6+Si/24+Ni/15+Cr/5+Mo/4+Cu/13+P/2\ (\%)$$

Applicable Object: the carbon steel and the low alloy high-tensile steel.

(2) Cold Crack Sensitivity (CCS)
$$P_{cm}=C+Mn/20+Si/30+Cu/20+Ni/60+Cr/20+Mo/15+V/10+5B\ (\%)$$

Applicable Object: $w_C=0.07\text{-}0.22\%$; $w_{Si}\leqslant0.60\%$; $w_{Mn}=0.4\text{-}1.40\%$; $w_{Cu}\leqslant0.50\%$; $w_{Ni}\leqslant1.20\%$; $w_{Cr}\leqslant1.20\%$; $w_{Mo}\leqslant0.7\%$; $w_V\leqslant0.12\%$; $w_{Nb}\leqslant0.04\%$; $w_{Ti}\leqslant0.05\%$; $w_B\leqslant0.005\%$; $\delta=19\text{-}50mm$; $[H]=1.0\text{-}5.0mL/100g$.

The parameters of cold crack sensitivity are shown in Table 6. 3.

δ——thickness (mm);

R——restraint intensity (MPa);

$[H]$——diffusive hydrogen content in weld joint (mL/100g);

$[H'_D]$——effective diffusive hydrogen content in the deposited metal (mL/100g);

λ——effective coefficient (low ydrogen basic electrode $\lambda=0.5$, $[H'_D]=[H]$; acid electrode $\lambda=0.48$, $[H'_D]=[H]/2$)

Table 6.3　parameters of cold crack sensitivity

Cold crack sensitivity formula(%)	Preheating temperature	Application conditions
$P_c=P_{cm}+[H]/60+\delta/600$	$T_0=1440P_c-392$	Y-Slit groove specimen, applying to low alloy steel, with $w_C<$
$P_w=P_{cm}+[H]/60+R/400000$		0.17%, $[H]=1-5$mL/100g,$\delta=19-50$mm
$P_H=P_{cm}+0.075\lg[H]+\delta/400000$	$T_0=1600P_H-408$	Y-Slit groove specimen, applying to low alloy steel with $w_C<$
		0.17%, $[H]>5$mL/100g,$R=500-33000$MPa
$P_{HT}=P_{cm}+0.088\lg[\lambda H'_D]+\delta/400000$	$T_0=1600P_H-330$	Y-Slit groove specimen, taking into consideration of the hydrogen accumulation nearby the fusion zone.

(3) Hot Crack Sensitivity

① Hot Crack Sensitivity (HCS)

$$HCS=\frac{C\times[S+P+(Si/25+Ni/100)]}{3Mn+Cr+Mo+V}\times10^3$$

When HCS$\leqslant4$, there's generally no crack generated. The greater the HCS, the higher hot crack sensitivity. This formula is applicable to the common low alloy steel, including the low-temperature steel and the pearlite heat resistant steel.

② Critical Strain Rate (CST)

$$CST=(-19.2C-97.2S-0.8Cu-1.0Ni+3.9Mn+65.7Nb-18.5B+7.0)\times10^{-4}$$

When CST$\geqslant6.5\times10^{-4}$, hot crack can be prevented.

(4) Stress Relief Crack Sensitivity Index

① ΔG

$$\Delta G=Cr+3.3Mo+8.1V-2\ (\%)$$

When $\Delta G<0$, there's no crack generated; When $\Delta G\geqslant0$, there's high crack sensitivity.

In respect to $w_C>0.1\%$ low alloy steel, the above formula can be amended to:

$$\Delta G'=\Delta G+10C=Cr+3.3Mo+8.1V+10C-2\ (\%)$$

When $\Delta G\geqslant2$, sensitive to crack; When $1.5\leqslant\Delta G\leqslant2$, crack sensitivity is medium. When $\Delta G\leqslant1.5$, there's low crack sensitivity.

② P_{SR}

$$P_{SR}=Cr+Cu+2Mo+5Ti+7Nb+10V-2\ (\%)$$

When $P_{SR}\geqslant0$, crack sensitivity is relatively high.

(5) Lamellar Tearing Sensitivity Index

$$P_L=P_{cm}+[H]/60+6S$$

(6) Highest Hardness of the Heat Affected Zone (HAZ)

Picking 7 or more points along the two sides of the tangency point seperatively (15 or more measuring points). The distance between the separate point is 0.5mm. The shape of hardness test is shown as Figure 6.2.

6.1.2.2　Direct test

Small tekken test (oblique Y type groove test): In order to evaluate the cold crack tend-

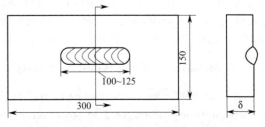

Figure 6.2　The shape of hardness test.

ency of base welding and HAZ, in Japan much use has been made of the Y-groove or Tekken cracking test. In the self-restraint form (illustrated in Figure 6. 3), a single weld bead is laid at the root of a gapped Y preparation (as shown) at a standard heat input rate of 1. 7kJ $\cdot$ mm^{-1}. The intensity of restraint is a function of plate thickness h, and is approximately

$$R_y = \begin{cases} 70h & \text{for } h \leqslant 40\text{mm} \\ 2800\text{kgf/mm} \cdot \text{mm} & \text{for } h > 40\text{mm} \end{cases} \tag{6.1}$$

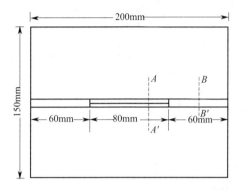 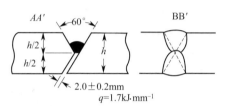

Figure 6. 3   The JIS Y-groove cracking test (Tekken test).

Test method:

core diameter, 4mm; welding current: 170A $\pm$ 10A; welding voltage: 24V $\pm$ 2V; welding speed: 150mm/min. 24h after welding, come into detect dissection

Calculation method:

$$\text{Root crack rate} = \frac{\text{the sum of crack length on longitudinal cross section}}{\text{the length of test weld}} \times 100\%$$

$$\text{surface crack rate} = \frac{\text{the sum of crack length on surface}}{\text{the length of test weld}} \times 100\%$$

$$\text{section crack rate} = \frac{\text{the sum of crack depth on horizontal cross section}}{\text{the length of test weld}} \times 100\%$$

Evaluating indicator: crack rate $\leqslant$ 20%, actual structure does not occur.

6. 2   Weldability of low carbon steel

Steel is basically Iron and Carbon with small amounts of other stuff like manganese. Low Carbon Steel has . 3 percent carbon. Not 3 percent but 0. 3 percent or point 3 percent. That's not much. For comparison sake, Cast iron has a full 3 percent and sometimes more. That's why cast iron is such a pain to weld and also why low carbon steel is the easiest metal to weld··· low carbon steel is also the cheapest metal to buy. Low Carbon Steel is what we use to learn to weld and low Carbon steel is what we compare all other metals to when we study metals. Why? Well it's easier to understand stuff if we can compare it to something we already know and understand. How you gonna weld anything else if you haven't learned welding steel? So, the weldability of low-car-bon steel will been discussed in this section.

6. 2. 1   Metallurgy of the liquid weld metal

It is probable that the results pertaining to gas absorption from arcs in argon-gas mixtures are broadly applicable to arc welding processes generally. In particular, gases are absorbed at the arc root more rapidly, and to a higher level, than would be the case in non-arc melting. Excess hydrogen that may consequently be present bubbles out at the rear of the weld pool and under steady welding conditions the surplus gas is purged before the metal solidifies, so that this process does not cause porosity. Nitrogen is less rapidly desorbed, and therefore is likely to be present at an undesirable level in the finished weld if protective measures are not taken. Oxygen, if absorbed to excess, combines with deoxidants and is rejected in the form of slag. If carbon dioxide is used as a shielding gas, it may add both carbon and oxygen to the weld pool. Details of individual gas-metal reactions are described below.

6. 2. 1. 1   Nitrogen

The amount of nitrogen absorbed in arc welding increases with the partial pressure of nitrogen in the arc atmosphere and with the amount of oxygen. The saturation level for nitrogen is about equal to the equilibrium solubility at 1 atm pressure and liquid metal temperature of 1600℃, which is 0. 045% by mass. The amount dissolved from a 50% N_2-50% O_2 arc atmosphere rises to 0. 16%, so that air is a particularly unfavorable atmosphere for the arc welding of steel. Hydrogen, conversely, reduces nitrogen absorption, so that in a nitrogen-hydrogen mixture the gas content is equal to the equilibrium value for the partial pressure of nitrogen in the arc atmosphere. Figure 6. 4 shows the nitrogen content of the transferring drops in self-shielded arc welding using cored wire. Wire A contains only iron powder, so this is effectively bare wire welding, and the nitrogen content falls with increasing current. Wire B has a rutile core, which is not adequate without additional shielding, and the nitrogen content increases slightly with current. Wire C is a typical self-shielded wire, containing a $CaCO_3$-CaF flux core with aluminium and magnesium. The transferring drops are surrounded with a blanket of volatile metal vapour, which keeps the nitrogen content below 0. 025%, regardless of current.

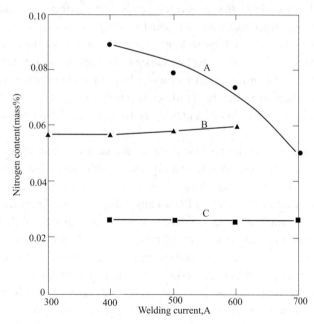

Figure 6. 4   The nitrogen content of transferring drops in self-shielded fluxcored DC arc welding: curve A, wire with iron power core; B, rutile core; C, $CaCO_3$-CaF_2 core plus Al and Mg.

Nitrogen is damaging in two ways, first by causing porosity, and second by embrittling the weld deposit. Porosity appears when the nitrogen content exceeds about 0. 045 mass %, as shown in Figure 6. 5, this would be expected from the saturation effect. Nitrogen porosity also occurs in the root pass of pipe welds when made with basic coated electrodes. The conditions here are unfavourable since the underside of the weld pool is in contact with air, and the arc atmosphere is oxidizing. Rutile and cellulosic electrodes do not suffer this defect, possibly because of the effect of hydrogen in the arc atmosphere. In self-shielded welding it is necessary to add about 1% aluminium in order to inhibit nitrogen porosity.

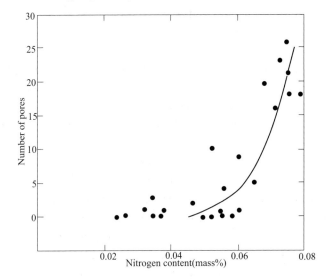

Figure 6. 5　The number of pores in the fractured surface of a tensile testpiece as a function of
nitrogen content; self-shielded flux-cored welding of carbon steel.

Nitrogen in the form of FeN has a severely embrittling effect on weld metal. Deoxidants normally added to welding filler materials are usually adequate to combine with nitrogen to form non-embrittling nitrides. In self-shielded welding, aluminium acts as both deoxidizer and nitride-former. However, aluminium has the effect of closing the gamma loop in the iron-carbon equilibrium diagram so that if too much is present a coarse, brittle ferritic structure results. This problem is overcome by the addition of austenite stabilizers such as manganese and by restricting the aluminium content. Where improved notch-ductility is required additions of 0. 5-2. 0% Ni may be made.

Nitrogen in a carbon or carbon-manganese steel may be responsible for strain-age embrittlement. If a nitrogen-bearing steel is subject to plastic strain and simultaneously or subsequently heated at a temperature of about 200℃, the notch ductility is reduced. Prior to World War II a number of welded bridges were erected in Belgium and Germany using steel made by the air-blown Bessemer process, and therefore of high nitrogen content. Several such bridges failed by brittle fracture, and these failures were ascribed to strain-age embrittlement. Subsequent testing has shown that if a small crack forms adjacent to the weld boundary and is then strained and reheated by successive weld passes, the tip of the crack can be sufficiently embrittled to initiate a brittle fracture. The root passes of a multipass weld are similarly strained and reheated, and this may also lead to a degree of embrittlement, as will be seen later. Strain-age embrittlement may be prevented by the addition of strong nitride-forming elements such as aluminium or titanium. This expedient was used successfully for plate material subsequent to the failures mentioned above, but is not normally possible for arc welding electrodes because Al and Ti burn out in the arc. However, in self-shielded welding the amount of Al in the weld deposit may be sufficient to prevent strain-age embrittlement of the root passes.

6. 2. 1. 2 Oxygen

Oxygen may be dissolved in the liquid metal either directly from the arc atmosphere or by reaction with a slag or flux. The arc atmosphere contains substantial amounts of oxygen in the gas metal arc welding of carbon and alloy steel, where it is added to stabilize the arc, in CO_2-shielded welding, and in self-shielded arc welding. Basic electrode coatings and basic submerged arc welding fluxes may also generate oxygen by decomposition of CO_2, but the dominant effect in these cases is the slag-metal reaction.

Oxygen in the arc atmosphere affects the weld metal properties in three ways: through the precipitation of non-metallic inclusions, by oxidizing alloying additions, and by causing CO porosity. Oxygen is present in weld metal as oxides, silicates or other chemical compounds, and in solution. The compound may be present as macroinclusions (slag inclusions) or microinclusions. Macroinclusions are usually the result of human error, but microinclusions are precipitated either at the rear of the weld pool or in the freshly solidified weld metal because of the fall in oxygen solubility with falling temperature. They are spherical in form, and appear as circular discs in microsections. They are composed of the oxides of silicon, manganese and any other deoxidants that may be present, together with manganese sulphide. Diameters are up to 10μm, and there are typically 1×10^4-3×10^4 inclusions per square millimetre, so that the volume fraction may be up to 1%.

In processes that employ a consumable electrode, oxidation of the alloying elements takes place in the droplets as they form at the electrode tip and transfer across the arc; there is little reaction with the weld pool. Silicon and manganese are commonly used as deoxidants for carbon steel in arc welding, and their oxidation loss in gas metal arc welding using argon-oxygen shielding is shown in Figure 6. 6 Manganese is lost by vaporization as well as oxidation, silicon by oxidation alone. Triple deoxidized wire containing titanium, zirconium and aluminium may be used in order to avoid porosity in the presence of surface contaminants. However, for most practical applications, deoxidization by silicon and manganese is adequate. The oxygen content of 9% Ni steel weld metal produced by gas metal arc welding with an Ar-O_2 shield is shown in Figure 6. 7. There is virtually no nitrogen pick-up, indicating that the shielding was good. The oxygen content with a 2% O_2-Ar mixture is 0. 025 mass$\%$, the maximum permissible carbon content to avoid CO blowholes would be 0. 1$\%$. For the most part gas metal arc wires have a carbon content below this level. However, in welding with coated electrodes with no added deoxidant (oxide-silicate coating), CO bubbles form in the drop at the electrode tip and eventually burst, generating a fine metal spray. Where deoxidants are present, the final oxygen content of the weld metal will be reduced as indicated by Figure 6. 7.

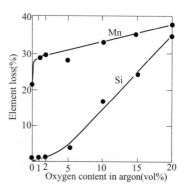

Figure 6. 6 The loss of manganese and silicon from carbon steel in gas metal arc welding, as a function of the oxygen content of the argon-oxygen atmosphere.

6. 2. 1. 3 Hydrogen

The hydrogen solubility at the arc root, S_a, is higher than the equilibrium value S_e, but that hydrogen evolution from the liquid metal surface outside the arc reduces the net amount absorbed to the equilibrium level at about 1600℃. An attempt has been made to measure S_a by producing an arc-melted pool in thin steel plate, the underside of which was kept solid by cooling. Argon-hydrogen mixtures were used for the arc atmosphere, and the pressure of hydrogen p_A dif-

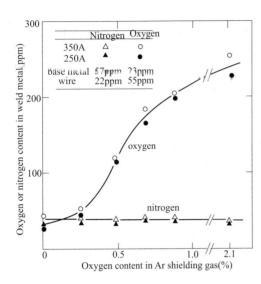

Figure 6.7 The oxygen and nitrogen contents in weld metal, as functions of the oxygen content in argon-oxygen shielding gas

fusing through the plate was measured and compared with the partial pressure of hydrogen in the arc atmosphere p_E. The arc solubility is then

$$\frac{S_a}{S_e} = \left(\frac{p_A}{p_E}\right)^{1/2} \qquad (6.2)$$

Results for carbon steel are given in Figure 6.8, from which $(p_A, p_E)^{-1/2}$ varies from 2.5 up to about 4. In such a test there is necessarily a hydrogen loss from the weld pool surface, so the true figure for S_a/S_e is probably higher.

Both testing and experience show that, under steady welding conditions, it is possible to obtain sound weld metal with up to 50% H_2 in the arc atmosphere. Under unsteady conditions (such as stops and starts), this is not the case, and hydrogen porosity is probable if the arc atmosphere is hydrogen-rich. Tunnel porosity can occur even when the hydrogen content is below the equilibrium solubility.

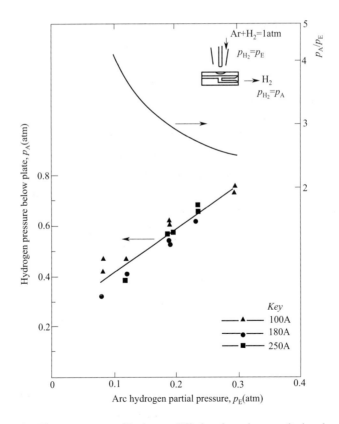

Figure 6.8 The pressure p_A of hydrogen diffusing through arc-melted carbon steel, as a function of hydrogen partial pressure p_E in arc atmosphere. Total pressure of $Ar+H_2$ is 1atm.

6. 2. 2　Solidification and solidification cracking

The primary structure of carbon and low-alloy steel weld metal is similar to that of other metals; it is epitaxial with elongated columnar grains extending from the fusion boundary to the weld surface. The substructure is cellular at low solidification rates and dendritic at higher rates. The phase structure at solidification depends mainly on the carbon and nickel contents. Figure 6. 9 shows the upper left-hand corner of the iron-carbon phase diagram. When the carbon content is below 0. 10%, the metal solidifies as δ ferrite. At higher carbon contents, the primary crystals are δ, but just below 1500℃ a peritectic reaction takes place and the remainder of the weld solidifies as austenite. The solubility of sulphur in ferrite is relatively high, but in austenite it is relatively low. Consequently, there is a possibility with C>0. 1 that sulphur will be rejected to the grain boundaries of primary austenite grains, promoting intergranular weakness and solidification cracking. Manganese tends to inhibit the effect of sulphur, but the higher the carbon content, the higher the manganese sulphur ratio required to avoid cracking, as shown in Figure 6. 10. Sulphur may also segregate to interdendritic regions and promote interdendritic cracks.

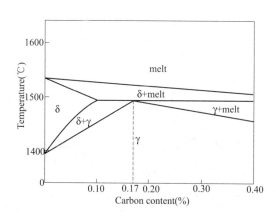

Figure 6. 9　A section of iron-carbon equilibrium diagram showing the peritectic reaction.

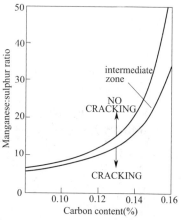

Figure 6. 10　The effect of manganese/sulphur ratio and of carbon content on the susceptibility of carbon steel weld metal to hot cracking.

Figure 6. 11 is part of the Fe-S binary phase diagram, which shows that the equilibrium maximum solubility of sulphur in 3 ferrite is 0. 18%, while in austenite the maximum solubility is about 0. 05%. Under continuous cooling a sulphur-rich liquid will be rejected at somewhat lower bulk concentrations than these, and at worst liquid sulphide can persist down to about 1000℃. In practice, the presence of sulphur has the effect of increasing the brittle temperature range. Figure 6. 12 shows the effect of sulphur and carbon contents on the brittle temperature range of carbon steel, as determined by the MISO technique. This diagram illustrates the cooperative action of increased sulphur and carbon contents in promoting solidification cracking.

It will also be seen from Figure 6. 12 that phosphorus has much the same effect on the brittle temperature range (and hence on solidification cracking). From the Fe-P equilibrium diagram (Figure 6. 13) the maximum solubility of phosphorus in δ ferrite is 2. 8 by mass%, and the formation of a phosphide eutectic is improbable. Phosphorus, however, segregates to grain boundaries and could act either by lowering the melting point in the interdendritic regions or by reducing intergranular cohesion.

The effect of other elements on the susceptibility to solidification cracking of carbon steel is shown in Figure 6. 14 Boron increases susceptibility in the same way as phosphorus; nickel, however,

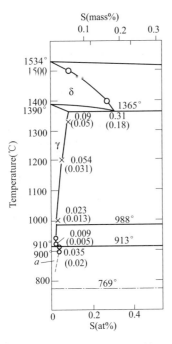

Figure 6. 11 Part of the Fe-S binary equilibrium diagram.

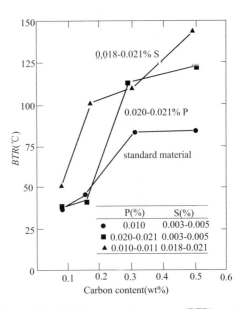

Figure 6. 12 Brittle temperature range (BTR) versus carbon content as determined by the MISO test.

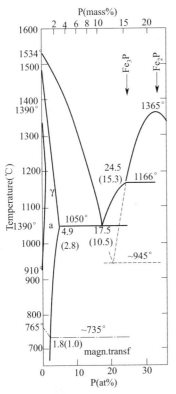

Figure 6. 13 Part of the Fe-P binary equilibrium diagram

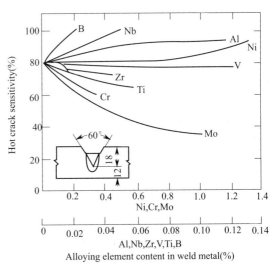

Figure 6. 14 The relationships between alloying element content and hot cracking sensitivity, measured as a percentage of weld run cracked with groove preparation as illustrated.

acts in the same way as carbon in promoting the formation of austenite as a primary structure. Because of a high risk of solidification cracking, manual metal arc welds containing more than 4% Ni are not normally possible; gas metal arc welding with 9% Ni wire is, however, practicable.

The probability of solidification cracking can be assessed for submerged arc welds in carbon-manganese steel by using a cracking index developed by Bailey and Jones:
$$U_{cs} = 230C + 190S + 75P + 45Nb - 12.3Si - 5.4Mn - 1 \qquad (6.3)$$
Where C, etc., are in mass%. Cracking of fillet welds is likely if $U_{cs} > 20$ and of butt welds if $U_{cs} > 25$. Bead shape and other factors may alter the cracking risk to some degree.

The risk of solidification cracking is minimized by:

① maintaining a low carbon content in the weld deposit;

② keeping sulphur and phosphorus contents as low as possible;

③ ensuring that the manganese content is high enough to allow for possible dilution (and ingress of sulphur) from the plate material.

It is normal practice to use low-carbon rimming steel as the core wire for carbon-steel and low-alloy-steel electrodes and a typical carbon-steel all weld metal deposit contains 0.05-0.10 C. In low-alloy (e.g. Cr-Mo) steel, carbon contents are usually about 0.1% but may be reduced below 0.06% by using low-carbon ferro-alloys in the coating or by using a low-carbon alloy core wire.

6.2.3 Stress intensification, embrittlement and cracking of fusion welds below the solidus

In exceptional cases, the degree of embrittlement so caused may be sufficient to result in cracking either during the welding operation or in service. Normally, however, some additional factor is required, either to augment the applied or residual stress or to increase the degree of embrittlement before any cracking will occur.

6.2.3.1 Embrittlement of fusion welds

Strain-age embrittlement may occur during the welding operation, but there are a number of mechanisms that may result in postwelding embrittlement. The most important of these are hydrogen embrittlement, secondary hardening and temper embrittlement. Cracking may result from poor transverse ductility in the plate material, and propagation of cracks in service may be due to a number of mechanisms, including stress corrosion and strain-age cracking. The mechanisms that may generate subsolidus cracks during or shortly after welding are discussed below.

6.2.3.2 The hydrogen embrittlement and cracking of welds in steel

Steel may suffer two types of embrittlement due to the presence of hydrogen. The first type occurs at elevated temperature and affects carbon and low-alloy steel. It results from chemical reaction between hydrogen and carbides, and causes permanent damage, either decarburization or cracking or both. The second type occurs at temperatures between $-100\,^{\circ}\text{C}$ and $200\,^{\circ}\text{C}$. This embrittlement is due to physical interactions between hydrogen and the crystal lattice, and is reversible in that after removal of the gas the ductility of the steel reverts to normal.

6.2.3.3 Hydrogen attack

The elevated-temperature effect, known as hydrogen attack, has been observed mainly in petroleum and chemical plant where hydrogen forms part of the process fluid. Initially the metal is decarburized, but at a later stage intergranular fissures appear and the metal is weakened as well as being embrittled. Dissolved hydrogen reacts with carbides to form methane (CH_4), which precipitates at the grain boundaries. There is an incubation period before any damage can be detected in normal mechanical tests. This incubation period may be very long (sometimes of the order of years) at low temperature, but it decreases sharply with increasing temperature. Increasing the chromium and molybdenum content of the steel raises the temperature above which hydrogen corrosion occurs, and austenitic chromium-nickel steels of the 18Cr-10Ni type are immune from attack. Decarburization and fissuring that resembles hydrogen attack has been observed in laboratory tests of high-tensile steel welded with cellulosic electrodes. Small areas around defects such as pores and inclusions were decarburized and cracked. It would appear, however, that the properties of the joint were not significantly affected, probably because of the small dimensions of the corroded areas. Of much greater importance in welding is the temporary form of hydrogen embrittlement, since this may cause hydrogen-induced cold cracking.

6. 2. 3. 4　The solution of hydrogen

The equilibrium solubility of hydrogen in ferritic iron below the melting point is

$$S = 47.66 p^{1/2} \exp(-2.72 \times 10^7 / RT) \tag{6.4}$$

Where S is in ppm by mass, p is in atmospheres, R is the gas constant (8. 134J $\cdot$ mol^{-1}) and T is temperature (K). For $p = 1$ atm and $T = 293$K, the solubility according to equation 1. 3 is 6. 7×10^{-4} ppm (7. 6×10^{-4} mL/100g).

The solubility is higher in austenite than in ferrite and is also modified by the presence of solute elements in the iron. It is also higher in a strained than in an unstrained lattice. If steel is strained to the yield stress σ_{ys}, then according to Oriani and Josephic (1974) the solubility is increased by a factor c/c_n

$$c/c_n = \exp(A\sigma_{ys}^{1/2} - B\sigma_{ys}) \tag{6.5}$$

where

$$A = \frac{2(1+\nu)\overline{V}}{3RT}\left(\frac{2E}{\pi}\right)^{1/2} \tag{6.6}$$

$$B = \frac{2(1+\nu)V}{RT}\left(\frac{2}{\pi}\right) \tag{6.7}$$

The ν is Poisson's ratio, V is the partial molar volume of hydrogen in iron, E is elastic modulus and other symbols are as before. At 20℃, $A = 6.926 \times 10^{-2}$ (MN $\cdot$ m^{-2})$^{-1/2}$ and $B = 3.242 \times 10^{-4}$ (MN $\cdot$ m^{-2})$^{-1}$. For a high-tensile steel where $\sigma_{ys} = 1 \times 10^3$ MN $\cdot$ m^{-2}, the solubility is increased by a factor of 6. 5. At the tip of a crack, the strain may be higher than that corresponding to uniaxial yield, and the solubility may be still further augmented.

Hydrogen separates out to grain boundaries and to the interfaces between phases in steel. Since hydrogen-induced cracking is intergranular at low and transgranular at high stress intensity factors, the degree of segregation is probably of the same order of magnitude as the increase of solubility due to moderate strain. Hydrogen recombination poisons such as P, S, S_a and S_b also separate out to grain boundaries and are thought to increase the segregation of hydrogen, thus acting in a cooperative way and enhancing intergranular embrittlement.

Where steel is strained, and particularly when it is subject to plastic strain, the dislocation density increases. Hydrogen diffuses preferentially to these discontinuities in the crystal lattice, and if present in

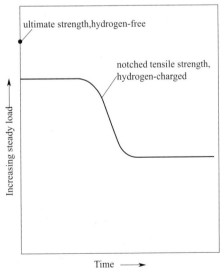

Figure 6. 15　The notched tensile strength of steel when charged with hydrogen.

sufficient quantity, precipitates to form microvoids.

In fusion welding the mean hydrogen content of steel weld metal immediately after solidification is in the range 1-50 ppm, which is four orders of magnitude higher than the equilibriium value at room temperature. Most of this hydrogen (diffusible hydrogen) diffuses out of the weld at room temperature, while the remainder can only be removed by vacuum fusion techniques, to give a measure of the total hydrogen content. Diffusible hydrogen is measured by plunging a weld sample into mercury and collecting the evolved gas in a burette. Traditionally, diffusible hydrogen contents have been expressed as ml per 100g or ppm of deposited metal. This method may cause difficulties in comparing submerged arc welding tests with those made using coated electrodes because the amount of dilution is higher with submerged arc. To overcome this problem results may be expressed as ppm or g/ton of fused metal (1ppm＝1g/ton＝1. 12ml/100g).

6. 2. 3. 5　Hydrogen embrittlement

The embrittlement of steel by hydrogen only manifests itself during processes that lead to the fracture of the metal; it does not, for example, increase the hardness as measured by an indentation test. The simplest way of assessing embrittlement is by comparing the reduction of area of a hydrogen-charged specimen δ_H with that of a hydrogen-free specimen δ_0. The degree of embrittlement E may then be expressed as

$$E = \frac{\delta_0 - \delta_H}{\delta_0} \tag{6. 8}$$

Alternatively, a V-notch may be machined around the circumference of a cylindrical specimen. If such a testpiece is charged with hydrogen and then subjected to a sufficiently high constant tensile load, it will fail after a lapse of time. The type of result obtained is illustrated in Figure 6. 15. The reduction of strength and the step in the strength-time curve both increase with increasing hydrogen content.

Other techniques employ precracked specimens of various geometry to obtain a measure of the stress intensity factor K_H for cracking of steel that has been charged with hydrogen or is exposed to a hydrogen atmosphere. The most direct method is to use a standard ASTM compact tension specimen and to load it in a hydrogen atmosphere so as to determine the critical stress intensity factor for crack propagation. At atmospheric and lower pressure, the solution of hydrogen in steel is inhibited by very small traces of oxygen, and to obtain reproducible results extreme measures must be taken to purify the hydrogen. In the tests carried out by Oriani and Josephic (1974) , which are discussed in the next section, the hydrogen pressure was increased to the point where the crack started to run, and then decreased to the point where it stopped. A small difference between these two pressures indicates that the degree of purification has been effective.

Other measurements have been made with cantilever beam specimens and with centre-cracked sheet metal testpieces. Hydrogen may be introduced by soaking in a hydrogen atmosphere at elevated temperature or, in a less controlled way, by cathodic charging. In such tests it is necessary to allow sufficient time for hydrogen to reach equilibrium level in the strained region at the crack tip. Not many investigators have observed this need, so that results quoted in the literature may be too high, particularly at low levels of stress intensity.

The effect of temperature is well illustrated in Figure 6. 16. This shows the notched tensile strength of a high-tensile material that has been precharged with hydrogen. Fracture occurs when a critical hydrogen content has accumulated in the strained region at the root of the notch. Above about 200℃ the material properties are such that hydrogen concentration and/or embrittlement are no longer possible. Below－100℃ the rate of diffusion of hydrogen is too low for the required amount of hydrogen to accumulate during the period of the experiment. The most severe embrittlement, it will be noted, is close to normal atmospheric temperature.

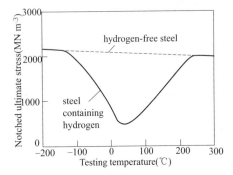

Figure 6. 16　The notched tensile strength of quenched and tempered low-alloy steel containing hydrogen in the quenched condition, as a function of testing temperature.

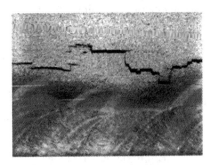

Figure 6. 17　A lamellar tear under T butt weld in C-Mn steel.

In general, the presence of hydrogen in steel causes a reduction of strain to failure and of the energy of fracture. This is reflected in the fracture morphology. For example, a ductile microvoid coalescence mode can alter to a brittle intergranular mode, or the extent of cleavage fracture in a mixed fracture mode may increase. Hydrogen-assisted crack growth can also occur by microvoid coalescence alone, and here the hydrogen affects the rate of nucleation of voids and reduces plasticity at the later stages of fracture.

6. 2. 4　Lamellar tearing

Lamellar tearing is a form of cracking that occurs in the base metal of a weldment due to the combination of high localized stress and low ductility of the plate in the through-thickness direction. It is associated with restrained corner or T joints, particularly in thick plate, where the fusion boundary of the weld is more or less parallel to the plate surface. The cracks appear close to or a few millimetres away from the weld boundary, and usually consist of planar areas parallel to the surface joined by shear failures at right angles to the surface. Figure 6. 17 illustrates a typical case.

The susceptibility to lamellar tearing depends upon the type of joint and the inherent restraint, on sulphur and oxygen contents, on the type and morphology of inclusions (which affect the through-thickness ductility) and on the hydrogen content of the weld.

Lamellar tearing has affected weld fabrication in the machine tool industry, where T and corner joints in heavy plate are required for frames and bed plates. It is also a hazard in the fabrication of offshore oil platforms, and in welded-on attachments to boilers and thick-walled pressure vessels.

Lamellar tears initiate by separation or void formation at the interface between inclusions and metal, or by shattering of the inclusion itself. The voids so formed link together in a planar manner by necking, microvoid coalescence or cleavage. Subsequently these planar discontinuities, when they exist at different levels, are joined by vertical shear walls. It would be expected that susceptibility to lamellar tearing would correlate with the number of inclusions as counted using a Quantimet apparatus, but this does not appear to be the case except in very broad terms. It is possible that submicroscopic inclusions play a part in generating this type of crack.

Silicate and sulphide inclusions both play a part in initiating lamellar tearing. Testing does not always show a clear correlation between sulphur and silicon content on the one hand and tearing susceptibility on the other, but reduction of sulphur content is generally regarded as one of the

124

methods of control. Cerium or rare-earth metal (REM) treatment is another means of control. Hydrogen has a significant effect on lamellar tearing. In high-strength steels that form martensite in the heat-affected zone, hydrogen-induced cold cracks will generally form preferentially, but in plain carbon steels of low hardenability, hydrogen increases the susceptibility to lamellar tearing quite markedly. There is little or no correlation between heat input rate and the incidence of lamellar tearing, but in the presence of hydrogen a low heat input rate might tip the balance towards hydrogen cracking.

Lamellar tearing may, in principle, be avoided by ensuring that the design does not impose through-thickness contraction strains on steel with poor through-thickness ductility. Some possible design modifications are illustrated in Figure 6. 18. Such changes will usually entail an increase in cost and therefore need to be justified by experience.

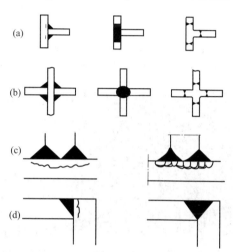

It is also possible to grind or machine away the volume of metal where tearing is anticipated, and replace the cut-away portion with weld metal, a process known as buttering. In severe cases the assembly is then stress-relieved before welding on the attachment. The risk of tearing may be further reduced by specifying a material of high through-thickness ductility, which is usually achieved by limiting the sulphur content to a low value, say less than 0. 007%. Preheating may also reduce the risk of lamellar tearing in some cases.

Figure 6. 18   Redesign to avoid lamellar tearing: (a) and (b) replace fillets with solid weld metal or forged sections; (c) buttering; (d) modify preparation of corner.

The most widely used test for susceptibility to lamellar tearing is the through-thickness ductility test. Plates are welded at right angles to and on opposite sides of the plate to be tested, or round bar may be friction welded thereto. Specimens are then cut out of this assembly and machined to a round test bar so that the original plate forms the central part of the gauge length. If the plate is thick enough the whole testpiece may be machined from it.

The ductility in a tensile test made on such a specimen is taken as a measure of susceptibility; material having a through-thickness ductility less than, say, 25% is regarded as susceptible. Other tests employ restrained or externally loaded welded specimens. Attenuation of an ultrasonic beam was at first considered to be a possible means of testing for lamellar testing susceptibility, but this proved not to be the case.

After the loss of the accommodation platform Alexander L. Kielland in 1980, it has become normal practice to specify that plates used in critical locations in North Sea offshore structures should have a minimum through-thickness ductility of 20 or 25%. This practice, combined with continued improvements in the cleanliness of steel, would appear to provide a reasonable security against such accidents.

6. 2. 5   Reheat Cracking

Reheat or stress relaxation cracking may occur in the heat-affected zone of welds in low-alloy steel during postweld heat treatment or during service at elevated temperature. The factors that contribute to reheat cracking are:

① a susceptible alloy composition;

② a susceptible microstructure;

③ a high level of residual strain combined with some degree of triaxiality;

④ temperature in the strain relaxation (creep) range.

Most alloy steels suffer some degree of embrittlement in the coarse-grained region of the heat-affected zone when heated at 600℃. Elements that promote such embrittlement are Cr, Cu, Mo, B, V, Nb and Ti, while S, and possibly P and Sn, influence the brittle intergranular mode of reheat cracking. Molybdenum-vanadium and molybdenum-boron steels are particularly susceptible, especially if the vanadium is over 0.1%. The relative effect of the various elements has been expressed quantitatively in formulae, due to Nakamura (6.9) and Ito (6.10):

$$P = Cr + 3.3Mo + 8.1V - 2 \tag{6.9}$$

$$P = Cr + Cu + 2Mo + 10V + 7Nb + 5Ti - 2 \tag{6.10}$$

When the value of the parameter P is equal to or greater than zero, the steel may be susceptible to reheat cracking. The cracks are intergranular relative to prior austenitic grains (Figure 6.19)

Figure 6.19 A typical reheat crack in Cr-Mo-v coarse-grain heat-affected zone.

and occur preferentially in the coarse-grained heat-affected zone of the weld, usually in the parent metal but also sometimes in the weld metal. There are two distinct fracture morphologies: low-ductility intergranular fracture and intergranular microvoid coalescence. The former is characterized by relatively smooth intergranular facets with some associated particles, and occurs during heating between 450 and 600℃, whereas the latter shows heavily cavitated surfaces and occurs at temperatures above 600℃ (Figure 6.20). The brittle intergranular mode is initiated by stress concentrators such as pre-existing cracks or unfavorable surface geometry; in the absence of stress intensifiers, the intergranular microvoid coalescence type of fracture is dominant. In the latter case, particles within cavities are either non-metallic inclusions containing sulphur or Fe-rich M_3C-type carbides. Microcracks that form during postweld heat treatment are likely to extend during service at elevated temperature.

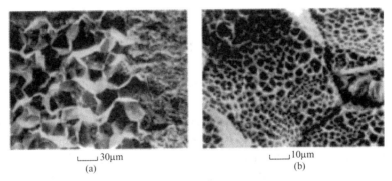

$\llcorner\!\!\lrcorner$30μm $\llcorner\!\!\lrcorner$10μm

(a)   (b)

Figure 6.20 Typical fracture morphologies of reheat cracks in alloy steel:
(a) low-ductility intergranular fracture; (b) intergranular microvoid coalescence.

There are indications that a structure having poor ductility (such as upper bainite) will be more susceptible to elevated-temperature embrittlement. Likewise coarse-grained material is more likely to crack than fine-grained. It follows that the use of low heat input processes will be better than submerged arc welding. The elevated-temperature strength may also be important. If the coarse-grained region of the heat-affected zone is stronger than the parent metal at the postweld heat treatment temperature, then relaxation takes place outside the heat-affected zone and the risk of cracking is reduced. The degree of restraint and the yield strength of the weld metal are important factors, as with hydrogen cracking. However, reheat cracking generally affects only thick sections (over about 50 mm), suggesting that a higher level of residual stress is required to cause failure. This would indeed be expected since the cracks form above 400℃ where the residual stress has already been reduced. High-pressure steam drums with closely spaced nozzles have failed owing to reheat cracking in the nozzle and plate material. Cracking of the same type may occur below stainless-steel weld-deposit cladding if the backing steel is susceptible and is given a heat treatment after cladding. The stress here is due to the differential expansion between austenitic and ferritic steel. The cracks generally occur during the heating cycle before reaching soaking temperature, probably in the 450-700℃ range. The heating and cooling rates do not appear to have any significant effect on the result.

There is evidence from Auger analysis of crack surfaces that, in the brittle intergranular mode, sulphur separates out to the crack tip. Two alternative models have been proposed to describe this behaviour. In the first model, it is assumed that solute atoms are driven to the crack-tip vicinity by elastic interaction with the crack-tip stress field. When sufficient concentration is reached, local embrittlement occurs and the crack jumps forwards by brittle fracture into a fresh region of unsegregated grain boundary, so that growth occurs in a stepwise manner (Hippsley, 1985). This model is similar to that for hydrogen-induced cracking, except that sulphur atoms occupy substitutional, not interstitial, locations and the detailed mechanism of migration is not the same.

The second proposal assumed that intergranular sulphides, which are originally precipitated by quenching from high austenitizing temperatures, dissolve when they are exposed on the crack surface. Elemental sulphur so formed then diffuses across the surface to the crack tip, enabling brittle fracture to progress at a steady rate. For both models, the rate of crack growth is governed by the rate of diffusion of sulphur.

Intergranular microcracking associated with sulphur segregation has been observed in gas tungsten arc 2. 25Cr-l Mo weld metal in the as-welded condition. The fracture surfaces were stepped, and there was evidence of sulphide precipitation during cooling through the austenitic range. Such a fracture appearance is consistent with the sulphur segregation mechanism discussed above, but in this instance the cracks must have formed on cooling and not during reheating. This type of cracking is rare, and is thought to be associated with an unusually low oxygen content (Allen and Wolstenholme, 1982).

Reheat cracks may also form or extend in service if the welded component is operating at elevated temperature and if joints are exposed to tensile stress, due to either inadequate stress relieving or service loads.

Reheat cracking tests may be divided into three types: self-restraint tests, high-temperature tensile tests and stress relaxation tests. One technique is to make up butt welds with about two-thirds of the weld completed. The samples are cut into strips, and the strips welded to an austenitic stainless-steel bar. This assembly is then heated and held for 2h at the postweld heat treatment temperature. The greatest length of sample in which no cracks are observed is a measure of susceptibility.

Hot tensile tests are made after first subjecting the specimen to a simulated weld thermal cycle. Subsequently a tensile test is made at 600℃ and both strength and reduction of area are measured. A combination of strength below that of the base metal and reduction of area below 20% indicates susceptibility to reheat cracking. Stress relaxation testing is carried out using a bar that is notched in the region of interest. The bar is loaded in four-point bending and maintained at constant radius during heating up to, say, 700℃ Load relaxation is measured, and the load-temperature curve can indicate the initiation and growth of cracks. The specimen is finally broken at low temperature for fractographic examination.

Reheat cracking is avoided and/or detected by the following means.

① Material selection: for heavy sections, limit alloy content as indicated by the Japanese formulae and limit vanadium to 0. 10% maximum.

② Designing to minimize restraint: where restraint is unavoidable, consider making a stress relief treatment after the vessel is part welded.

③ Using a higher preheat temperature; dressing the toes of fillet and nozzle attachment welds; using a lower-strength weld metal.

④ Carrying out ultrasonic and magnetic particle testing after postweld heat treatment.

Austenitic chromium-nickel steels and some nickel-base alloys may also suffer reheat cracking.

6. 3　Weldability of Magnesium and Its Alloys

6. 3. 1　Alloys and Welding Procedures

Magnesium finds its widest application in the aircraft industry and for launch vehicles and satellite structures, where its excellent strength/weight ratio can be used to full advantage. The pure metal has too low a strength for engineering use. The alloys may be divided into three main groups: aluminium-zinc, zinc-zirconium and thorium respectively. The Mg-Al-Zn alloys were the earliest in development and have the disadvantage of being susceptible to stress corrosion cracking; nevertheless, the 3Al-1Zn-0. 4Mn alloy remains one of the most generally applicable and readily welded types. The Mg-Zn-Zr alloys with 2 % zinc or less also have good weldability, as do the thorium alloys, which are designed specifically for good strength at elevated temperatures. A 2. 5Zn-1Mn alloy is used for aerospace duties.

There are a number of casting alloys that may be joined into structures by welding or may be repaired by welding. The principles outlined below apply to these alloys also.

6. 3. 2　Oxide Film Removal

Like aluminium, magnesium forms a refractory oxide that persists on the surface of the molten metal and tends to interfere with welding. However, magnesium oxide recrystallizes at high temperature and becomes flaky, so that the surface film breaks up more easily than that which forms on aluminium. The mechanism of oxide removal by means of a flux in welding is probably similar to that in aluminium welding. Fluxes are typically mixtures of chlorides and fluorides of the alkali metals (e. g. 53% KCl, 29% CaCl$_2$, 12% NaCl and 6% NaF), and are highly corrosive to the base metal. For this and other reasons, gas welding is little used for magnesium and its alloys, the most important fusion welding process being gas tungsten arc welding with alternating current. Oxide is removed from the surface by arc action during the half-cycle when the workpiece is negative. Mechanical cleaning of the weld edges is essential for fusion welding. For spot welding, chemical pickling is necessary, combined with mechanical cleaning (with steel wool) immediately before welding.

6. 3. 3　Cracking

Zinc and calcium additions both increase the susceptibility of magnesium alloys to solidification cracking during welding. Zinc is a constituent of a substantial proportion of the alloys; in amounts of up to 2% it is not deleterious, but alloys containing larger quantities, particularly those with 4-6% Zn, have poor weldability. Aluminium, manganese and zirconium have little effect on this characteristic, but thorium and rare-earth elements are beneficial and tend to inhibit solidification cracking. Generally speaking, the most crack-sensitive magnesium alloys are the higher-strength high-alloy types, which suffer from cracking both in the weld and at the weld boundary.

6.3.4 Mechanical Properties

Weld deposits of magnesium alloys solidify with fine grain and have a tensile strength frequently higher than that of the equivalent wrought material. Thus welded joints tested in tension commonly fail in the heat-affected zone, which may be embrittled by grain growth. Alloys that have been hardened by cold-working, and age-hardened material, soften in the heat-affected zone. Generally, however, the joint efficiency of fusion welds in magnesium alloys is good, and it is possible to use a relatively low-melting filler metal (e.g. the 65Al-1Zn type) for a wide range of alloys and achieve 80-100% joint efficiency'as-welded'.

6.3.5 Corrosion Resistance and Fire Risk

Magnesium alloys are commonly protected against atmospheric corrosion by means of a chromate dip. The green chromate layer must, of course, be removed from the vicinity of the joint before welding. Aluminium-containing magnesium alloys are susceptible to stress corrosion cracking in the heat-affected zone of the welds and must be stress-relieved (generally at about 250℃) after welding to prevent this type of attack. The zirconium-and thorium-bearing alloys are not susceptible to stress corrosion and do not require stress relief after welding. There is a risk of fire if magnesium is allowed to accumulate in finely divided form, and proper attention must be paid to cleanliness in all operations involving cutting, machining and grinding. Except in the joining of foil, there is no direct risk of fire due to either fusion or resistance welding of magnesium.

Chapter 7　Residual Stresses, Distortion and Fatigue

7.1　Residual stresses

Residual stresses are stresses that would exist in a body if all external loads were removed. They are sometimes called internal stresses. Residual stresses that exist in a body that has previously been subjected to nonuniform temperature changes, such as those during welding, are often called thermal stresses.

7.1.1　Development of residual stresses

7.1.1.1　Three-Bar Arrangement

The development of residual stresses can be explained by considering heating and cooling under constraint. Figure 7.1 shows three identical metal bars connected to two rigid blocks. All three bars are initially at room temperature. The middle bar alone is heated up, but its thermal expansion is restrained by the side bars (Figure 7.1a). Consequently, compressive stresses are produced in the middle bar, and they increase with increasing temperature until the yield stress in compression is reached. The yield stress represents the upper limit of stresses in a material, at which plastic deformation occurs. When heating stops and the middle bar is allowed to cool off, its thermal contraction is restrained by the side bars (Figure 7.1b). Consequently, the compressive stresses in the middle bar drop rapidly, change to tensile stresses, and increase with decreasing temperature until the yield stress in tension is reached. Therefore, a residual tensile stress equal to the yield stress at room temperature is set up in the middle bar when it cools down to room temperature. The residual stresses in the side bars are compressive stresses and equal to one-half of the tensile stress in the middle bar.

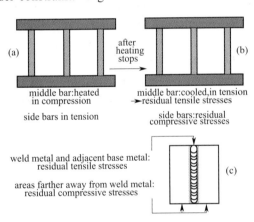

Figure 7.1　Thermally induced stresses:
(a) during heating; (b) during cooling;
(c) residual stresses in weld.

7.1.1.2　Welding

Roughly speaking, the weld metal and the adjacent base metal are analogous to the middle bar, and the areas farther away from the weld metal are analogous to the two side bars (Figure 7.1c). This is because the expansion and contraction of the weld metal and the adjacent base metal are restrained by the areas farther away from the weld metal. Consequently, after cooling to the room temperature, residual tensile stresses exist in the weld metal and the adjacent base metal, while residual compressive stresses exist in the areas farther away from the weld metal. Further explanations are given as follows.

Figure 7. 2 is a schematic representation of the temperature change (ΔT) and stress in the welding direction (σ_x) during welding. The crosshatched area $M—M'$ is the region where plastic deformation occurs. Section $A—A$ is ahead of the heat source and is not yet significantly affected by the heat input; the temperature change due to welding, ΔT, is essentially zero. Along section $B—B$ intersecting the heat source, the temperature distribution is rather steep. Along section $C—C$ at some distance behind the heat source, the temperature distribution becomes less steep and is eventually uniform along section $D—D$ far away behind the heat source.

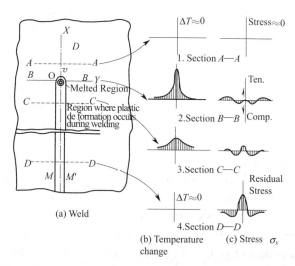

Figure 7. 2   Changes in temperature and stresses during welding.

Consider now the thermally induced stress along the longitudinal direction, σ_x. Since section $A—A$ is not affected by the heat input, σ_x is zero. Along section $B—B$, σ_x is close to zero in the region underneath the heat source, since the weld pool does not have any strength to support any loads. In the regions somewhat away from the heat source, stresses are compressive (σ_x is negative) because the expansion of these areas is restrained by the surrounding metal of lower temperatures. Due to the low yield strength of the high-temperature metal in these areas, σ_x reaches the yield strength of the base metal at corresponding temperatures. In the areas farther away from the weld σ_x is tensile, and σ_x is balanced with compressive stresses in areas near the weld.

Along section $C—C$ the weld metal and the adjacent base metal have cooled and hence have a tendency to contract, thus producing tensile stresses (σ_x is positive). In the nearby area σ_x is compressive. Finally, along section $D—D$ the weld metal and the adjacent base metal have cooled and contracted further, thus producing higher tensile stresses in regions near the weld and compressive stresses in regions away from the weld. Since section $D—D$ is well behind the heat source, the stress distribution does not change significantly beyond it, and this stress distribution is thus the residual stress distribution.

7. 1. 2   Analysis of Residual Stresses

Figure 7. 3 shows typical distributions of residual stresses in a butt weld. According to Masubuchi and Martin, the distribution of the longitudinal residual stress σ_x can be approximated by the equation

$$\sigma_x(y) = \sigma_m \left[1 - \left(\frac{y}{b}\right)^2 \right] \exp\left[-\frac{1}{2}\left(\frac{y}{b}\right)^2 \right] \tag{7.1}$$

Where σ_m is the maximum residual stress, which is usually as high as the yield strength of the weld metal. The parameter b is the width of the tension zone of σ_x (Figure 7.3a).

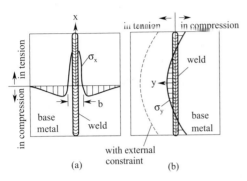

(a)　(b)

with external constraint

Figure 7.3　Typical distributions of longitudinal (σ_x) and transverse (σ_y) residual stresses in butt weld.

The distribution of the transverse residual stress σ_y along the length of the weld is shown in Figure 7.3b. As shown, tensile stresses of relatively low magnitude are produced in the middle part of the weld, where thermal contraction in the transverse direction is restrained by the much cooler base metal farther away from the weld. The tensile stresses in the middle part of the weld are balanced by compressive stresses at the ends of the weld. If the lateral contraction of the joint is restrained by an external constraint (such as a fixture holding down the two sides of the workpiece), approximately uniform tensile stresses are added along the weld as the reaction stress. This external constraint, however, has little effect on σ_x.

Figure 7.4 shows measured and calculated distributions of residual stresses σ_x in a butt joint of two rectangular plates of 5083 aluminum (60cm long, 27.5cm wide, and 1cm thick) welded by GMAW. The calculated results are based on the finite-element analysis (FEA), and the measured results are from Satoh and Terasaki. The measurement and calculation of weld residual stresses have been described in detail by Masubuchi and will not be repeated here. Residual stresses can cause problems such as hydrogen-induced cracking and stress corrosion cracking. Postweld heat treatment is often used to reduce residual stresses. Figure 7.5 shows the effect of temperature and time on stress relief in steel welds. Table 7.1 list the temperature ranges used for postweld heat treatment of various types of materials. Other techniques such as preheat, peening, and vibration have also been used for stress relief.

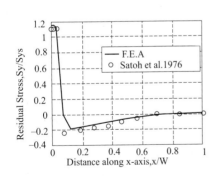

Figure 7.4　Measured and calculated distributions of residual stress in butt joint of 5083 aluminum.

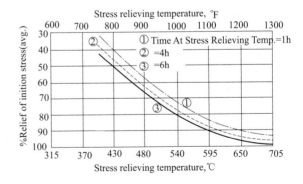

Figure 7.5　Effect of temperature and time on stress relief of steel welds.

Table 7.1　Typical thermal treatments for stress relieving weldments

Material	Soaking Temperature(℃)	Material	Soaking Temperature(℃)
Carbon steel	595-680	1% Cr-1/2% Mo steel	620-730
Carbon-1/2% Mo steel	595-720	11/4% Cr-1/2% Mo steel	705-760
1/2% Cr-1/2% Mo steel	595-720	2% Cr-1/2% Mo steel	705-760

continue

Material	Soaking Temperature(℃)	Material	Soaking Temperature(℃)
21/4% Cr-1% Mo steel	705-770	11/4% Mn-1/2% Mo steel	605-680
5% Cr-1/2% Mo (Type 502)steel	705-770	Low-alloy CrNi-Mo steels	595-680
7% Cr-1/2% Mo steel	705-760	2-5% Ni steels	595-650
9% Cr-1% Mo steel	705-760	9% Ni steels	550-585
12% Cr(Type 410)steel	760-815	Quenched and tempered steels	540-550
16% Cr(Type 430)steel	760-815		

7.2　Distortion

7.2.1　Cause

Because of solidification shrinkage and thermal contraction of the weld metal during welding, the workpiece has a tendency to distort. Figure 7. 6 illustrates several types of weld distortions. The welded workpiece can shrink in the transverse direction (Figure 7. 6a). It can also shrink in the longitudinal direction along the weld (Figure 7. 6b). Upward angular distortion usually occurs when the weld is made from the top of the workpiece alone (Figure7. 6c). The weld tends to be wider at the top than at the bottom, causing more solidification shrinkage and thermal contraction at the top of the weld than at the bottom. Consequently, the resultant angular distortion is upward. In electron beam welding with a deep narrow keyhole, the weld is very narrow both at the top and the bottom, and there is little angular distortion. When fillet welds between a flat sheet at the bottom and a vertical sheet on the top shrink, they pull the flat sheet toward the vertical one and cause upward distortion in the flat sheet (Figure 7. 6d). Figure 7. 7 shows angular distortions in butt welds of 5083 aluminum of various thicknesses. As shown, angular distortion increases with workpiece thickness because of increasing amount of the weld metal and hence increasing solidification shrinkage and thermal contraction. The quantitative analysis of weld distortion has also been described in detail by Masubuchi and hence will not be repeated here.

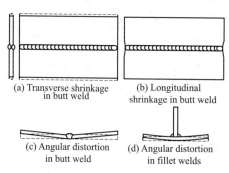

(a) Transverse shrinkage in butt weld　(b) Longitudinal shrinkage in butt weld

(c) Angular distortion in butt weld　(d) Angular distortion in fillet welds

Figure 7. 6　Distortion in welded structures.

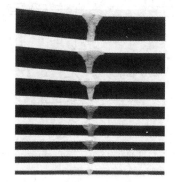

Figure 7. 7　Distortion in butt welds of 5083 aluminum with thicknesses of 6. 4-38mm.

7.2.2　Remedies

Several techniques can be used to reduce weld distortion. Reducing the volume of the weld metal can reduce the amount of angular distortion and lateral shrinkage. Figure 7. 8 shows that

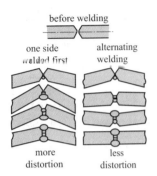

Figure 7. 8　Reducing angular distortion by using double-V joint and welding alternately on either side of joint.

welding alternately on either side of the double-V joint is preferred. Placing welds about the neutral axis also helps reduce distortion. Figure 7. 9 shows that the joint preparation angle and the root pass should be minimized. The use of electron or laser beam welding can minimize angular distortion. Balancing welding by using a double-V joint in preference to a single-V joint can help reduce angular distortion. Figure 7. 10 shows that the shrinkage forces of an individual weld can be balanced by placing another weld on the opposite side of the neutral axis. Figure 7. 11 shows three other techniques to reduce weld distortion. Presetting (Figure 7. 11a) is achieved by estimating the amount of distortion likely to occur during welding and then assembling the job with members preset to compensate for the distortion. Elastic prespringing (Figure 7. 11b) can reduce angular changes after the removal of the restraint. Preheating (Figure 7. 11c), thermal management during welding, and postweld heating can also reduce angular distortion.

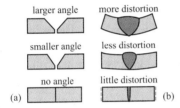

Figure 7. 9　Reducing angular distortion by reducing volume of weld metal and by using single-pass deep-penetration welding.

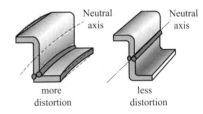

Figure 7. 10　Reducing distortion by placing welds around neutral axis.

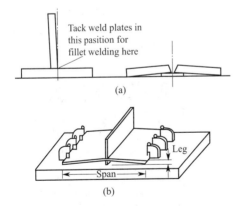

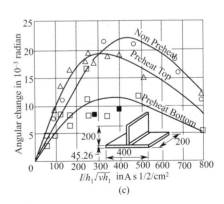

Figure 7. 11　Methods for controlling weld distortion: (a) presetting; (b) prespringing; (c) preheating.

7. 3　Fatigue

7. 3. 1　Mechanism

Failure can occur in welds under repeated loading. This type of failure, called fatigue, has three phases: crack initiation, crack propagation, and fracture. Figure 7. 12 shows a simple type of fatigue stress cycling and how it can result in the formation of intrusions and extrusions at the surface of a material along the slip planes. A discontinuity point in the material (e. g. , inclusions, porosity) can serve as the source for a slip to initiate. Figure 7. 13 shows a series of intrusions and extrusions at the free surfaces due to the alternating placement of metal along slip planes. Eventually, these intrusions and extrusions become severe enough and initial cracks form along slip planes. The direction of crack propagation is along the slip plane at the beginning and then becomes macroscopically normal to the maximum tensile stress.

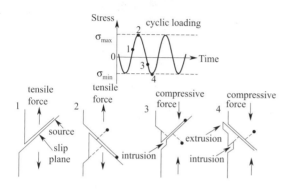

Figure 7. 12   Fatigue stress cycling (top) and formation of intrusions and extrusions (bottom).

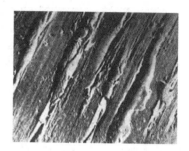

Figure 7. 13   Fatigue surface showing extrusions and intrusions.

7. 3. 2   Fractography

As pointed out by Colangelo and Heiser, the appearance of fatigue failures is often described as brittle because of the little gross plastic deformation and the fairly smooth fracture surfaces. Fatigue failures are usually easy to distinguish from other brittle failures because they are progressive and they leave characteristic marks. Macroscopically, they appear as "beach, " "clam-shell, " or "conchoidal" marks, which represent delays in the fatigue loading cycle. Figure 7. 14 shows a fatigue fracture surface, where the arrow indicates the origin of fracture.

7. 3. 3   S-N Curves

Fatigue data are often presented in the form of S – N curves, where the applied stress (S) is plotted against number of cycles to failure (N). As the applied stress decreases, the number of cycles to failure increases. There are many factors that affect the fatigue behavior, such as material properties, joint configuration, stress ratio, welding procedure, postweld treatment, loading condition, residual stresses, and weld reinforcement geometry. Figures 7. 15-Figures 7. 17 show the effect of some of these factors observed by Sanders and Day in aluminum welds.

Figure 7. 14   Fatigue fracture surface showing beach marks and origin of fracture.

7. 3. 4   Effect of Joint Geometry

As pointed out by Sanders and Day, in developing any fatigue behavior criteria for welding, the severity of joint geometry is probably the most critical factor. The more severe the geometry, the lower the fatigue strength, as shown in Figure 7. 16. The severity level of the longitudinal butt weld is lowest because both the weld and the base metal carry the load. The severity level of the cruciform, on the other hand, is highest since the welds alone carry the load and the parts are joined perpendicular to each other.

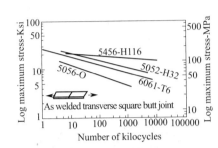

Figure 7.15　Effect of alloy and material properties on fatigue of transverse butt joint.

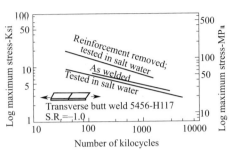

Figure 7.16　Effect of reinforcement removal and saltwater environment on fatigue of 5456-H117 aluminum.

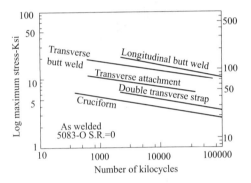

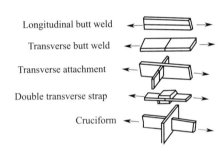

Figure 7.17　Effect of joint configurations on fatigue of 5083-O aluminum.

7.3.5　Effect of Stress Raisers

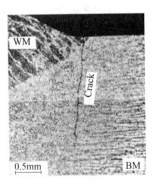

Figure 7.18　Fatigue crack originating from weld toe of gas-metal arc weld of carbon steel.

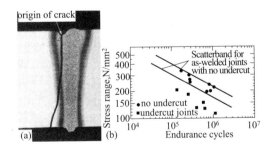

Figure 7.19　Effect of undercutting on fatigue in electron beam welds of carbon steel: (a) photograph; (b) fatigue life.

It is well known that stress raisers tend to reduce fatigue life, namely, the so-called notch effect. Stress raisers can be mechanical, such as toes with a high reinforcement, lack of penetration, and deep undercuts. They can also be metallurgical, such as microfissures (microcracks), porosity, inclusions, and brittle and sharp intermetallic compounds. Figure 7.18 shows a fatigue crack originating from the toe of a gas-metal arc weld of a carbon steel. Figure 7.19 shows a fatigue failure originating from an undercut at the top of an electron beam weld in a carbon steel and how undercutting can reduce fatigue life.

7.3.6　Effect of Corrosion

As also shown in Figure 7.17, a corrosive environment (salt water in this case) can often reduce fatigue life. This is called corrosion fatigue. It has been reported that the damage can be almost always greater than the sum of the damage by corrosion and fatigue acting separately.

7.3.7　Remedies

7.3.7.1　Shot Peening

Welding and postweld grinding can create tensile residual stresses at the weld surface and promote fatigue initiation when under cyclic loading. Shot and hammer peening, on the other hand, can introduce surface compressive stresses to suppress the formation of intrusions and extrusions and hence fatigue initiation. In shot peening, the metal surface is bombarded with small spherical media called shot. Each piece of shot striking the surface acts as a tiny peening hammer, producing a tiny indentation or dimple on the surface. Overlapping indentations or dimples develop a uniform layer of residual compressive stresses. Figure 7.20 shows the residual stresses as a function of depth, namely, the distance below the surface. It is clear that tensile residual stresses (>0) in the as-welded condition can be reduced by stress-relieving heat treatment and reversed to become highly compressive residual stresses (<0) by shot peening.

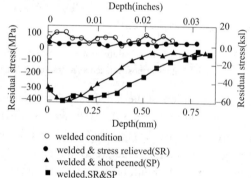

○　welded condition
●　welded & stress relieved(SR)
▲　welded & shot peened(SP)
■　welded,SR&SP

Figure 7.20　Effect of stress relieving and shot peening on residual stresses near the metal surface.

7.3.7.2　Reducing Stress Raisers

Figure 7.21 shows stress raisers caused by improper welding and how they can be reduced or eliminated. Figure 7.17 shows that removing the reinforcement improves the fatigue life. This is consistent with the results of Nordmark et al. shown in Figure 7.22 for concentration lack of penetration transverse butt welds of 6.4mm (1/4in.) thick 5456-H116 aluminum. However, in the case of incomplete penetration, removing the reinforcement can dramatically reduce the fatigue life.

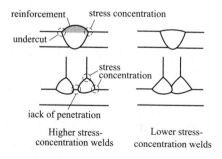

Figure 7.21　Stress raisers in butt and T-welds and their corrections.

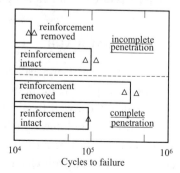

Figure 7.22　Effect of weld reinforcement and penetration on fatigue life of transverse butt welds of 5456 aluminum.

7.4 Case Studies

7.4.1 Failure of a Steel Pipe Assembly

Figure 7.23 (a) is a sketch showing a steel pipe of 10mm wall thickness bent to turn in 90° and welded at the ends (b) to connecting flanges. The pipe – flange assembly was connected to a bottle-shaped container (a) and a heavy overhanging valve weighing 95kg (e). The working pressure was 425 kg/cm^2 and the operating temperature was 105℃. The assembly was subjected to vibrations from the compressors provided at intervals along the pipe system. Graphical recorders showed evidence of the vibrations. The assembly failed after a service time of about 2500h.

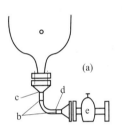

Figure 7.23 Failure of a steel pipe assembly: (a) pipe system; (b) fracture A caused by craters at position c; (c) fracture B at weld at position d; (d) surface of fracture B.

Examination of the failed assembly showed two fractures: fracture A at position c and fracture B at the weld at position d. Both fractures exhibited radial lines and striations typical of a fatigue fracture. Fracture A (Figure 7.23b) originated in small craters accidentally formed in the flange during arc welding. Fracture B (Figure 7.23c) started at the weld toe, namely, the junction between the weld reinforcement and the base metal surface. The fracture surface (Figure 7.23d) shows the radial lines and striations of fatigue.

The composition of the steel was unavailable, though metallography showed that it had a ferrite-pearlite structure, and the grains are fine and equiaxed. Regarding fracture A, many cracks were observed in the fused metal in the craters and in the martensitic structure of the heat-affected zone. Under the cyclic loading from the vibrations, these cracks served as the initiation sites for fatigue. As for fracture B, the notch effect due to reinforcement of the weld promoted the fatigue failure.

7.4.2 Failure of a Ball Mill

Figure 7.24 shows part of a ball mill used for ore crushing. The cylindrical shell of the ball mill was 10.3m in length, 4.4m in diameter, and 50mm in thickness.

A flange with 100mm wall thickness was welded to each end of the cylindrical shell ⌈left half of Figure 7.24 (a) ⌋. Both the cylindrical shell and the flanges were made from a killed steel with the composition of the steel being 0.19% C, 0.25% Si, 0.65% Mn, 0.025% P, and 0.028% S. The entire weight of the mill charge was approximately 320 tons and the drum operated at a rotation speed of 14rpm. After about 3000h of operation, long cracks appeared on the outside surface of the drum ⌈Figure 7.24 (b) ⌋.

The failed drum was emptied, its inside inspected, and cracks ranging from 100 to 1000mm

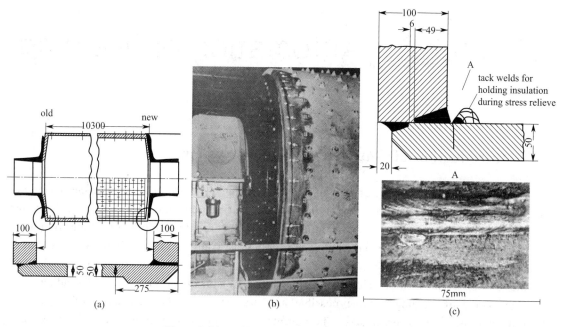

Figure 7. 24　Failure of a ball mill: （a）design;
（b）fatigue cracks（indicated by white arrows）;　（c）origin of fatigue cracks.

long were observed.　It was found that these cracks had originated from nearby tack welds,　which had been made for holding insulation during stress relieving of the drum ［Figure 7. 24（c）］.　Apparently,　the high notch effect has greatly reduced the fatigue life of the drum.　It was subsequently suggested that the new joint design shown in the right half of Figure 7. 24（a）be used and a new stress relief method be employed in order to avoid the use of similar tack welds.

Chapter 8   Automation of Welding

8.1   Introduction of Automatic Welding System

The need to reduce the cost of welding is never ending. The use of larger-diameter electrodes and higher welding currents reduce costs somewhat, but not enough. The quest for improved productivity and lower production costs continues. This has brought about the transition from manual to semiautomatic to machine applications of welding that continued until robotic welding with adaptive control became available. This has reduced the involvement of the individual welder and provides an improvement in operator factor, which has a major effect on the cost of welding.

Automation of welding became possible and practical with the acceptance of continuous electrode wire arc welding processes. The advantages of automatic welding are well known and include the following:

① Increased productivity through higher operator factor;

② Increased productivity through higher deposition Rates;

③ Increased . productivity through higher welding speeds;

④ Good uniform quality that is predictable and consistent;

⑤ Strict cost control through predictable weld time;

⑥ Minimized operator skill and reduced training requirements;

⑦ Operator removed from the welding arc area for safety and environmental reasons;

⑧ Better weld appearance and consistency of product.

The shift from manual to automatic welding and the resulting cost reduction has been known for many years. However, the automation of welding has lagged behind other metalworking operations. This is because arc welding is a much more complex process. Another reason is the lack of incentive to develop automatic welding since the welded product can still be produced by manual or semiautomatic welding.

The major deficiency of automatic welding is its inability to compensate for variations in welding joints in any but the simplest weldment designs. There are two potential solutions: ① make the piece parts perfect in every respect, or② develop welding equipment that will compensate for these variations and still produce high-quality welds.

The first solution seems contrary to normal production operations. In the past, variations have been allowed to collect in manufacturing processes, and the welder would overcome the accumulated tolerances and still produce a good-quality weldment. The welder would compensate for variations, using human skill and attention. This closed loop welding system overcomes the problems of variations in material and in piece part preparation. This is an expensive option.

Automatic welding is an open-loop system unable to make needed compensating changes. The solution is a closed-loop system to produce a good-quality weld in spite of variations. This requires a new method of application called *adaptive control welding*. It is a step beyond automatic welding since it involves complete control of the operation, including accommodations for poorly fitted joints, joint preparation errors, and warpage problems. The difference between adaptive control welding, which is a closed-loop system, and automatic welding, which is an open-loop system, is the use of feedback sensing devices and adaptive controls.

Use of the computer to control process motion and the retention of this data in memory; the development of power electronics, making welding equipment computer controllable; the development of robot and precision motion devices; and the development of sensors that detect changes led initially to robotic arc welding, but also to the overall automation of welding.

The chart shown in Table 8.1 describes the functions involved in making a weld. It also shows that manual, semiautomatic, and mechanized welding methods are closed-loop systems because of the human involvement. Automatic welding is not under constant supervision of an individual and so is an open-loop system. The functions involved in making an arc weld are expanded and show whether they are controlled by the individual or by the machine. These functions affect the level of fatigue of the individual. When more of these functions are taken over by the machine, fatigue levels are reduced and productivity increases.

Table 8.1 Person-machine relationship for arc welding with automation

Method of Application Arc Welding Elements/Function	MA Manual (closed loop)	SA Semiautomatic (closed loop)	ME Mechanized (closed loop)	AU Automatic (closed loop)	RO Robotic(open or closed loop)	AD Adaptive control (closed loop)
Start- maintains, and controls the arc	Person	Machine	Machine	Machine	Machine	Machine
Feeds- and directs the electrode in the arc	Person	Machine	Machine	Machine	Machine	Machine
Manipulates- the arc to control the molten metal weld pool	Person	Person	Machine	Machine	Machine(robot) with or without sensor	Machine with sensor
Moves-the arc along joint(travel)	Person	Person	Machine	Machine via prearranged path	Machine(robot) with or without sensor	Machine with sensor
Guides- the arc along joint	Person	Person	Person	Machine via prearranged path	Machine(robot) with or without sensor	Machine with sensor
Corrects- the arc to overcome deviations	Person	Person	Person	Does not correct hence potential weld imperfection	Machine(robot) with or without sensor	Machine with sensor

The functions are:

① *Starts*, maintains, and controls the arc.

② *Feeds* and directs the electrode into the arc (to control the placement of the weld deposit and fill the joint).

③ *Manipulates* the arc to control the molten metal weld pool.

④ *Moves* the arc along the joint (travels to provide motion at proper speed to make the weld joint).

⑤ *Guides* the arc along the joint (to track the weld joint).

⑥ *Corrects* the arc to overcome deviations (to compensate for improper fitup).

Closed loop means that real-time observations made during welding and immediate correction are made to compensate for deviations.

In "automatic" welding the welding apparatus is programmed to provide the exact taught motion patterns and the exact preset welding parameters. In many cases the weldment is simple and the parts are sufficient accurate so that changes are not required in the welding conditions or the taught motion pattern. Good-quality welds will result because the inherent tolerance of the welding process accommodates minor variations. If the joint location or geometry is beyond established variation a defective weld may result.

An automatic or automated welding system consists of at least the following:

① *Welding arc*: requires a welding power source and its control, an electrode wire feeder and its control, the welding gun assembly, and necessary interfacing hardware.

② *Master controller*: controls all functions of the system. It can be the robot controller or a separate controller. It is the overall controller.

③ *Arc motion device*: can be the robot manipulator or a dedicated welding machine, or a standardized welding machine. It may involve several axes.

④ *Work motion device*: can be a standardized device such as a tilt-table positioner, a rotating turntable, or a dedicated fixture. It may involve several axes.

⑤ *Work bolding fixture*: must be customized or dedicated to accommodate the specific weldment to be produced. It may be mounted on the work motion device.

⑥ *Welding program*: requires the development of the welding procedure and the software to operate the master controller to produce the weldment.

⑦ *Consumables*: includes the electrode wire or filler metal, the shielding media (normally gas), and possibly a tungsten electrode.

The *automatic-adaptive control* arc welding system is shown in Figure 8. 1. Changing the top block from "master control with welding program plus human" to "master control with welding program and feedback and adaptive control," and changing the bottom right from human monitoring and supervising to multisensors, changes this from an automatic to an adaptive control welding system.

There are differences in the degree of automation of a welding system. This depends on the number of sensors employed to monitor conditions. Sensors are needed to find the joint, provide root penetration, provide bead placement, follow the joint, and ensure joint fill. Adaptive control requires sensing devices and computerized circuits that alter the motion and value of a particular variable in order to compensate and satisfy the new requirements. Many sensing devices will be required to provide total adaptive controlled or automated welding. Sensing devices and adaptive controls are expensive, and only a few "real-time" sensors are used.

The subject of automated welding is changing due to new developments. The methods of application of welding are listed as follows.

(a) *MA*, *Manual welding*: welding with the torch, gun, or electrode holder held and manipulated by hand.

(b) *SA*, *Semiautomatic welding*: manual welding with equipment that automatically controls one or more of the welding conditions.

(c) *ME*, *Mechanized welding*: welding with equipment that requires manual adjustment of the equipment controls in response to visual observation of the welding, with the torch, gun, or electrode holder held by a mechanical device.

(d) *AU*, *Automatic welding*: welding with equipment that requires only occasional or no

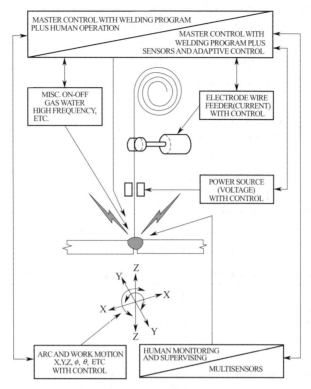

Figure 8.1   Automatic-adaptive control arc welding systems.

observation of the welding and no manual adjustment of the equipment controls.

(e) *RO*, *Robotic welding*: welding that is performed and controlled by robotic equipment.

(f) *AD*, *Adaptive control welding*: welding with a process control system that determines changes in welding conditions automatically and directs the equipment to take appropriate action.

In robotic welding the weld sequence and the path, once established, will always be followed identically. Robots will make weldments successfully with well prepared piece parts over and over. This is an open-loop system. However, robotic welding equipment can use sensors with feedback capabilities so that the path can be followed even if it is not the original memorized path. Welding conditions can change if the sensors detect a change such as in the joint configuration. This is a closed-loop system and can be as complicated as necessary to control all parameters to make a perfect weld in every situation. This system approaches the ability of a human welder to compensate for changes during the welding operation. The adaptive controller with appropriate sensors automatically determines changes in process conditions and directs the equipment to take appropriate action to ensure a high-quality weld. Automated welding is becoming widely used.

8. 2   Flexible Automation of Welding

Today the manufacturing industry faces greater demands than ever before. Customers want shorter delivery time and require a greater variety of products. At the same time, the product's lifetime is shorter, and manufacturing batch or lot sizes are smaller. A response to these demands has been the development of flexible manufacturing systems (FMSs). Flexible manufacturing systems are being used to replace small batch and continuous manufacturing operations without losing the economies of volume production. The flexible manufacturing system was developed during the 1960s by the machine tool industry with government and customer assistance.

A study by the U. S. Congress, Office of Technology Assessment ("Computerized Manufacturing Automation· Employment Education and the Workplace" OTA CIT-235) indicated that discrete manufacturing could be divided into three categories, based on the volume and variety of products, shown by Table 8. 2.

① Single-piece parts or an extremely low volume of similar items.

② Batch production of medium lot sizes.

③ Continuous production or a high volume of similar parts.

Job shop production is low-volume production with a lot size as small as one piece - that is, custom production of 1 to 10 parts if it is a large complex part, or a volume of 1 to 300 units if it is a small simple part. Batch production is a moderate to medium lot size of 10 to 300 large, complex parts, or over 15000 small, simple parts. This usually means continuous operation of dedicated production equipment. These may be arbitrary figures, but are based on this study.

Table 8. 2   Characteristics of metal working production by lot size

Type of production	Job Shop	Batch	Mass
Lot size(volume)	Low volume	Medium volume	High volume
Large complex parts	1-10	10-300	Over 300
Small simple parts	1-300	300-1500	Over 15000
Weld setup	Manual setup	Fixture,manual loading	Fixture,automatic loading
Welded production	Manual or semiauto weld	Standardized welding machine	Dedicated welding machine
Estimated percentage of U.S.production	10-20%	60-80%	20-30%

Job shop production involving single units or small lot sizes is very labor intensive. The parts produced are very expensive. There is insufficient volume to justify special machines or dedicated equipment.

Batch production involves medium-volume lot sizes. This type of production can justify simple filtering and standardized machines to make weldments with less labor. This category is still relatively labor intensive but produces parts at a lower cost.

Mass production involves high-volume or continuous production. This type of production justifies customized welding equipment. The amount of labor per part is minimum, labor efficiency is maximum, and the end product is the least expensive.

The flexible automation of welding that makes use of flexible manufacturing systems can make batch manufacturing as efficient and productive as mass production. Carried to its ultimate, it could even make job shop production much more efficient and productive and greatly reduce the cost of "one-only" production.

Robotic arc welding is the obvious answer for flexible automation of welding. The use of a robot and a welding fixture that can be mounted on a work motion device is the key to reducing welding costs. A computer program is placed in memory and used every time the particular part is manufactured. The setup time is minimal, and the robot is kept busy welding many small lot sizes of parts all day long. It allows the capability of changing from one part to another quickly and needs only a positive locating point to align the robot's welding torch with the parts being welded. Extremely small or medium-sized lots can be processed economically in this manner. A different locating fixture is used for each part and for welding the lot size required.

Robots are expensive and must be kept busy on a fulltime basis to be economically acceptable.

There is another way of accomplishing the economy of mass production of small parts produced in small lot sizes. Typical parts are shown in Figure 8. 2. This can be done with a flexible welding system that is computer controlled. A flexible automatic welding station for welding small simple parts is shown in Figure 8. 3. This workstation costs less than half that of a robot cell. The welding sequence for each workpiece is programmed and stored in the computer memory. A simple holding and locating fixture is provided for each weldment. When the part is to be produced, the operator places the fixture on the table and

Figure 8. 2 Typical parts manufactured with flexible welding equipment.

calls up the program from memory. This takes very little time. For production welding the operator unloads the finished weldment. This machine can be programmed for linear arc motion using one or two torches. It can be arranged for rotating work or arc motion with the axis of rotation vertical or for head and tail stock rotary motion with the axis horizontal. Figure 8. 4 shows modular components for a welding station and actual components.

Figure 8. 3   Flexible welding workstation with microprocessor controller.

Figure 8. 4   Modular components for welding system.

The equipment is quickly changed over from one type of motion to another. It is easily adapted to product mix changes and to small batch sizes. This is flexible automation of welding. It is used for more and more short-run applications on simple parts. It will eliminate complex dedicated fixtures and is finding increasing acceptance in volume production plants. This equipment is much less expensive than a robot, yet will make the welds at the same production rate.

8. 3   ARC Welding Robots

8. 3. 1   Introduction

Arc welding robots have become very popular in the last few years; however, robots have been around for many years. Joseph Engleburger, the father of modern robots, developed a machine in the mid-1950s and gave it the name robot. This was based on the Czech word *robota*, which connotes forced labor that was depicted as a kind of automation in Karel Capek's 1920 play entitled R. U. R. Today the Robot Industries Association defines a robot as a "reprogrammable, multifunctional manipulator designed to move materials, parts, tolls, or specialized devices, to variable programmed motions for the performance of a variety of tasks." The Japanese define the robot as a three axis programmable tool. This difference in definition might explain why there are more robots in Japan than in the United States.

Robots were introduced to North American industry in the early 1960s; however, not until the mid 1970s was robotic arc welding used in production. Robotic welding grew rapidly in the early 1980s because of the emphasis by the automobile industry. In the mid 1980s other manufacturing companies started using welding robots, and today their use is widespread and growing.

The Robot Industries Association started keeping track of robots in early 1990. In 1994, approximately 8000 robots were shipped; in 1995, approximately 12000. In 1998 there was a slight downturn to 11000, but in 1999 it increased to over 15000 units shipped. Today there are more than 120000 robots in use in North America. The pie chart shown in Figure 8. 5 shows that most robots are used for material handling, including machine loading and unloading applications. However, spot weld-ing robots, representing approximately 30%, are close behind. Arc welding robots represent 18% to 20%. Other applications, including painting, coating, and inspection, represent about 10%, whereas assembly and dispensing represent approximately 8% of the robot applications.

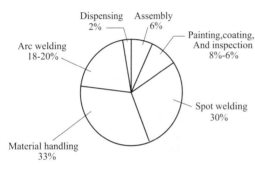

Figure 8. 5   Robot application.

Figure 8. 6   Robots handling spot welding guns on autobody line.

The automotive industry first used robots for spot welding (Figure 8. 6). The robot replaced a person using spot welding guns, this has completely changed the automobile body production line. Today, almost every automobile body production line, today, almost every automobile body produced is spot welded with a robot.

All arc welding robot systems consist of a number of major components (Figure 8. 7). The part referred to as the robot is known as the *manipulator* or *mechanical unit*, which performs the manipulative functions. The brain of the robot is the controller, and many auxiliary devices make the robot more productive.

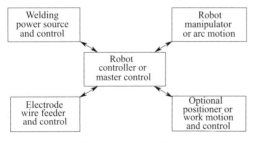

Figure 8. 7   Robot arc welding system.

The robot manipulator is a series of mechanical linkages and joints capable of moving in various directions in order to provide motion. The mechanisms are driven by linear actuators, which may be hydraulic or pneumatic, or by rotary motors, which may be hydraulic or electric. They are coupled together by mechanical links and may be direct driven or driven indirectly through gears, chains, or screws.

There are different designs of manipulators, ranging from three axes to multiple axes. The mechanical manipulator can be categorized by its general design.

The more common types of manipulators are the ① cartesian coordinate, ② cylindrical coordinate, ③ spherical coordinate, ④ anthropomorphic coordinate, ⑤ gantry, and ⑥ SCARA type. Each type has specific advantages and features, but all can be used to move a welding torch to make welds.

The complexity of the robot is usually described by the number of axes or freedom of motion, most robots have a two- or three-axis-of-wrist motion in addition to their basic motions. In selecting robot manipulator has a different work envelope configuration. The shape and size of the work envelope relates to the motions and size of linkages of the robot. Arc welding robots were originally designed to match the working area of a human being.

8. 3. 2   Robot Manipulator Configuration

Four of the six types of robots are shown in Figure 8. 8. The first is the cartesian coordinate robot, based on the three-plane drawing system used for blueprints. It is often called the rectangular coordinate system since it moves within a box-shaped volume based on the x, y, and z directions. The direction X stands for longitudinal notion in a horizontal plane. Y stands for transverse or "in or out" motion in a horizontal plane, and Z stands for up-and-down motion in a vertical plane. It has sliding motion in all three directions. It has three motion axes: longitudinal, transverse, and vertical. Its work envelope is a rectangular box.

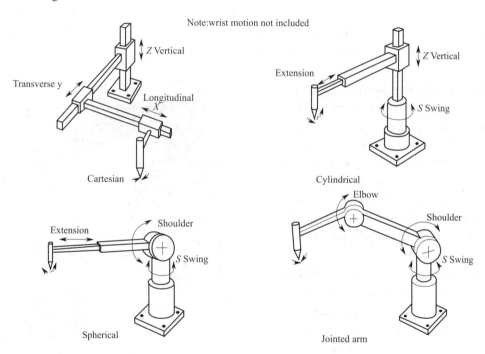

Figure 8. 8   Four types of robots.

The second is the cylindrical coordinate robot. This robot type is similar since it uses sliding motion for two directions, the vertical and one extension, but has one rotational or swing motion. The work envelope is cylindrical in the plan view and rectangular in the elevation. The arm holding the welding torch moves up and down the mast and swings about the mast with less than a full circle. The torch extends and retracts.

The third is the spherical coordinate robot, also known as a polar coordinate robot. This robot type has one sliding motion and two rotational motions. One is around the vertical post, and the other is around a shoulder joint. The mechanism holding the arm swings about a vertical axis and rocks up and down about a horizontal axis. The arm slides to extend and retract. The work envelope is spherical, with a similar plan view as the cylindrical coordinate motion robot, but with an elevation view showing the rotational motions based on the shoulder rotation.

Figure 8. 9   Gantry robot having eight axes of motion.

The fourth robot is the anthropomorphic robot, or revolute or jointed arm robot. The motions are all rotational with no sliding motion. The work envelope is irregularly shaped in the vertical plane and about two-thirds of a circle in the horizontal plane. This type of robot swings about its base to sweep the arm in a circle. It bends the upper arm forward and backward at the shoulder and raises and lowers the lower arm at the elbow.

The fifth robot, which can be considered as having a cartesian coordinate motion, is the gantry robot (Figure 8. 9). The gantry is only part of the total motion since a jointed arm robot or a two or three axis wrist is attached to the gantry carriage to provide maximum movement within the work envelope. Its work envelope is a large rectangular box.

The sixth robot is the SCARA. SCARA is an acronym for *selection compliance assembly robot arm*, also known as a horizontal articulate robot. Some SCARA robots have four axes of motion, but do not have much vertical travel. They are used for welding primarily in a single plane. Their work envelope is a flat rectangular box. The SCARA robot is not popular for welding.

There can be combinations of these types of motion systems for special appli-cations. The work envelopes of different makes of robots of the same type are similar. The variations are due to different lengths of arms and links. The jointed arm or anthropomorphic robot is the most popular. The basic movements are shown in Figure 8. 10. The work envelope of a typical jointed arm robot is shown in Figure 8. 11.

The method for attaching a welding torch or gun is by means of an adapter attached to the wrist. Two different methods of attachment are shown in Figure 8. 12. The adapter may have a breakaway feature, which avoids damage if the torch crashes into the work or fixtures. The wrist,

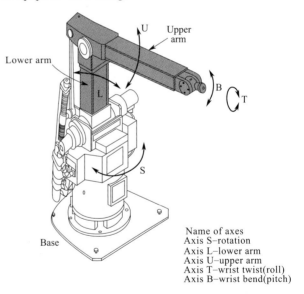

Name of axes
Axis S—rotation
Axis L—lower arm
Axis U—upper arm
Axis T—wrist twist(roll)
Axis B—wrist bend(pitch)

Figure 8. 10   Basic movements of a jointed-arm robot manipulator.

which is attached to the work end of the robot upper arm, allows two or three additional axes of motion. They are very similar to the human wrist. These motions are known as pitch, roll, and yaw, which are boating terms, or bend, twist, and tilt. Figure 8. 13 shows the wrist motions with a welding torch attached. Two or three axis wrists are used with arc welding robots.

The body motions and wrist motions allow the welding torch to be manipulated in space in almost the same fashion as a human being would manipulate it. This allows the torch angle and travel angle to change to make good-quality welds in all positions. They are also required in order to reach difficult-to-reach areas. Even so, a robot cannot provide the same manipulative motions as a human being, but it can come extremely close.

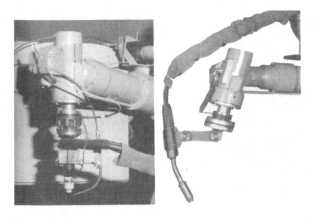
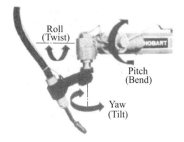

Figure 8. 11　Methods of welding gun attachment.　　　　　Figure 8. 12　Wrist motions.

Additional axes are added when the robot is mounted on a moving carriage. This will add an additional axis of motion. A work-holding device can add an additional axis of motion. This is usually rotation and/or tilt, which will add two more axes of motion. A jointed arm robot with a three-axis wrist working with a two-axis manipulator would have eight axes of motion.

In selecting a robot it is necessary to determine its work envelope and reach and the number of axes of torch motion. This will allow you to determine if the robot will weld the weldment in question. This is difficult to determine without making tests; however, computer design programs are available that will help decide whether the robot can accommodate the weldment. An actual test is the positive method.

An important factor is the repeatability of the robot. This is the closeness of agreement of repeated position movements under the same conditions to the same location this means to move the welding torch to the same point every time it goes through its program. Most electric robots provide a maximum variation of 60. 015 in. in robot movement for repeated returns to a programmed point. This is affected by operating speed and is acceptable for gas metal arc welding. For gas tungsten arc or plasma arc welding, a tighter tolerance is required and a repeatability of 60. 008 in. is desired. This information is provided by manufacturers, specifications; however, a test provides positive data.

Accuracy of robot movement is also very important. This is the degree to which the actual position corresponds to the desired command position. This is measured by comparing the command position to the actual position.

Resolution is also very important. This is a measure of the smallest possible increment of change in variable output of the robot. It is determined by the ability of the position feedback encoders or resolvers to determine the location of a particular joint and the position of the endpoint, called the tool center point.

Another factor is the weight-carrying capacity of the robot. This is the weight it will accommodate in its normal operating envelope at normal travel velocities on the end of the wrist. Weight-carrying capacity should accommodate the welding torch, the torch breakaway devices, water and gas hoses, current-carrying cable, and in some cases the electrode wire feeder or feed head and the electrode wire.

The type of motion drive system is extremely important, as is the type of position feedback

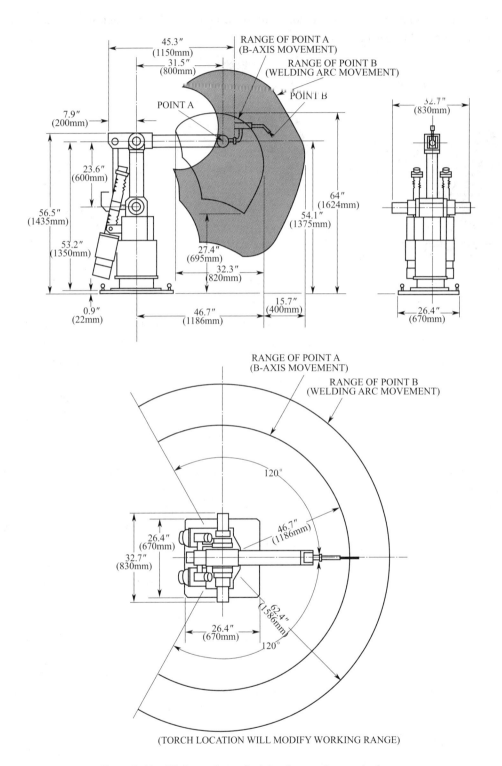

Figure 8. 13 Work envelope of a jointed-arm robot manipulator.

sensors. The motion should be smooth at all times in all positions. Electric drive robots are most widely used for arc welding. Hydraulic drives can be used for painting or spot welding since accuracy or repeatability is less critical. The electrical robots are more repeatable since hydraulic systems tend to drift during warm-up and during operation. In addition, hydraulic robots may have oil leaks. Finally, consideration should be given to mounting position, base height adjustment, manipulator weight, environmental limits, and approvals.

A typical robot cell installation is shown in Figure 8.14. This shows the robot manipulator, workpiece positioner, and necessary equipment in a safety enclosure.

Figure 8.14 Typical robot cell with 180° index positioner.

8.3.3 Robot Welding Application

Robots are welding many, many different products. They can weld just about anything that a human being can weld. An interesting application that shows the robot, s capability of welding a complex structure can be seen in Figure 8. 3. 11a. This is the welded frame of a large motorcycle; a finished motor-cycle is shown in Figure 8. 15 (b). The following are examples to show the diversity of types of welds made by robots.

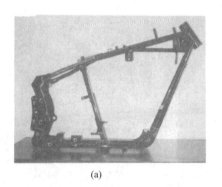

(a)

(b)

Figure 8. 15   Robot-welded motorcycle frame.

8. 3. 3. 1   Case Study: Tubular Welded Product

The need was to handle more different varieties of frames and to increase production. The company took the following approach: Fixtures were modified to handle more than one size of frame. Robots and positioners were installed. The fixtures were mounted on positioners, and two positioners were used with each robot. Five parts are required. The major part is thin-wall, small-diameter tubing. The other parts are sheet metal stampings. Tack welding is not used. The operator loads the fixture, and the frame is completely welded before removing from the fixture. One operator tends to two robots loading and unloading workpieces on one positioner, while the robot welds on the other. Six robots are producing over 60, 000 frames per month. Improved quality, reduced production costs, virtually eliminated scrap, and minimized inspection time resulted from changing from semiautomatic to robotic welding of this application, shown in Figure 8. 16.

8. 3. 3. 2   Case Study: Sheet Metal Assembly

This manufacturer of health care equipment wanted to remove welders from routine work and from the welding environments and to reduce costs and improve quality. The weldment is a large sheet metal part (Figure 8. 17). The work cell consisted of one robot and three workstations, all within the robot work envelope. One operator mans all three workstations; how ever, an operator start-and-stop control panel is located in each station. Each fixture is firmly fixed. The operation

151

Figure 8. 16   Tubular product.

operates three shifts a day and has reduced production costs by using less electrode wire, less CO_2 shielding gas, and increased welding speed. The quality of welds is good and consistent, so that fillet weld sizes can be reduced. The productivity has increased over 200%.

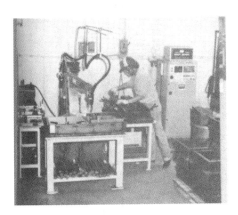

Figure 8. 17   Sheet metal assembly.

8. 3. 3. 3   Case Study: Pipe Welded Assembly

A manufacturer was seeking to reduce costs with small lot sizes and short production runs. Its work involved pipe fittings that required high-quality welds. Short runs are from 25 to 200 parts, and there are 35 different welded assemblies. The company installed a two-station, five-axis work positioner and elected to have different fixtures on each end of the turnaround positioner. An assembly is shown in Figure 8. 18. This is a flange-to-welded assembly. Switching to robotic welding has increased productivity, since the operator sets up workpieces of various size and types on one end of the turntable, while the robot is welding at the other end. The robot utilizes through-the-arc seam tracking, which provides good quality for every weld, even though fit up may not be perfect. The pipe assemblies are welded to code requirements.

Figure 8. 18   Pipe welded assembly.

8. 3. 3. 4   Case Study: Gas Tungsten Arc Welds

Gas tungsten arc is being used for more and more applications. This aerospace supplier produces accessories for jet engines. The material is thin and medium-thick stainless steel and nickel alloys. This company installed a dual-station positioner and an inverter power source. The material thickness ranged from 0. 032 to 0. 215 in. , which required a wide range of welding currents. The robot was equipped with an automatic arc length control (AVC) operating through the robot software. Precision and repeatability has been excellent and the resulting weldments are more consistent than those produced previously. Cold wire feed is used for heavier materials but not for the thin materials. This application is shown in Figure 8. 19.

8. 3. 3. 5　Case Study: Automotive Front Cross Member

Automotive companies have scheduled model changeover. Changeover expense can be minimized by using robots and dedicated holding fixtures rather than dedicated welding machines. The product is an automobile front cross member made from two head, sheet metal stampings and miscellaneous smaller stampings. This assembly, shown in Figure 8. 20, requires 56 in. of intricate curved welds. It is first spot welded together and then arc welded. The operation is completely automated, including transporting the workpiece from station to station. The conveyor transports the workpiece under the positioner, which clamps it and rotates it 180° for welding position. Following the weld cycle, the finished workpiece is automatically released onto the conveyor and transported to the next workstation.

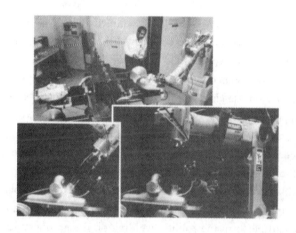

Figure 8. 19　Gas tungsten arc welding.

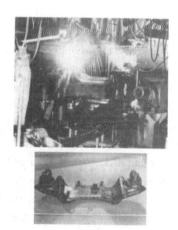

Figure 8. 20　Auto front cross member.

8. 3. 3. 6　Case Study: Aluminum Gas Metal Arc Welding

A supplier to the defense industry is producing aluminum louvered grill assemblies. The company selected a five-axis robot with a five-axis, double-ended, dual-station work positioner. The parts were self-jigging but required holding fixtures to keep parts in proper alignment. The holding fixtures were attached to the turntables on each end of the positioner. The system uses a push-pull wire feeding system with a water-cooled torch. Approximately 150 in. of weld is required to produce each louver. With the robot, weld quality has greatly improved, warpage has been greatly reduced, and productivity has increased. Welding these louvers is shown in Figure 8. 21.

Figure 8. 21　Aluminum gas metal arc welding.

8.3.4　Buying a Welding Robot

Careful economic analysis is required to justify the purchase of automated equipment. This may be aggravated by the fact that it is difficult to hire qualified, skilled welders. Once the decision has been made to adopt automatic or robotic welding, the problem becomes how to select the most suitable arc welding system. Only a handful of companies worldwide produce arc welding robots and automatic arc welding equipment. However, many robot sales representatives and integrators can assist you in selecting the best solution for your automated welding problem. In general, it might be advantageous to select a preengineered arc welding robot cell. These are engineered to use continuous wire welding systems, gas tungsten arc welding systems, or cutting or resistance welding. Preengineered robotic cells are available from basic units with minimum size capabilities to complex cells covering larger weldments. The advantage of the robot cell is that it can be installed and immediately will go to work to produce your parts. Robot cells are engineered with compatible equipment and built-in safety devices that meet national standards. Robot companies will also engineer special cells for your requirements, or you can purchase the necessary parts to construct your own cell for automated welding stations. When going this route, it is necessary that all components be matched for the ultimate requirement. For the do-it-yourself company it is recommended that you refer to American National Standard ANSI/AWS D16. 2, entitled "Guide for Components of Robots and Automated Welding Installations. " This document applies to the recommended design, integration, installation, and use of industrial welding robotic and automatic systems. It includes the various components such as the manipulator. Power source, torch accessories, wire feed system, and shielding gas system. It does not contain information standardizing the control system. Control computer systems are designed and provided by the manipulator producer for their particular machine. Each control system and control software system are based on a particular manufacturer's robot and may not be compatible with other controllers. This problem is being considered by the robot industry; in fact, universal robot controllers are now available for reworked robots and to provide uniformity throughout the entire factory. They may allow a universal programming system that will standardize the programming of various makes of robots.

It is strongly suggested that the first robot installation be in the form of an integrated cell. It is important to make sure that the cell you order will perform the robotic welding on the products you manufacture.

8.3.5　Robot Safety

Robots were originally designed to duplicate the job functions of a human being. They were designed to relieve human beings of the drudgery of unpleasant, fatiguing, or repetitive tasks and to remove them from a potentially hazardous environment. In this regard, robots can replace people in the performance of dangerous jobs and are considered beneficial for preventing industrial accidents. However, robots have caused fatal accidents.

The best document relating to robot safety is the "American National Standard for Industrial Robots and Robot Systems—Safety Requirements ANSI/RIA R15. 06. " This standard provides guidelines for industrial robots. It covers manufacturing, remanufacturing, insulation, safeguarding, maintenance, testing, and startup requirements. A copy should be obtained from the Robot Industries Association, and it should be followed.

Robots work beyond their base area and have large work envelopes that may overlap with adjacent machinery. The travel speed is fast. And robots are multidirectional, operating with as many as six or more axes. Additionally, they start up suddenly and change direction abruptly during motion.

Due to the variable nature of robot applications, specific safety hazards for each installation must be studied on an individual basis. For a robot to be truly effective, it must maintain a high degree of flexibility. This implies that the working envelope must be unrestricted to allow for programs and path changes. Robots work best when they stand where a person once stood, next to other people.

Unfortunately, a robot performing the same function as a human will occupy more space than the human. The primary safety rule is that the person and the robot should not occupy the same working space at the same time. The nature of arc welding requires a person to be close to the arc while programming or analyzing a program. To remove the person from the arc area limits the robot's flexibility and accuracy. Hence one of the major problems associated with robotic arc welding is the presence of a human programmer in close proximity to the welding torch held by the robot. For small weldments, this is not a major problem. For very large weldments, the parts are heavy and a completed weldment will require cranes for loading and unloading. These introduce the normal problems of safety with respect to materials handling. However, they also introduce the problem of bringing heavy pieces of material into the robot's work envelope.

One of the best solutions for robot safety is to purchase the robot as a complete welding cell. A complete cell includes barriers, all necessary safety devices, and a method of loading and unloading the workstation. It is best used for the production of smaller weldments. In general, a turntable, turnover, or shuttle device is used for loading parts outside the robot's work envelope. The parts are then presented to the robot inside the barrier where the welding is performed. After the welding is completed, the parts are then transferred to outside the barrier, where they are unloaded and sent to their next destination. Figure 8. 22 shows a pictorial view of a robot cell with a rotary 180° indexing table for the workstation.

This cell is for small weldments that can be loaded and unloaded outside the barrier. Different index fixtures can be used for larger weldments. A robotic welding cell layout with two pneumatic indexing shuttle positioners and two robots is shown in Figure 8. 23. Work-holding devices can also be loaded and unloaded automatically, in which case they must work with a material motion device that presents additional safety hazards. This becomes a special engineered project.

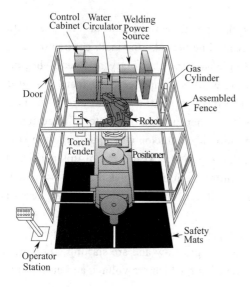

Figure 8. 22　Layout of a robot cell
with 180° index positioner.

Figure 8. 23　Robot cell with two
shuttle index positioner.

Figure 8. 24 Danger
warning sign.

The robot industry has adopted special safety graphics. Although these have not yet been accepted as a national standard, they are used by many robot suppliers. They should be posted at appropriate locations. One warning sign that is agreed upon by all is shown in Figure 8. 24: DANGER—DO NOT ENTER—MACHINE MAY START AT ANY TIME. This should be posted at the cell access door.

8. 4　Controls for Automatic Arc Welding

When making a weld, it is always the intent to produce a perfect weld. In any of the application methods, except manual welding, a control system is required to run the welding program. A welding program is always employed consciously or unconsciously whenever a weld is made. The program or welding procedure is the basis for making the weld. In manual welding these are established and controlled by the welder. In semiautomatic welding a control mechanism in the wire feeder actuates electrode wire feed and starts the welding current and shielding gas flow when the welder presses the gun trigger.

Mechanized and automatic welding have more complicated programs and control additional functions, in-duding travel or motion, torch position, and fixture motion. All motion functions are sequential. A-daptive welding, which varies weld parameters in accordance with actual conditions, has a complicated computer control system that includes sensing devices and adaptive feedback.

8. 4. 1　Automatic Welding Controllers

Programmers are designed to execute a welding program. As the welding program becomes more complex, the controller must include more electrical circuits. A typical program for gas metal arc welding is shown in Figure 8. 25. It can also be used for flux-cored arc welding or submerged arc welding. The top three lines represent welding current (or wire feed speed) and arc voltage . The next two lines rep-resent auxiliary activities shielding gas and cooling water flow. The bottom line represents travel or relative motion.

At the cycle start point, the operation begins and the specific activities occur. First is preflow of shielding gas and flow of cooling water. After a preset time period, the main contractor closes. The arc starts and the electrode wire feed begins. Single-axis travel, rotary or linear, begins at this point or after a preset delay. Travel occurs until the weld is completed, but many end at different points, de-pending on the welding program. The travel or motion control circuit includes a motor speed control circuit. When the weld is completed, there is time for crater fill and time for burn back prior to terminating the weld. The welding circuit contractor will open, the arc stops, but shielding gas continues to flow during a preset postflow period. At the end of this period, the shielding gas and water-cooling valves close and the welding cycle is completed. The cycle can be made to repeat for arc spot welds or for skip welds, or it can only repeat when new pieces are placed in the machine and the cycle is reinitiated.

To fully understand a welding program, it is necessary to understand the terms used:

① *Preflow time*: the time between start of shielding gas flow and arc starting (prepurge) .

② *Start time*: the time interval prior to weld time during which arc voltage and current reach a preset value greater or less than welding values.

③ *Start current*: the current value during the start-time interval.

④ *Start voltage*: the arc voltage during the start-time interval.

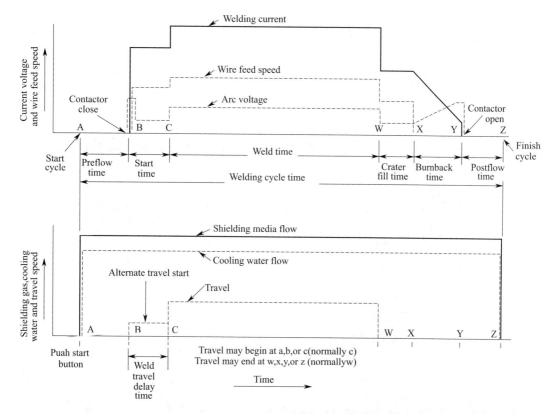

Figure 8. 25   GMAW welding program.

⑤ *Hot start current*: a brief current pulse at arc initiation to stabilize the arc quickly.

⑥ *Initial current*: the current after starting but prior to upslope.

⑦ *Weld time*: the time interval from the end of start time or end of upslope to beginning of crater fill time or beginning of downslope.

⑧ *Travel start delay time*: the time interval from arc initiation to the start of work or torch travel.

⑨ *Crater fill time*: the time interval following weld time but prior to burn back time, during which arc voltage or current reach a preset value greater or less than welding values. Weld travel may or may not stop at this point.

⑩ *Crater fill current*: the arc current value during crater fill time.

⑪ *Burnback time*: the time interval at the end of crater fill time to arc outage, during which electrode feed is stopped. Arc voltage and arc length increase and current decreases to zero to prevent the electrode from freezing in the weld deposit.

⑫ *Downslope time*: the time during which the current is changed continuously from final taper current or welding current to final current.

⑬ *Upslope time*: the time during which the current changes continuously from initial current value to the welding value.

⑭ *Postfiow time*: time interval from current shutoff to shielding gas and/or cooling water shutoff (postpurge) .

⑮ *Weld cycle time*: the total time required to complete the series of events involved in making a weld from beginning of preflow to end of postflow.

The controller for running the program in Figure 8. 25 is shown in Figure 8. 26. Controllers of this type include meters for arc voltage, for welding current, and some times for electrode wire feed speed. It also includes pilot lights for other activities, such as an " arc on" signal to indicate that the arc has been established. This type of controller usually has input voltage compensation and will compensate for welding cable voltage drops, and so on. The controller includes motor speed control circuits, which accurately regulate the wire feed speed motor and the travel speed motor. Time-delay circuits are included whenever a delay period is required.

Figure 8.26   Welding controller for single-axis motion.

Other activities, such as welding head positioning and fixture clamping, can be included. A relay controller of this type can only provide one function at a time in a prearranged sequence. Two on/off functions can be simultaneous, and sequenced functions can be in rapid order. This type of controller does not have the capability to ramp or gradually change the welding current during operation. This function is included, however, in controllers for gas tungsten welding and plasma arc welding. Adaptive feedback signals cannot be accommodated with this type of controller. Controllers of this type can be preprogrammed to provide specific delays for shielding gas preflow and postflow time, travel start time, crater fill time, and burn hack time. Welding current and arc voltage at different levels can be preprogrammed, as well as the total weld cycle time. This same type of programmer can be used with limit or proximity switches, to use motion as a control base rather than time.

This controller can control more than one axis of travel motion, and it has extra contacts so that it can control other motions, such as fixture clamp and torch advance. However, it cannot control coordinated or simultaneous motion of two or more axes. Motion must be sequential so that one activity immediately follows the previous one. Coordinated motion requires microprocessor-type controllers.

Controllers are simple or complex, depending on the number of activities that must be controlled. The one shown is for a semiautomatic wire feeder. A relay logic system requires some operator skill because the control provides the sequencing of operation but still requires the operator to establish parameters, delays, and decision-making capabilities to ensure a good-quality weld.

Controls and timers can be standard or precision, depending on the needs of the welding procedure pro-gram. Tachometer feedback of wire speed and travel speed motors can be included to provide for more precision and repeatability. The more precise controller ensures consistent high weld quality and repeatability.

The weld control systems described are relatively simple but are well suited for many, many applications using arc motion and work motion devices. They can be used for standardized and dedicated automatic arc welding machines with not more than two axes of simultane-0us (not coordinated) motion. Controllers such as those mentioned here and more complex control units are available from different manufacturers.

8. 4. 2　Robot Controllers

For robotic arc welding systems, a much more complex controller is required. Controllers include a high-speed microprocessor since coordinated, simultaneous, continuous motion of up to eight axes and all welding parameters may be required. As the number of axes increases, the a-mount of computer capacity must increase.

The machine tool industry introduced numerical controls (NC) years ago. Automatic shape cutting machines use the same type of controller for directing the path of cutting torches. These are known as *point-to-point* (PTP) control systems. Points are locations in two dimensions in one plane. For arc welding robots the arc is moved from one point to the next in space. A typical robot arc welding controller is shown in Figure 8. 27. The location of the arc is known as the *tool center point* (TCP). The path of the TCP is programmed and stored in memory. For spot welding, pick and place, and machine loading, point-to-point playback is used.

For arc welding, playback of the arc motion is a continuous path in space. The robot controller must be coordinated so that each axis movement begins and ends at the same time. The programmer's function is to accept the input of many point

Figure 8. 27　Robot controller.

locations, relate welding parameters to the path taught, and store this information in memory, then play it back to execute a welding program. It is beyond the scope of this book to explain its inner workings; however, we will explain how it is used to make welds. The major points of interest are the teach mode, memory, and playback or execution.

8. 4. 3　Teaching the Robot

There are at least four methods of teaching or programming a robot controller: manual methods, walk through, lead through, and off-line programming. The manual method is not used for arc welding robots. It is used mainly for pick-and-place robots.

The walk-through method requires the operator to move the torch manually through the desired sequence of movements. Each move is recorded into memory for play back during welding. The welding parameters are controlled at appropriate positions during the weld cycle. This method was used in a few early welding robots.

The lead-through method is a popular way of programming a robot. The robot welding operator accomplishes this by using a teach pendant (Figure 8. 28). By means of the keyboard on the teach pendant, the

Figure 8. 28　Teach pendant.

torch is power driven through the required sequence of motions. In addition, the operator inputs electrode wire feed speed, arc voltage, arc on, counters, output signals, job jump functions, and much more. All of these functions are related to a particular point along the taught path. In this way, if the robot speed is changed, it is not necessary to change the time for certain actions to happen. This/means that actions are sequence and position related rather than time related. The travel speed of the torch Is independently programmed between specific points by the keyboard.

The path of the arc or tool center point is taught by moving the TCP to a particular point using the teach pendant keyboard. The machine axes locate the torch, and the wrist axes control the angle of the torch. There is a control for each drive motor (i. e., one for each axis). When the desired position is reached, it is necessary to record the position by pushing the record button. This same operation is repeated for the next location point, until the complete path is taught. The robot controller must be coordinated to control all the axes simultaneously. The normal arc welding robot has five or six axes, including two or three in the wrist. The controller should have additional capacity to control the axes of positioning equipment. Robot positioners increase overall efficiency and the range of the robot and improve weld accessibility. The robot controller should be able to control the positioner and provides total coordinated motion.

In the playback mode the robot will follow the path between each point according to its interpolation function. Normally, linear interpolation is used, which means that the arc or TCP will move in a straight line between taught points. Circular interpolation means that the arc or TCP will move in a circle. Three points will designate and locate a circle. It is useful for developing a curved path and reduces the number of points required. The playback mode must be a continuous path.

The controller should allow revision of one taught point without reteaching the entire path. It should allow deletions or additions of taught points. Also, it should al-low changes of travel speed or of welding parameters. The operator should be able to check the taught path and welding parameters without welding. The speed of the arc may be set in absolute values or by transverse runtime (TRT) or time between points. These tasks are done in an edit mode so that the taught path can be modified or shortened, speed changed, or welding parameters changed.

Older robots require an interface panel between the robot controller and the welding power source and electrode wire heater. The panel allows the programmer to control the wire feeder and power source in exact volts and amperes. Some interface panels also provide subroutines such as weld termination. The controller usually has many steps from minimum to maximum to control current and voltage, and these must be converted to absolute current and voltage values to conform with the program. The newer robot controllers have more capabilities, and with newer power sources avoid the need for an interface panel.

The robot controller must program welding parameters to have a truly automatic welding system. They must be stored and retrieved the next time the job is run, without the necessity of adjusting the welding equipment.

The robot controller must have a diagnostic system built in to allow a quick check when problems occur. Most robot controllers offer other features, which may be built in or optional. Linear and circular interpolation, mentioned previously, is important. Other features available as options could be:

Automatic acceleration and deceleration.

① Three-dimensional shift.

② Simultaneous control of extra axes.

③ Scale-up and scale-down.

④ Mirror image.

⑤ Software weave.

All of these are useful for an arc welding robot. The software weave is very useful since it allows the robot to manipulate the weld pool like a human welder. It allows a larger weld cross section and better bead contour and enables the weld to bridge gaps. Different patterns can be programmed, from simple sideway oscillation to triangular patterns. This is taught in three steps. Frequency of the weaving oscillation, amplitude, and dwell at each end are taught. Once the weaving pattern is taught, welding will continue through changes of path in all planes without reteaching the weaving pattern. Other options include through-the-arc seam tracking and other tracking functions. A thorough study of the robot is necessary to determine and learn what these features include.

Off-line programming involves the preparation of the program on a computer. An appropriate language must be used. The program is entered into the robot memory very quickly. This increases the use of the robot, since lead-through teaching ties up the robot during programming. Off-line programming is becoming more widely used, but requires experienced personnel.

8.4.4 Robot Memory

The amount of memory of the controller is usually indicated by the number of steps and instructions that can be programmed with the number of axes involved. This is often described as having a memory capacity of 2, 200 steps and 1, 200 instructions. Memory should have at least 32K bytes with battery backup. There should be a programming terminal with keyboard and screen displays in addition to the teach pendant.

The controller usually has one or more microprocessors. Faster execution, response time to better in-Put/output control, and overall flexibility is possible when two or more processors are used. Controller soft-ware that provides all the control features is stored in RAM (random-access memory) and ROM (read-only memory). Memory can be expanded with external cassette tapes, diskettes, or disk drives. External stored information must be read into the RAM prior to execution.

The computer must have communication ports so that it can talk to the overall controller. The robot memory should be selected based on the work to be done. Controllers allow feedback signals from various sensors.

8.4.5 Weld Execution

Welds can be made only when the power is on all components, electrode wire is installed, and the controller is in the playback or operate mode. The material must be in the fixture and ready. Pushing the start button will initiate the operation. The robot will move the torch to the start point. The welding equipment will begin its cycle of operation (i. e., gas preflow, start the arc, etc.). The robot controller will determine that the arc has started and then start motion. Points along the taught path will initiate other activities programmed. At the end of the taught path, the welding equipment will terminate the weld program and the robot controller will determine that the electrode wire has separated from the work. After this the robot will return to its home position, ready for another cycle. At this point the weld should be checked for quality. The program should be checked and edited to improve the weld ff necessary and to minimize the air cut path and increase air cut speed. When the weld quality is acceptable and cycle time is at a minimum, it is time to freeze the program and start production.

8.5 Sensors and Adaptive Control

8.5.1 Introduction

The ultimate automated welding system will simulate the human welder and provide a closed-loop system that compensates for all variations to produce a high-quality weld. This is true adaptive control welding. The components of an automatic welding system shown in Figure 8.1 are changed to adaptive control as shown in Figure 8.29. Adaptive control welding can be applied to robotic welding systems or to complex automatic welding systems, which are open-loop systems until adaptive control is added.

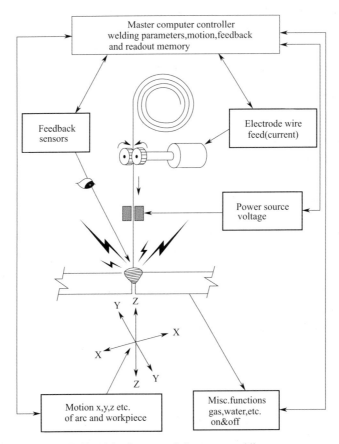

Figure 8.29　Adaptive control for an arc welding system.

True adaptive control for automatic or robotic welding closes the loop because sensing devices can replace the human operator for almost every function required, as shown in Table 8.1.1 in the three right-hand columns. In practice, however, sensors should be provided only for the functions that require surveillance and control. The number of sensors indicates the level of completeness of a closed-loop system.

Two components must be added to a system to provide adaptive control:

① A controller with a high-powered microprocessor that will accept signals from sensors and make the necessary changes in the welding parameters in real time.

② Sensing devices that provide real-time information to cause parameter changes.

The controller for a welding robot or for a multiaxis automated welding machine was described in Section 8. 4. An advanced controller coordinates additional movements and has the ability to accept feedback sensor signals.

An adaptive controller for a robotic arc welding sys-tem must control all functions and accommodate feedback signals. The controller's central processing unit (CPU) controls and monitors arc motion and workpiece motion, torch location and angular position, welding parameters, parts location, shielding gas supply, and other functions. The advanced controller eliminates the need for an interface panel and provides necessary analog-to-digital conversion for inputs and outputs. The processor must have high speed with the ability to process vast amounts of data. The unit should contain at least 4 MB of RAM and a 20-MB hard disk for program storage and weld history. A floppy drive or a tape drive should be included for making copies of welding procedures or taking historic real-time data. The robot controller should communicate with other factory processors and fit the CAD equipment used. It should provide a warning alarm system that is adjustable for variations in parameters if they exceed previously set tolerances.

Configuration editors should be included for different procedures and applications. The CPU should have a color display monitor with a touch-sensitive screen so that the operator can correct operations easily and accurately The controller should have a logical menu-driven program with color icons and sound, written in plain English to lead the operator through the weld procedure. Only selections that make sense at a given time should be presented to the operator. If an error occurs, the controller should suggest solutions. The controller memory should contain hundreds of welding schedules in its library that can be recalled and applied as required. The controller should allow procedures to be checked by the system for logical consistency before the actual weld is made. Password routines should be used to allow a procedure to be viewed but changed only by personnel with the authority to do so. A lightweight portable pendant with a single connector to the main processor console should be provided. The pendant should contain an emergency stop button, individual trim knobs for each weld parameter, jog buttons for each motion axis, wire feed, and subroutines. It should have a display screen that displays messages and actual weld parameters. The programmer controller should be able to gather data on all activities, provide printouts of pro-cedures and parameter values, and so on. Printouts should provide the date, time, operator iden-tification, weld procedure, and part identification. Programmers should be sufficiently flexible that the operator working at the main menu can touch the screen and review the welding procedure or select a new one from the library. It should be possible to make a dry run to determine the pro-cedure without the arc on. The operator's pendant, which displays parameter values, can be used to modify and control the weld. The master robot controller should be able to communicate with other computers in the factory. Two typical modern controllers are shown in Figure 8. 30.

The other components necessary for adaptive control are sensors. A sensor is a device that de-termines or measures a function in real time during the welding operation. Sensors are used to de-termine actual conditions so that the welding procedure can be modified if necessary. They provide signals that are used to modif3' the motions of the arc as well as for changing welding parameters. Feedback of sensor variations causes the adaptive controller to change parameters and travel path to produce a quality weld despite problems that may be encountered. Sensors close the loop and make truly automatic welding possible.

A variety of sensing devices are commercially available. Special software or a special comput-er may be required to match a sensor to the robot controller. New and improved sensors are continually being developed, with their use becoming more widespread.

Figure 8. 30   Advanced robot controllers.

8. 5. 2   Contact Sensors

The two major categories of sensors for scare tracking are the contact (tactile) and the noncontact. Tactile sensors have been used for joint tracking for many years. They range from simple mechanical systems to complex electrical-mechanical contacting sensors. The simplest seam tracker is a spring-loaded roller with a floating welding torch. The roller fits against a reference surface and causes the head to maintain a specific dimensional relationship with the joint. The head will follow the motions generated by the roller.

Figure 8. 31   Electromechanical contact-type seam.

The electromechanical system is more versatile. In this system, a wheel or a stylus probe will contact the surface, which can be the plate surface, the edge of a groove, the edge of a T-joint, or similar surface, and provide a signal that operates a motorized cross slide to adjust the torch for making the weld. A second axis can be provided to maintain accurate torch-to-work dimensions. The probe and torch are mounted on the carriage (Figure 8. 31). This system is used for long, straight seams. Probes wear and must be replaced. They are connected to switches that provide the correction signal. The probe must be sufficiently distanced from the arc to prevent spatter buildup. Tack welds and the start and end of welds pose a problem. This type of equipment is not suited for robotic arc welding.

The distance from the arc to the sensing location can pose a problem for a mechanical probe or wheel. If the distance is too great, deviations can occur; if it is too short, the arc will interfere with the probe and cause rapid wear and deterioration. These systems are not able to accommodate abrupt changes of direction at welding speeds.

A different type of touch system is employed in conjunction with through-the-arc tracking systems for a robot. This system uses the electrode wire, which protrudes beyond the current pickup tip, as the contact. The robot is programmed to move the electrode wire and touch the work surface at different points to determine the location of the start of the joint. It can also be programmed to measure the weld geometry and establish the size of the weld groove. It uses a complex motion system. This computer-driven system may employ an expert system with a memory. It is capable of sensing the joint path in three dimensions and storing it in memory. The calculation of the weld joint detail in connection with the expert data bank will establish a new welding procedure and modify the welding parameters.

8. 5. 3 Noncontact Sensor Systems

Noncontact sensor systems have become very popular. There are three basic types: (1) sensor systems that rely on physical characteristics of materials or energy output relationships, (2) through-the-arc systems that use electrical signals generated in the arc, and (3) optical-visual systems that attempt to duplicate the human eye.

Acoustics can be used to control the length of a gas tungsten arc and the standoff distance for laser heads. The sound energy is linearly proportional to arc voltage. An acoustical waveguide close to the arc leads to a microphone. The signal is amplified, filtered, and rectified and is used to control the torch movement and thus to control the standoff distance and the arc length. It is used for pulsed current gas tungsten arc welding and for laser cutting.

Capacitance is the property used by some proximity switches. The capacitance limit switch has been used in automatic equipment for years. It can be adjusted for different distances. It is also used to detect the presence or absence of material, such as if a clamp is closed or not.

Eddy currents are currents set up ill the base metal by an adjacent AC field that is generated by a coil located dose to the base metal. Another coil acts as the pickup and detects the eddy current. Electronic circuitry produces a voltage dependent on the distance from the base metal. The output changes when a joint interrupts the metal surface. The sensor is oscillated across the joint to produce control signals, which are processed to give the position of the joint centerline. Different types are required for ferrous metal and for nonferrous metal. Thickness is not a major factor. This system is for noncontact seam-tracking systems.

Inductance or induced current in the base metal can be detected and measured and used for seam tracking. In this case the sensor contains two coils, which scan the seam and provide signals that give information on the location of the joint. This is similar to the eddy current system. The sensor must be at a given distance above the base metal and placed ahead of the arc because of its sensitivity to heat and spatter.

Infrared radiation can be picked up by sensors that are used for penetration control . The infrared sensor is focused on the underside of the weld pool to detect the color of the metal under the weld. This system's accuracy is subject to surface conditions and exact target location. It is not considered extremely reliable as a penetration control system and has limited applications.

Through-the-arc seam tracking is a noncontact system with many advantages. It does not need accessory items attached to the torch. It is a real-time system that can be used for most types of welds. Monitoring occurs while the weld is being made. There are several types of through-the-arc systems and they are used both when metal crosses the arc and when metal does not cross the arc.

The earliest through-the-arc sensing system was the arc length control system for gas tungsten arc welding. Such a system is called an *arc voltage control* (AVC) *system*; however, *arc length control* is a more appropriate name. The starting mechanism of some AVC systems operates such that when the cold tungsten electrode touches the work, it initiates the arc and immediately withdraws to the preset voltage. Arc length control systems are very reliable and are widely used.

The major use of through-the-arc systems is for seam tracking. The welding torch is oscillated and the arc voltage and/or welding current are monitored before and after each oscillation. Mechanical oscillation is normally used, but magnetic oscillation can be used for gas tungsten arc welding but not for gas metal arc welding. Through-the-arc systems can be used for fillet or groove

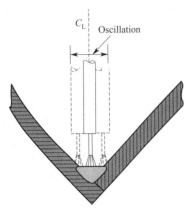

Figure 8. 32 Through-the-arc guidance system.

welds. Figure 8. 32 illustrates the principle of operation. Control circuits measure the voltage and/or current and reference the left- and right-hand values to equalize them. The control circuit moves the torch to the center point between the two equal points. This adjusts the path automatically. This system also has a corner recognition mode that allows tracking around a 90° change of direction and is capable of sensing the joint path in three dimensions. It can be used with all modes of metal transfer. Welding speeds of up to 40 in. /min (1025 mm/min) can be attained. Oscillation can vary from 1/8 in. (3. 2 mm) to 1 in. (25 mm) , and the frequency is from 1 to $4\frac{1}{2}$ Hz. The controls can be integrated into the controller. The final pass of a groove weld is attained by using the previous passes to establish the torch path in memory. This system can be coupled with the electrode contact system mentioned previously, where the electrode wire is used to find and measure the weld joint. If the root opening or gap in the groove joint is excessive, the machine can be programmed to select a different procedure from the memory bank and make alternate layers for each layer rather than a single pass.

Optical-visual sensor systems are based on an analysis of the manual welding operation, which states that the welder derives the bulk of the information required to make a high-quality weld through visual input. Optical-visual systems provide real-time signals for fully automated arc welding. Optical-visual systems find the seam, follow it, and identify and define the joint detail so that welding parameters can be adjusted to produce a high-quality weld. Optical-visual systems are extremely fast and do not become fatigued. However, they are extremely complex. A system flowchart is shown in Figure 8. 33.

Optical-visual systems have overcome the problem of viewing different colors and surfaces: bright, rusty, smooth, rough, that tend to confuse the sensor. They can pick up a very small joint in thin material, even when the joint separation is minimal. Many optical-visual systems are operating suc-cessfully, but no single system can be applied universally to robotic welding applications. Different systems are designed for particular applications.

The image to be viewed can be the weld joint ahead of the arc, the arc itself, the weld pool under and behind the arc, or the light generated by the arc. The image selected depends on the viewing area and how it is lighted. The image can be picked up by means of a TV camera as shown in Figure 8. 34 or by photodiodes arranged in a matrix array. The pickup method affects the image display and processing system. Two images are usually required. In some cases, images are triangulated to determine the exact location. Fiber optics is used to transmit the image to the camera. The angle of viewing depends on the image processing method. Images can also be picked up by a system operating through the torch.

The picked-up image must be enhanced for better visibility. One method uses structured light, usually a pattern of bright and no light that can be directed from an oblique angle, as illustrated in Figure 8. 35. The light source is usually a laser, which is more useful because it is monochromatic and can be highly focused. The incident arc light can be filtered out, which simplifies processing. If structured light from a point source is used, it is sometimes augmented by a beam from another direction, to facilitate triangulation for precise positioning. The image from the pickup device must be processed to provide a display. Digitizing the image is normal.

166

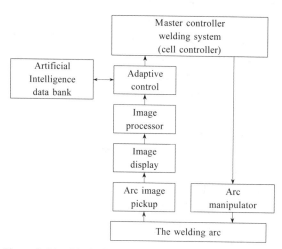

Figure 8. 33   Block diagram of visual guidance system.

Figure 8. 34   TV camera to pick up image.

The most common image display device is the cathode ray tube, as shown by Figure 8. 36. Image analysis requires the use of high-speed microprocessors. It also requires an extremely complex program to analyze all the data received and put them into a useful form so that the image can be used to make real-time changes based on variations in the weld.

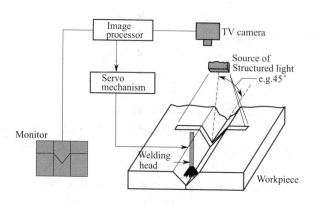

Figure 8. 35   Structured light for seam tracking.

Figure 8. 36   Image displayed
on cathode ray tube.

Adaptive control systems require an interface between the sensor and the robot controller. It normally uses a database and an expert system to provide weld parameters when conditions change. The complete system will provide the necessary input and close the loop to produce the perfect weld.

Each optical-vision system has advantages and disadvantages. Each system is useful for certain applications. he following is a brief list of optical-visual systems:
① Reflecting light with the photodiode pickup.
② Viewing the welding arc with a TV camera.
③ Viewing the molten weld pool either through the torch or adjacent to the torch.
④ Viewing the joint ahead of the arc.
⑤ Laser range-finding techniques (rastering) .

Optical-visual sensing systems are continually being improved and are being more widely used for automated arc welding applications.

Figure 8.37   Torch-to-work distance for laser cutting.

The economics of sensors must be considered. Only sensors needed to detect a repeatable problem should be used. For example, in a simple weldment, if the piece parts are always made accurately and holding devices are accurate, there is no need for a seam follower. If the location of the equipment, tooling, and piece parts is always accurate, there is no need for a seam-finding sensor. The more sensors involved, the more expensive and potentially troublesome the system becomes. Sensors must be small, robust, and durable. They must be able to withstand the hostile environment near the arc. They must be easy to connect to the controller. They must immediately and routinely send a correction signal to the controller for immediate weld parameter correction.

The more commonly used systems are the electrode touch system for finding the joint combined with through-the-arc system for seam tracking. An optical-visual system is used for seam tracking when welding with GMAW. A system for maintaining the torch-to-work (standoff) distance with feedback from a capacitance sensor is used for laser cutting (see Figure 8.37). The robot control system must accommodate the different types of sensors. The selected system should fit the work.

8.6   Tooling and Fixtures

A weldment is an assembly of piece parts. Automated assembly should be anticipated in the future. Parts should be designed so they can be inserted with a straight-line up-and-down motion. Robots with appropriate grippers will be used to assemble weldment parts in the properly designed holding fixture. If specific welds must be made prior to adding another piece part, consideration should be given to building the weldment in subassemblies and using a final welding operation to combine the subassemblies.

Fixturing for weldments should be coengineered by the product designer and the fixture designer. The weldment design should allow assembly of the weldment on a base with additional parts added to the top side. Self-jigging should be incorporated if at all possible. The addition of parts after a welding operation should be held to an absolute minimum.

Both designers must take into consideration and anticipate shrinkage and warpage inherent to weldments. When a weld cools, it shrinks and this causes warpage. One advantage of robotic welding is that distortion will normally be more uniform because the robot makes the weld in the same sequence every time. The designer should anticipate the pattern in which the welds will be made and attempt to balance welding to minimize warpage. The work-holding fixture for arc welding must accurately locate and hold the component parts of the weldment in their proper location for welding. It must locate the joints accurately and maintain the correct fitup. It speeds up the operation and improves the dimensional accuracy of the weldment. There are many types of welding fixtures, and there are many reasons for employing them.

Originally, welding fixtures were used for manual shielded metal arc welding (stick welding) to eliminate the time-consuming hand layout and tack welding of parts. With manual welding, if a sufficient number of weldments were made, the cost of the fixture would be recovered quickly due to the elimination of the setup and tack welding operation. The fixture also increased the accuracy of the weldment by eliminating the errors that could occur during the setup operation. With the advent of mechanized, automated, or robotic arc welding, the advantages of fixtures became even more pronounced. Efficient fixtures allow unattended welding. Once the parts are in the fixture and it is properly located, the automated or robotic welding process can start and operate without observation, monitoring, or supervision.

It is important to keep the fixture in operation as much of the time as possible to quickly recover its cost. In addition to the savings provided by the elimination of the layout operation, productivity is greatly increased because fixtures can be loaded and unloaded while the welding machine is making welds. Arc-on time is much higher, running as high as 90%. It also improves the safety of robotic welding since double-ended indexing positioners are normally used. Two fixtures are placed on the indexing positioner, which can rotate to position one fixture inside the welding cell, and the operator remains on the outside of the cell unloading and loading the other fixture.

There are basically two types of fixtures used for robotics arc welding: ①those used for tack welding parts together, and②those that hold the weldment during the complete welding operation. The second type, sometimes called *strongbacks*, is heavier and more robust than tacking fixtures. They are used to hold the parts, maintain accurate alignment, and resist warpage of the weldment. The work-holding fixture is customized for each weldment. It is unique and must be reworked if the design of the weldment is changed.

For automated or robotic arc welding, the work-holding fixture is placed on an indexing positioner. This provides operator safety and increased productivity. Each end of the positioner may have two axes of motion, such as horizontal-vertical and/or tilt motion, which can be integrated by the controller. This allows the fixture and the work to move so that the welds can be made in the flat position and also maintains accessibility for the welding torch. The work-holding device on each end of an indexing positioner need not be for the same weldment. The robot can be programmed to weld different products on the two ends of the positioner. The exception to this practice is when rotary tables are used for loading, moving the work to the welding station, and moving the weldment to the unload station; in this case the fixture must be for the same weldment.

The time required for unloading a finished weldment, loading the next weldment's piece parts, properly locating them, and clamping them must be less than the arc welding time for either weldment. This allows the operator time for inspecting and moving material. The total time from beginning to load parts to unloading the weldment is the factor that determines the robot system's production rate. Indexing Fixtures change the index position when instructed by the operator rather than by the pro-gram of the robot.

Good fitup is required to obtain high-quality welds. The size of the root opening relates to the speed of welding. If the root opening is excessive, the root pass will burn through, resulting in the need to rework the joint. The piece part should be remade. Often a third type of fixture is used to attach the tack welded weldment to the positioner table to hold it in the proper location for the robotic program. It can also be used to facilitate quick attachment and easy removal. Clamping might not be necessary if the worktable of the positioner remains horizontal. Attention must be given to the positioner's weight capacity, which must also include the fixture.

In contrast to the previous information, keep in mind that extremely simple work-holding devices can be made quickly and will pay back after being used for a few batch runs of production. These fixtures can be built around a finished weldment. Assuming that the weldment is dimensionally accurate, the parts produced in the fixture will be accurate. Fixtures used for manual welding can be upgraded for automatic welding, They must be properly identified, stored, and called up again for the next production run of the same part. This keeps the automatic welding system running at full capacity, pays back quickly, and produces good-quality weldments.

It is essential that the weldment and the fixture ph3vide accessibility for the welding gun to make the necessary welds. It may be necessary to redesign the fixture orweldment to allow weld location. This is why coengineering is essential.

Fixtures are normally purchased from a fixture builder or system company. The fixture builder or designer should be selected based on experience of bulleting similar types of fixtures. Responsibility must be established and accepted. There must be complete understanding of the entire project by the fixture user and the fixture producer. This is best accomplished in a meeting of the weldment designers, the welding production department, and the fixture designer or producer. It is necessary to agree on the productivity expected from the fixture, which would include welding time cycle, load time, unloading time, the annual quantity required, and the production lot size. The result is an agreement with all concerned to obtain the desired fixture at a reasonable price. Written specifications are often used.

It is necessary to provide information concerning the weldment and its weight and size. If possible, show the exact weldment or a similar weldment to the fixture designer. It is necessary to agree on the dimensional tolerances that will be permitted. Show the dimensions and indicate which are critical and which are not. This allows the designer to determine how every piece part must be located and held, how much distortion can be allowed, and how much material is allowed for finish machining. At the same time, it is worthwhile to review previous fixtures produced by the designer and producer.

The welding process to be used must be specified, as well as the size and type of each weld, the position of welding each joint, the type of work motion device that will be used, the work envelope of the equipment or robot that is contemplated, the type of welding gun or torch, and the decision whether multiple-pass welds will be required. Groove welds versus fillet welds should also be discussed along with the weld details and weld quality expected.

It is also desirable to indicate the target budget allowed for the fixture. Welding fixtures are expensive and can represent up to 50% of the total cost of the automatic welding cell. The fixture designer and producer should be able to provide an estimate of the fixture's cost. Specifications should be understood and agreed to by all parties. Also, it is worthwhile to enter into a design-and-build contract between the parties. This would identify the fixture and weldment and finalize the specifications. The prelim-design should be reviewed and approved by the buyer. The fixture should then be manufactured and proven. This is done by making weldments with the mechanized equipment; the resultant weldment must meet the specifications.

In view of this process, particularly on complex welding fixtures, complete trust must be established and responsibility accepted. Both parties must be satisfied. As the weldments become more complex, the fixture becomes more complex, and the cost goes up accordingly. Weld fixtures or work-holding devices should be designed and built by people with experience. Properly used, fixtures will pay for themselves quickly.

Chapter 9   Welding Quality Inspection

Weld quality inspection is the use of technological methods and actions to test or assure the quality of welds, and secondarily to confirm the presence, location and coverage of welds. In manufacturing, welds are used to join two or more metal surfaces. Because these connections may encounter loads and fatigue during product lifetime, there is a chance they may fail if not created to proper specification.

Methods of weld testing and analysis are divided into destructive and non-destructive methods. A few examples of destructive testing include macro etch testing, fillet-weld break tests, transverse tension tests, and guided bend tests. Other destructive methods include acid etch testing, back bend testing, tensile strength break testing, nick break testing, and free bend testing. Non-destruc-tive methods include fluorescent penetrate tests, magnaflux tests, eddy current (electromagnetic) tests, hydrostatic testing, tests using magnetic particles, X-rays and gamma ray based methods and acoustic emission techniques. Other methods include ferrite and hardness testing.

The purpose of testing is to determine whether a material or part is free enough of voids or defects to perform its intended function. It must be realized that the desired properties or qualities must be built into a product; they cannot be inspected into it. The primary purpose of inspection is to determine the existing quality or state of the material with a view to acceptance or rejection.

9. 1   Welding Defects

9. 1. 1   Definition and Types

A welding defect is any flaw that compromises the usefulness of the finished weldment. It can be defined as irregularities in the weld metal produced due to incorrect welding parameters or wrong welding procedures or wrong combination of filler metal and parent metal.

Weld defect may be in the form of variations from the intended weld bead shape, size and desired quality. Defects may be on the surface or inside the weld metal. Certain defects such as cracks are never tolerated but other defects may be acceptable within permissible limits. Welding defects may result into the failure of components under service condition, leading to serious accidents and causing the loss of property and sometimes also life.

Various welding defects can be classified into groups such as cracks, porosity, solid inclusions, lack of fusion and inadequate penetration, imperfect shape and miscellaneous defects. Any of these defects are potentially disastrous as they can all give rise to high stress intensities which may result in sudden unexpected failure below the design load or in the case of cyclic loading, failure after fewer load cycles than predicted.

9. 1. 2   Cracks

Cracks may be of micro or macro size and may appear in the weld metal or base metal or base metal and weld metal boundary. Different categories of cracks are longitudinal cracks, transverse cracks or radiating/star cracks and cracks in the weld crater. Cracks occur when localized stresses exceed the ultimate tensile strength of material. These stresses are developed due to shrinkage during solidification of weld metal.

Cracks may be developed due to poor ductility of base metal, high sulpher and carbon contents, high arc travel speeds i. e. fast cooling rates, too concave or convex weld bead and high hydrogen contents in the weld metal (see Figure 9. 1).

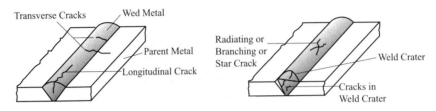

Figure 9. 1　Various types of cracks in welds.

9. 1. 3　Porosity

Porosity results when the gases are entrapped in the solidifying weld metal. These gases are generated from the flux or coating constituents of the electrode or shielding gases used during welding or from absorbed moisture in the coating. Rust, dust, oil and grease present on the surface of work pieces or on electrodes are also source of gases during welding. Porosity may be easily prevented if work pieces are properly cleaned from rust, dust, oil and grease. Furthermore, porosity can also be controlled if excessively high welding currents, faster welding speeds and long arc lengths are avoided flux and coated electrodes are properly baked. Different Forms of Porosities are shown in Figure 9. 2.

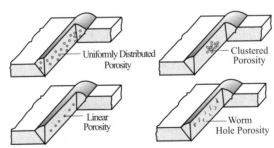

Figure 9. 2　Different forms of porosities.

9. 1. 4　Solid Inclusion

Solid inclusions may be in the form of slag or any other nonmetallic material entrapped in the weld metal as these may not able to float on the surface of the solidifying weld metal (see Figure 9. 3). During arc welding flux either in the form of granules or coating after melting, reacts with the molten weld metal removing oxides and other impurities in the form of slag and it floats on the sur-face of weld metal due to its low density. However, if the molten weld metal has high viscosity or too low temperature or cools rapidly then the slag may not be released from the weld pool and may cause inclusion.

Slag inclusion can be prevented if proper groove is selected, all the slag from the previously deposited bead is removed, too high or too low welding currents and long arcs are avoided.

9. 1. 5　Lack of Fusion and Inadequate or incomplete penetration

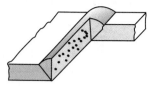

Figure 9. 3　Slag inclusions in weldments.

Lack of fusion is the failure to fuse together either the base metal and weld metal or subsequent beads in multipass welding because of failure to raise the temperature of base metal or previously deposited weld layer to melting point during welding (see Figure 9. 4). Lack of fusion can be avoided by properly cleaning of surfaces to be welded, selecting proper current, proper welding technique and correct size of electrode.

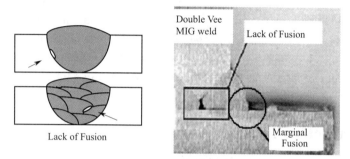

Figure 9. 4　Examples of lack of fusion.

Penetration is also one of the most important factors. There is correct penetration when the weld completely crosses the joint thickness, leaving a small seam of continuous penetration well-fused at the back.

Insufficient penetration consists in discontinuity between the two edges of the bevel due to the fact that the filler metal has not completely penetrated the joint (see Figure 9. 5). This takes place as, during welding, the groove starts to close; the seam becomes narrow and the welding bath stagnant. To prevent this problem, a possible remedy is to decrease feed speed or reduce the electrode drive angle to increase the temperature of the bath and therefore the penetration. If this is not sufficient, interrupt welding and increase the current or use the grinder to reduce the root face.

The opposite defect is excessive penetration, which is marked by an excessive reinforcement on the back of the joint, higher than required (see Figure 9. 5). In this case, during welding the groove becomes too wide and the weld pool control is difficult due to its size and fluidity. To reduce penetration and eliminate this problem feed speed may be increased, possibly also increasing the electrode drive angle. If this is not sufficient, interrupt welding and reduce the current.

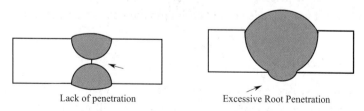

Figure 9. 5　Examples of improper penetration.

9. 1. 6　Imperfect Shape

Imperfect shape means the variation from the desired shape and size of the weld bead. During undercutting a notch is formed either on one side of the weld bead or both sides in which stresses tend to concentrate and it can result in the early failure of the joint. Main reasons for undercut are the excessive welding currents, long arc lengths and fast travel speeds.

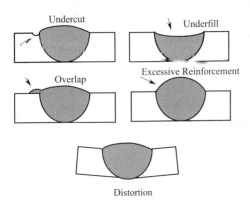

Figure 9. 6   Various imperfect shapes of welds.

Underfill may be due to low currents, fast travel speeds and small size of electrodes. Overlap may occur due to low currents, longer arc lengths and slower welding speeds. Excessive reinforcement is formed if high currents, low voltages, slow travel speeds and large size electrodes are used. Excessive root penetration and sag occur if excessive high currents and slow travel speeds are used for relatively thinner members. Distortion is caused because of shrinkage occurring due to large heat input during welding. Various Imperfect Shapes of Welds are shown in Figure 9. 6.

9. 2   Non-destructive Testing

Nondestructive testing or Non-destructive testing (NDT) is a wide group of analysis techniques used in science and industry to evaluate the properties of a material, component or system without causing damage. The terms Nondestructive examination (NDE), Nondestructive inspection (NDI), and Nondestructive evaluation (NDE) are also commonly used to describe this technology. Because NDT does not permanently alter the article being inspected, it is a highly-valuable technique that can save both money and time in product evaluation, troubleshooting, and research. Common NDT methods include ultrasonic, magnetic-particle, liquid penetrant, radiographic, remote visual inspection (RVI), etc.

Non-destructive testing is the use of physical methods which will test materials, components and assemblies for flaws in their structure without damaging their future usefulness. NDT is concerned with revealing flaws in the structure of a product. It, however, cannot predict where flaws will develop due to the design itself.

All NDT methods have the following common characteristics:

① The application of a testing medium to the product to be tested.

② The changes in the testing medium due to the defects in the structure of the product.

③ A means by which it detects these changes.

④ Interpretation of these changes to obtain information about the flaws in the structure of the product.

9. 2. 1   Radiographic Testing

Radiographic testing is used to detect internal defects in welds. Although it can find planar (two-dimensional) defects such as cracks or lack of fusion it will not find them in all orientations. It will, however, more easily find volumetric defects such as porosity or slag inclusions or shape defects such as undercut or excess root penetration. It can also be used for pro file surveys of pipework and components to check for loss of wall thickness caused by corrosion and/or erosion. Figure 9. 7 shows the basic technique.

9. 2. 1. 1　Rays

Gamma rays (from a radioactive isotope) or X-rays (from a machine) are passed through the material and strike a film causing it to darken. The film gets darker the more radiation that hits it so volumetric defects such as porosity that allow more radiation through the material will show as areas darker than the surrounding area. Conversely, areas such as excess penetration, where more radiation is absorbed by the material, will show as lighter than the surrounding area.

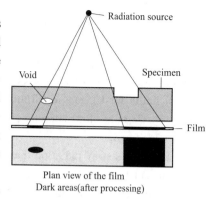

Figure 9. 7　Making a radiograph.

Gamma radiography is commonly used on site because it is portable and does not require a power source. It is inherently dangerous, though, because the radioactive isotope (source) cannot be 'turned off' and is always radiating. Storage, transportation and use of the source must therefore be closely controlled to ensure the safety of the radiographers and work-place personnel.

9. 2. 1. 2　Isotope

The type of isotope used will depend on the thickness of material to be tested. The most common Gamma isotope is iridium 192 but thinner materials may use other isotope such as yturbium and (for thicker materials 40 mm) cobalt 60. Cobalt 60 is incredibly dangerous and should only really be used when iridium 192 is impracticable. It is a good idea to finish having all the children you want before using cobalt 60 or, better still, get someone else to use it and keep well back.

On a more serious notetreat it with great respect. The sources are contained in carriers made from depleted uranium and are only wound out for the required exposure time.

9. 2. 1. 3　Quality

Quality of the radiographic film is measured using four main parameters:

(1) Density

Density is a measure of how much light passes through the film. The higher the density number, the darker the film. Normal acceptance levels are densities of between 1. 8 minimum to 4. 0 maximum for X-ray and 2. 0 to 4. 0 for gamma, but it varies between standards. The density meas-urement is normally taken along the area of interest (i. e. the weld length) using a piece of equip-ment called a densitometer.

(2) Sensitivity

Sensitivity is an indication of the smallest defect that can be seen on the image. A wire type or hole type image quality indicator (IQI) is used to determine the smallest defect visible on the image. The wire type IQI is the more common type used and consists of either six or seven wires depen-ding on the standard used (see Figure 6. 5). The American ASTM standard speci fies six wires but the European standard specifies seven. Sensitivity is expressed as a percentage derived from the thinnest wire visible divided by the material thickness. The acceptable percentage will vary depen-ding on material thickness. To save calculations ASME V and EN standards give tables specifying the smallest wire that must be visible to give the correct sensitivity value for different material thick-nesses and different radiographic techniques.

(3) Geometric unsharpness (Ug)

Geometric unsharpness (Ug), also known as penumbra, is a measure of the 'fuzziness' of the radiographic image. Geometric unsharpness (Ug) is calculated from the formula

$$U_g = Fd/D$$

Where, F is effective source size or focal spot.

d is object to film distance.

D is source to object distance.

Acceptance is based on the relevant code requirement, ASME V Section 2 gives recommended maximum limits for U_g ranging from 0. 020 in (0. 51mm) for material thicknesses below 2 in to 0. 070 in (1. 78 mm) for materials greater than 4 in.

(4) Backscatter

Backscatter is stray radiation that can expose the film. A lead letter 'B' is placed on the back of the film and if excessive backscatter is present a light image 'B' will be visible on the film, which should then be rejected. A darker image, on the other hand, is not a cause for rejection.

① Application Range Radiographic Testing encompasses sources such as X-rays, Gamma rays as well as newer methods such as real time radiography, computed radiography (CR) and computed tomography (CT). Not one solution can meet all radiographic needs; the right choice depends upon the application. Radiographic Testing is mainly used to test new welds and verify compliance but it is also used to detect corrosion in life plants.

② Safety Industrial radiography appears to have one of the worst safety profiles of the radiation professions, possibly because there are many operators using strong gamma sources in remote sites with little supervision when compared with workers within the nuclear industry or within hospitals.

The radiographic testing method is used for the detection of internal flaws in many different materials and configurations. An appropriate radiographic film is placed behind the test specimen Figure 9. 7 and is exposed by passing either X-rays or gamma rays (Co-60 & Ir-192 radioisotopes) through it . The intensity of the X-rays or gamma rays while passing through the product is modified according to the internal structure of the specimen and thus the exposed film, after processing, reveals the shadow picture, known as a radiograph, of the product. It is then interpreted to obtain data about the flaws present in the specimen.

③ Application range This method is used on wide variety of products such as forgings, castings and weldments. Some of the advantages of radiographic testing include:

(a) It can be used to inspect large areas at one time.

(b) It is useful on wide variety of materials.

(c) It can be used for checking internal malstructure, misassembly or misalignment.

(d) It provides permanent record.

(e) No calibration needed on the job site.

(f) Devices for checking the quality of radiograph are available.

(g) Interpretation of radiographs can be done in comfortable conditions.

Some of the limitations of this method are:

(a) X-rays and Gamma-rays are hazardous to human health.

(b) It cannot detect planar defects readily.

(c) Access to both sides of the specimen is required.

(d) Thickness range that can be inspected is limited.

(e) Certain areas in many items cannot be radiographed because of the geometric consideration.

(f) Sensitivity of inspection decreases with thickness of the test specimen.

(g) It is more costly.

(h) It cannot be easily automated.

(i) It requires considerable skill for the interpretation of the radiographs.

(j) Depth of discontinuity not indicated.

9. 2. 2　Ultrasonic Testing（UT）

9. 2. 2. 1　How it works

Ultrasonic testing is used to find internal defects within a weld or body of a component being tested. A probe emits a sound wave that is passed through the material. If this sound wave hits a defect then all or part of it gets rebounded back to a receiver in the probe and the size and position of the defect can be plotted on a graph by a skilled operator. Figure 9. 8 shows the arrangement of base A-scan pulse technique.

Angled probes send the wave into a weld at angles suitable for the weld preparation bevel angles used. A zero degree 'compression' probe is used first to check for any laminations in the parent material that could deflect angled waves and mask defects in the weld.

The surface of the component must be clean and smooth and a couplant applied to exclude air from between the probe and com-po-nent. The couplant must be suitable for use on the material being tested and then be thor-ough-ly cleaned off afterwards to prevent any risk of corrosion or degradation of the compo-nent in

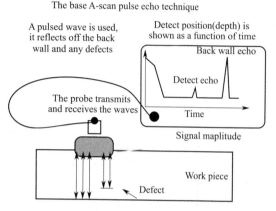

Figure 9. 8　The arrangement of base A-scan pulse technique.

service. Wallpaper paste is often used as a couplant because when it dries it can be easily peeled off.

In ultrasonic testing a short burst of acoustic energy is transmitted into the piece being tested, and echoes from various reflecting boundaries of defects are received. Flat surfaces produce reflections similar to light reflections on polished mirrors, whereas rough surfaces scatter the beam. Thus defects limited in sonic reflecting ability by their rough contour or small size are difficult to detect.

The frequency of the sound waves used for weld inspection is generally in the order of 1 to 10 MHz. Most testing is done with a frequency of 2. 25MHz. the lower frequencies provide great pen-etrating power for the sound beam, but create greater divergence which tends to bypass small iso-lated reflectors such as scattered porosity, whereas the high frequencies are much more directive.

9. 2. 2. 2　Advantages

① High penetrating power, which allows the detection of flaws deep in the part.

② High sensitivity, permitting the detection of extremely small flaws.

③ Only one surface need be accessible.

④ Greater accuracy than other nondestructive methods in determining the depth of internal flaws and the thickness of parts with parallel surfaces.

⑤ Some capability of estimating the size, orientation, shape and nature of defects.

⑥ Nonhazardous to operations or to nearby personnel and has no effect on equipment and ma-terials in the vicinity.

⑦ Capable of portable or highly automated operation.

9. 2. 2. 3　Disadvantages

① Manual operation requires careful attention by experienced technicians

② Extensive technical knowledge is required for the development of inspection procedures.

③ Parts that are rough, irregular in shape, very small or thin, or not homogeneous are difficult to inspect.

④ Surface must be prepared by cleaning and removing loose scale, paint, etc., although paint that Is properly bonded to a surface need not be removed.

⑤ Couplants are needed to provide effective transfer of ultrasonic wave energy between transducers and parts being inspected unless a non-contact technique is used. Non contact techniques include Laser and Electro Magnetic Acoustic Transducers (EMAT).

⑥ Inspected items must be water resistant, when using water based couplants that do not contain rust inhibitors.

9.2.3　Magnetic Particle Inspection (MPI)

Magnetic particle testing is used to find mainly surface breaking defects in ferromagnetic materials. Sometimes it is possible to find slightly subsurface defects when used with a permanent magnet or D. C. electromagnet. A magnetic flux (or field) is introduced into the material and any defects cutting across the magnetic flux can be detected when ink or powders containing ferromag-netic particles (iron flings) are applied to the material. What happens is that a flux leakage occurs at the defect, which effectively makes the defect a magnet in its own right. This "magnet" attracts the ferromagnetic particles, which take the shape of the defect.

The magnetic flux can be introduced from:

① a permanent magnet.

② an electromagnet (either A. C. or D. C.).

③ electric prods (either A. C. or D. C.) between which a current flows (and the current flow is surrounded by a magnetic field).

Ferromagnetic particles can be applied to the material as:

① a black ink (viewed against a pre-applied white contrast paint).

② fluorescent ink (viewed under UV light conditions).

③ red or blue dry powders (used at higher temperatures). This method will detect surface discontinuities including those too fine to be seen with the naked eye, and those that lie slightly below the surface.

In magnetic particle inspection, a magnetic field is established in a piece of ferro-magnetic material. At discontinuities in the path of the magnetic flux, minute poles are set up at each side which has a stronger attraction for the magnetic particles sprinkled on the work for the test than the surrounding surface of the material.

The inspector must be able to interpret the indications given by the magnetic particles to decide which discontinuities require repair. Among the defects that can be detected are surface cracks of all kinds both in the weld and in the adjacent case metal, incomplete fusion, shallow subsurface cracks, and lack of penetration.

Magnetic particle inspection cannot be used to inspect nonmagnetic non-ferrous materials or austenitic steels, and false indications may occur where the magnetic characteristics of the deposited metal and base plate are appreciably different. Excessively coarse grained areas create magnetic discontinuities that produce indications even in a sound joint.

Magnetic particle testing is used for the testing of materials which can be easily magnetized. This method is capable of detecting open to surface and just below the surface flaws. In this method the test specimen is first magnetized either by using a permanent or an electromagnet or by passing electric current through or around the specimen. The magnetic field thus introduced into the specimen is composed of magnetic lines of force. Whenever there is a flaw which interrupts the flow of magnetic lines of force, some of these lines must exit and reenter the specimen. These points of exit and re-entry form opposite magnetic poles. Whenever minute magnetic particles are sprinkled onto the surface of such a specimen, these particles are attracted by these magnetic poles to create a visual

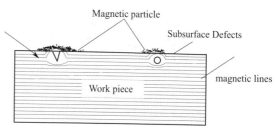

Figure 9. 9　Basic principle of magnetic particle testing.

indication approximating the size and shape of the flaw. Figure 9. 9 illustrates the basic principles of this method.

Direct current, rectified current or alternating current may be used for magnetizing the parts to be inspected. High-amperage low voltage direct current is usually employed. Direct current produces a field that penetrates throughout the part and is, therefore, more sensitive than alternating current for the detection of subsurface discontinuities. Only a thin surface layer of the metal is magnetized by alternating current.

Depending on the application, there are different magnetization techniques used in magnetic particle testing. These techniques can be grouped into the following two categories: ① Direct current techniques: These are the techniques in which the current flows through the test specimen and the magnetic field produced by this flow of current is used for the detection of defects. These techniques are shown in Figure 9. 10(a), (b) &(c). ②Magnetic flux flow techniques: In these techniques magnetic flux is induced into the specimen either by the use of a permanent magnet or by flowing current through a coil or a conductor. These techniques are shown in Figure 9. 10(d)-(g).

(1) Advantages of magnetic particle testing include the following

① It does not need very stringent pre-cleaning operation.

② Best method for the detection of fine, shallow surface cracks in ferromagnetic material.

③ Fast and relatively simple NDT method.

④ Generally inexpensive.

⑤ Will work through thin coating.

⑥ Few limitations regarding the size/shape of test specimens.

⑦ Highly portable NDT method.

⑧ It is quicker.

(2) Some of the limitations of magnetic particle testing include the following

① Material must be ferromagnetic.

② Orientation and strength of magnetic field is critical.

③ Detects surface and near-to-surface discontinuities only.

④ Large currents sometimes required.

⑤ "Burning" of test parts a possibility.

⑥ Parts must often be demagnetized, which may be difficult.

9. 2. 4　Liquid Penetrant Testing（PT）

Liquid penetrant examination, often called dye penetrant or penetrant testing (PT), is used to find surface breaking defects only. It involves the use of a cleaner (degreaser), a liquid penetrant and a developer. The most common PT system on site involves the use of these three materials from cans and is referred to as the 'three can system'.

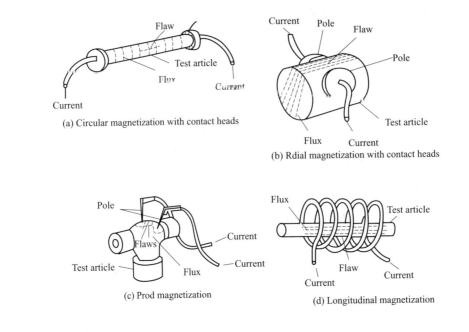

(a) Circular magnetization with contact heads

(b) Rdial magnetization with contact heads

(c) Prod magnetization

(d) Longitudinal magnetization

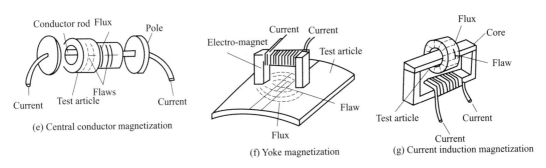

(e) Central conductor magnetization

(f) Yoke magnetization

(g) Current induction magnetization

Figure 9. 10   Different magnetizations used in magnetic particle testing.

A typical color contrast procedure involves preparing the surface to remove any spatter, slag or other imperfections that could retain the penetrant and mask relevant indications. The surface is then thoroughly cleaned, using the cleaner, to remove any surface oil or grease, which could prevent the red liquid penetrant being drawn into surface breaking cracks or indications. It is then dried using air or lint free cloths. The penetrant is then applied by spray or brush and left for a dwell time as speci fied in the procedure. This dwell time must be long enough to enable the penetrant to be drawn into surface breaking defects by capillary action. Excess penetrant is then removed using cloths dampened with the cleaner. The cleaner must not be sprayed directly on to the component otherwise penetrant could be washed out of relevant indications. Developer (a white chalk like substance) is then lightly sprayed on to the surface causing the red penetrant to be drawn out of any indications by reverse capillary action and the blotting effect of the developer. Any indication high-lighted by the red penetrant against the white developer can then be assessed. The penetrant which remains in the discontinuity is absorbed by the developer to indicate the presence as well as the location, size and nature of the discontinuity. The process is illustrated in Figure 9. 11.

Penetrants used are either visible dye penetrant or fluorescent dye penetrant. The inspection for the presence of visible dye indications is made under white light while inspection of presence of indications by fluorescent dye penetrant is made under ultraviolet (or black) light under darkened conditions. The liquid penetrant processes are further sub-divided according to the method of washing of the specimen. The penetrants can be: ① water-washable, ② postemulsifiable, i. e. an emulsifier is added to the excess penetrant on surface of the specimen to make it water-washable, and ③ solvent removable, i. e. the excess penetrant is needed to be dissolved in a solvent to remove it from the test specimen surface.

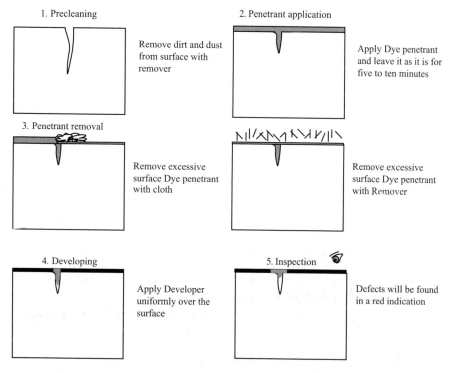

Figure 9. 11   Different stages of liquid penetrant process.

In order of decreasing sensitivity and decreasing cost, the liquid penetrant processes can be listed as:

    ① Post emulsifiable fluorescent dye penetrant.
    ② Solvent removable fluorescent dye penetrant.
    ③ Water washable fluorescent dye penetrant.
    ④ Post emulsifiable visible dye penetrant.
    ⑤ Solvent removable visible dye penetrant.
    ⑥ Water washable visible dye penetrant.

9. 2. 4. 1   Some of the advantages of liquid penetrant testing are as follows

    ① Relatively low cost.
    ② Highly portable NDT method.
    ③ Highly sensitive to fine, tight discontinuities.
    ④ Fairly simple method.
    ⑤ Can be used on a variety of materials.
    ⑥ All surface discontinuities are detected in one operation, regardless of orientation.

9. 2. 4. 2   Some of the limitations of liquid penetrant testing are as follows

    ① Test surface must be free of all contaminants (dirt, oil, grease, paint, rust, etc.).

② Detects surface discontinuities only.

③ Cannot be used on porous specimens and is difficult to use on very rough surfaces.

④ Removal of all penetrant materials, following the test, is often required.

⑤ There is no easy method to produce permanent record.

9.3 Destructive Test

9.3.1 Tension Tests

The main objective of a tension test on a welded joint is to measure the yield and tensile strengths of the sample under test. A pulling force (load) is applied to the sample and the yield and ultimate tensile strength (UTS) are measured and recorded on the test form along with the material type, specimen type, specimen size and location of the fracture. Weldments are normally subjected to a reduced transverse tensile test (see Figure 9.12).

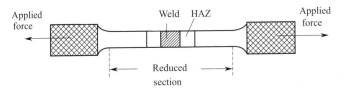

Figure 9.12 Tensile specimen: reduced section transverse test.

Manufacturers of welding consumables carry out a longitudinal "all weld metal" tensile test to measure the tensile strength, yield point and percentage elongation ($E\%$) of the deposited weld metal. The sample is taken from the centre of the weld and consists of weld metal only.

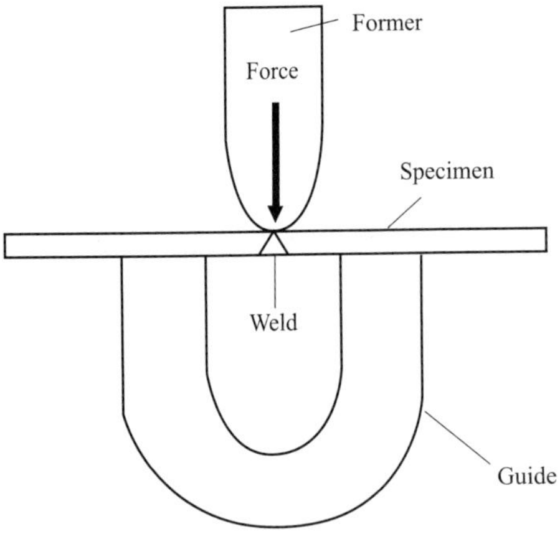

9.3.2 Bend Tests

Bend tests give an indication of weld quality and a rough indication of ductility by putting the weld and HAZ under tension. The weld and HAZ must be included within the bent portion and a limit given to the size of linear openings permitted on the surface under test. Bend tests are normally transverse tests taken across the weld and include the weld, HAZ and base material. Longitudinal tests are more unusual but can be used where dissimilar base materials with widely differing properties are welded or where the weld metal

Figure 9.13 Guide bend test.

is of greatly differing properties to the base metal. Guided bend tests are those that have the sample bent into a guide (see Figure 9.13).

Bend tests are classed as face, root or side bends depending on which surface is under tension; a face bend will have the face under tension while a root bend will have the root under tension. A side bend test is used where the sample is too thick to form a face or root bend. With a side bend test the cross-section of the whole weld is put under tension and checked for internal defects such as lack of sidewall fusion or inter-run fusion. It is worth keeping in mind that the side bend is just a snapshot of the weld at one particular point within the weld length.

9.3.3 Charpy Tests

Material impact toughness can be measured by various types of test such as the Charpy V-notch impact test, Izod test or KIC test. The most commonly used test is the Charpy impact test (see Figure 6.9), which gives an indication of the toughness of a material at a specified temperature. It is not a particularly accurate test but can give a general indication of the ability of a material to resist brittle fracture at its minimum design material temperature. The test consists of holding a machined specimen, of a specified size (normally 55mm×10mm×10mm) containing an accurately machined notch of specific dimension, at both ends as a simple beam. A pendulum impacts on the specimen and the start and finish heights of the pendulum are measured. The difference in height equates to the energy absorbed by the specimen before it fractures. This absorbed energy is usually measured in joules on a scale attached to the machine.

Three Charpy specimens are tested at each specified temperature and the final result taken as an average of the three. Tests can be done at various temperatures and recorded in a graph to form the Charpy curve (see Figure 9.14) and determine the ductile-to-brittle transition temperature. The ductile-to-brittle transition temperature is the temperature at which the test specimen will start to become more brittle than ductile. You would therefore not want to use the material at design temperatures below this as it would have an increased risk of failing in a brittle manner.

Remember that this is not an accurate test reflecting the material behavior under actual service conditions, so the results should therefore be used with caution.

A more accurate test to check a material's likelihood of failing in a brittle manner is the crack tip open displacement (CTOD) test, sometimes referred to as a KIC test.

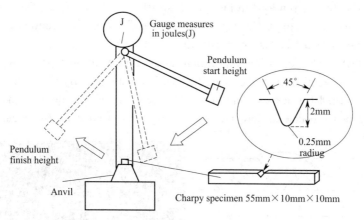

Figure 9.14   Charpy V-notch impact test.

9.3.4   Hardness Testing

The most common hardness tests are Vickers, Rockwell and Brinell. Hardness is defined as the ability of a material to resist indentation on its surface. Hardness tests consist of impressing a ball (Brinell or Rockwell) or diamond shape (Vickers or Rockwell) into the material under a specified loading and measuring the width of the indentation to give a relative hardness reading (Figure 9.15). The smaller the width of the indentation, the harder the material will be. Hardness testing normally encompasses the weld and HAZ and is usually done to confirm that PWHT has been carried out correctly. When hardness testing is done for weld procedure qualification purposes it is often done through the weldment thickness as hardness levels can vary considerably through the thickness.

The various types of hardness testing have their own units:

① Vickers test: HV (Vickers hardness).

② Brinell test: HB (Brinell hardness).

③ Rockwell: HR (Rockwell hardness).

A Shore Schlerescope is a portable dynamic hardness test using equipment similar in size to a ballpoint pen. It drops a weight from a height on to the test surface and measures the height of the rebound. The higher the rebound the higher the hardness value, which can be read off in any selected unit. It may be used by the welding inspector to gauge hardness values on site, but the accuracy depends on the condition of the test surface and the support of the test piece during the test.

9.4   Radiograph Interpretation

In addition to producing high quality radiographs, the radiographer must also be skilled in ra-di-ographic interpretation. Interpretation of radiographs takes place in three basic steps which are① detection, ②interpretation, and③evaluation. All of these steps make use of the radiographer's visual acuity. Visual acuity is the ability to resolve a spatial pattern in an image. The ability of an individual to detect discontinuities in radiography is also affected by the lighting condition in the place of viewing, and the experience level for recognizing various features in the image. The following material was developed to help students develop an understanding of the types of defects found in weldments and how they appear in a radiograph.

9.4.1   General Welding Discontinuities

Discontinuities are interruptions in the typical structure of a material. These interruptions may occur in the base metal, weld material or "heat affected" zones. Discontinuities, which do not meet the requirements of the codes or specification used to invoke and control an inspection, are referred to as defects. The following discontinuities are typical of all types of welding.

① Cold lap is a condition where the weld filler metal does not properly fuse with the base metal or the previous weld pass material (interpass cold lap). The arc does not melt the base metal sufficiently and causes the slightly molten puddle to flow into base material without bonding (see Figure 9.15).

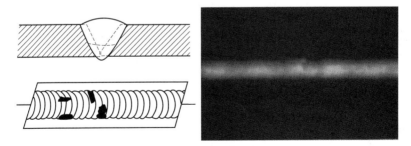

Figure 9.15

② Porosity is the result of gas entrapment in the solidifying metal. Porosity can take many shapes on a radiograph but often appears as dark round or irregular spots or specks appearing singularly, in clusters or rows. Sometimes porosity is elongated and may have the appearance of having a tail. This is the result of gas attempting to escape while the metal is still in a liquid state and is called wormhole porosity. All porosity is a void in the material it will have a radiographic density more than the surrounding area (see Figure 9.16).

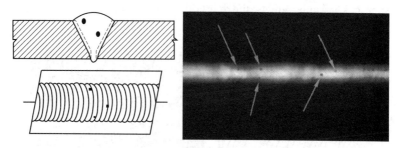

Figure 9. 16

③ Cluster porosity is caused when flux coated electrodes are contaminated with moisture. The moisture turns into gases when heated and becomes trapped in the weld during the welding process. Cluster porosity appears just like regular porosity in the radiograph but the indications will be grouped close together (see Figure 9. 17).

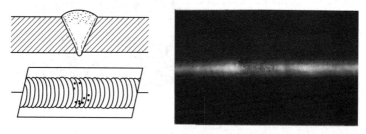

Figure 9. 17

④ Slag inclusions are nonmetallic solid material entrapped in weld metal or between weld and base metal. In a radiograph, dark, jagged asymmetrical shapes within the weld or along the weld joint areas are indicative of slag inclusions (see Figure 9. 18).

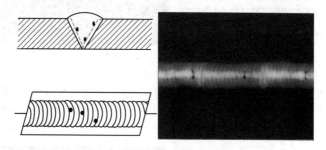

Figure 9. 18

⑤ Incomplete penetration (IP) or lack of penetration (LOP) occurs when the weld metal fails to penetrate the joint. It is one of the most objectionable weld discontinuities. Lack of penetration allows a natural stress riser from which a crack may propagate. The appearance on a radiograph is a dark area with well-defined, straight edges that follows the land or root face down the center of the weldment (see Figure 9. 19).

⑥ Incomplete fusion is a condition where the weld filler metal does not properly fuse with the base metal. Appearance on radiograph: usually appears as a dark line or lines oriented in the direction of the weld seam along the weld preparation or joining area (see Figure 9. 20).

⑦ Internal concavity or suck back is condition where the weld metal has contracted as it cools and has been drawn up into the root of the weld. On a radiograph it looks similar to lack of penetra-tion but the line has irregular edges and it is often quite wide in the center of the weld image (see Figure 9. 21).

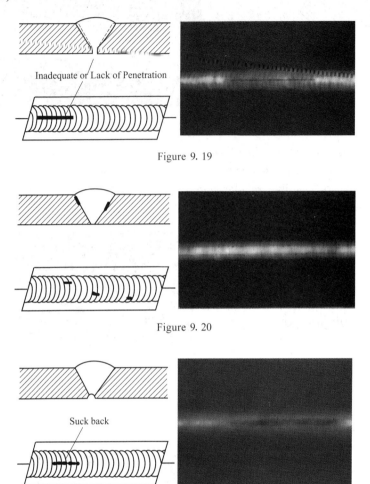

Figure 9. 19

Figure 9. 20

Figure 9. 21

⑧ Internal or root undercut is an erosion of the base metal next to the root of the weld. In the radiographic image it appears as a dark irregular line offset from the centerline of the weldment. Undercutting is not as straight edged as LOP because it does not follow a ground edge (see Figure 9. 22).

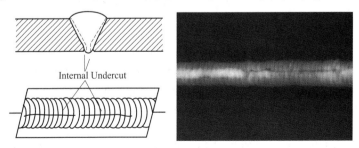

Figure 9. 22

⑨ External or crown undercut is an erosion of the base metal next to the crown of the weld. In the radiograph, it appears as a dark irregular line along the outside edge of the weld area (see Figure 9. 23).

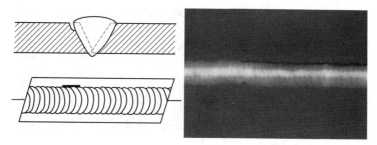

Figure 9. 23

⑩ Offset or mismatch is terms associated with a condition where two pieces being welded together are not properly aligned. The radiographic image is a noticeable difference in density between the two pieces. The difference in density is caused by the difference in material thickness. The dark, straight line is caused by failure of the weld metal to fuse with the land area (see Figure 9. 24).

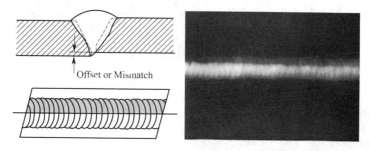

Figure 9. 24

⑪ Inadequate weld reinforcement is an area of a weld where the thickness of weld metal deposited is less than the thickness of the base material. It is very easy to determine by radiograph if the weld has inadequate reinforcement, because the image density in the area of suspected inadequacy will be more (darker) than the image density of the surrounding base material (see Figure 9. 25).

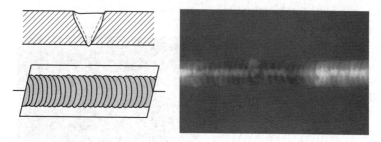

Figure 9. 25

⑫ Excess weld reinforcement is an area of a weld, which has weld metal added in excess of that specified by engineering drawings and codes. The appearance on a radiograph is a localized, lighter area in the weld. A visual inspection will easily determine if the weld reinforcement is in excess of that specified by the individual code involved in the inspection (see Figure 9. 26).

Cracking can be detected in a radiograph only the crack is propagating in a direction that produced a change in thickness that is parallel to the x-ray beam. Cracks will appear jagged and often very faint irregular lines. Cracks can sometimes appearing as "tails" on inclusions or porosity (see Figure 9. 27).

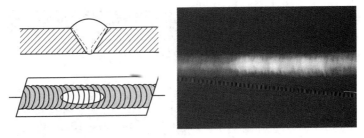

Figure 9. 26

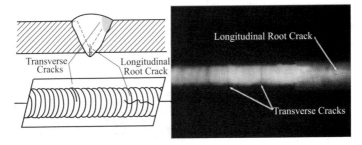

Figure 9. 27

9. 4. 2　Other Discontinuities

9. 4. 2. 1　Discontinuities in TIG Welds

The following discontinuities are peculiar to the TIG welding process. These discontinuities occur in most metals welded by the process including aluminum and stainless steels. The TIG method of welding produces a clean homogeneous weld which when radiographed is easily interpreted.

① Tungsten inclusions Tungsten is a brittle and inherently dense material used in the electrode in tungsten inert gas welding. If improper welding procedures are used, tungsten may be entrapped in the weld. Radiographically, tungsten is denser than aluminum or steel; therefore, it shows as a lighter area with a distinct outline on the radiograph (see Figure 9. 28).

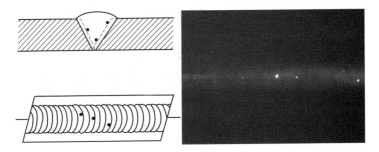

Figure 9. 28

② Oxide inclusions are usually visible on the surface of material being welded (especially aluminum). Oxide inclusions are less dense than the surrounding materials and, therefore, appear as dark irregularly shaped discontinuities in the radiograph (see Figure 9. 29).

9. 4. 2. 2　Discontinuities in Gas Metal Arc Welds (GMAW)

The following discontinuities are most commonly found in GMAW welds.

① Whiskers are short lengths of weld electrode wire, visible on the top or bottom surface of

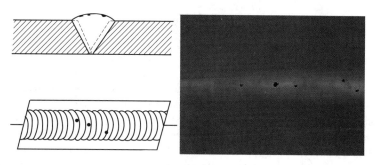

Figure 9. 29

the weld or contained within the weld. On a radiograph they appear as light, "wire like" indications.

② Burn through will result when too much heat causes excessive weld metal to penetrate the weld zone. Lumps of metal sag through the weld create a thick globular condition on the back of the weld. On a radiograph, burn through appears as dark spots surrounded by light globular areas.

References

[1] Charlotte Weisman, *Welding Handbook*. Seventh ed. Fundamental of Weldings. Vol. 1: American Welding Soceity.

[2] Donald R. Askeland, *The Science and Engineering of Materials*. 1998: Nelson Thorned Ltd.

[3] Geogre Linnert, *Welding Metallurgy*. Third ed. Vol 1: American Welding Society.

[4] R. L. O'Brien. *Welding Handbook*. 8 ed. Welding Processes. Vol. 2. 1991, American Welding Society.

[5] A. F. Manz. *Welding Power Handbook*. 1973, New York: Union Carbide Corporation.

[6] Robert L. O'Brien. *Jefferson's Welding Encyclopedia*. American Welding Society, 1997.

[7] Rajiv S. Mishra, Murray W. Mahoney. *Friction Stir Welding and Processing*. 2007 ASM International.

[8] G. G. Saunders et al. *Influence of welding and postweld heat treatment on the heat-affected zone fracture toughness of carbon-manganese and low alloy steels*. The Toughness of Weld Heat-affected Zones. National Seminar, Mar., 1974, The Welding Institute.

[9] 王勇, 王引真, 张德勤. 材料冶金学与成型工艺. 东营: 石油大学出版社, 2005.

[10] J. F. Lancaster. *Metallurgy of Welding*. George Allen & Unwin, London. Third Edition, 1980.

[11] Christensen, N. V. de L. Davies and K. Gjermundsen. Distribution of temperatures in arc welding. *Brit. Welding J*. 1965, (12) : 54-74.

[12] Robert D. Stout. *Weldability of Steels*. Welding Research Council. USA New York. Fourth Edition, 1987, p94-99.

[13] Chubb, J. P. and J. Billingham. *Metals Technology* 5, part 3, March, 1978, p100-103.

[14] Harujiro Sekiguchi. *Fundamental Research on the Welding Heat-affected Zone of Steel*. The Nikkan Kogyo Shimbun, Ltd. 1976, Tokyo. p3-15, p204-209.

[15] T. Kobayashi. Effects of electrodes on heat-affected zone and distortion of arc welded steel specimens. *Journal of J. W. S.*, Vol. 18 (1949), p177-183.

[16] S. A. Herres. Arc welding of alloy steels. *Trans. A. S. M.*, 33 (1944), p535-563.

[17] G. L. Hopkin. A suggested cause and a general theory for the cracking of alloy steels on welding. *Welding J.*, 23 (1944) No. 11, 606-s~608-s.

[18] H. W. Mallet and P. J. Rieppel. Arc atmospheres and underbead cracking. *Welding J.*, 25 (1946) No. 11, 748-s~759-s.

[19] Masubuchi, K., *Analysis of Welded Structures*, Pergamon, Elmsford, NY, 1980.

[20] *Welding Handbook*, 7th ed., Vol. 1, American Welding Society, Miami, FL, 1976.

[21] TWI Job Knowledge for Welders, Part 34, Welding Institute, Cambridge, UK, March 21, 1998.

[22] Hertzberg, R. W., *Deformation and Fracture Mechanics of Engineering Materials*, Wiley, New York, 1976, p. 422.

[23] Colangelo, V. J., and Heiser, F. A., *Analysis of Metallurgical Failures*, Wiley, New York, 1974.

[24] Wulpi, D., *Understanding How Components Fail*, American Society for Metals, Metals Park, OH, 1985, p. 144.

[25] Uhlig, H. H., Corrosion and Corrosion Control, 2nd ed., Wiley, New York, 1971.

[26] Fontana, M. G., and Greene, N. D., Corrosion Engineering, 2nd ed., McGraw-Hill, New York, 1978.

[27] Fatigue Fractures in Welded Constructions, Vol. II, International Institute of Welding, London, 1979, p. 56.

[28] Howard B. Cary, Scott C. Helzer. *Modern Welding Technology*. Sixth Edition. Pearson Prentice Hall, 2005

[29] Steven E. Hughes, Clifford Matthews. *Quick Guide to Welding and Weld Inspection*. 2009, Matthews Engineering Train-ing Limited. Oxford Cambridge New Delhi.

[30] Robert D. Stout, W. Dorville Dorty. *Weldability of steels* (second edition). Welding Research Council. 1971, New York.

[31] Sindo Kou. *Welding Metallurgy* (second edition). John Wiley & Sons, Inc., Publication. Hoboken, New Jersey. 2002.

[32] Cartz, Louis. Nondestructive Testing. *A S M International*, 1995.

[33] Charles Hellier. *Handbook of Nondestructive Evaluation*. McGraw-Hill, 2003.